Scripture in the World Religions

A SHORT INTRODUCTION

OTHER BOOKS IN THIS SERIES:

Buddhism: A Short History, Edward Conze, ISBN 1–85168–221–X
Buddhism: A Short Introduction, Klaus K. Klostermaier, ISBN 1–85168–186–8
Hinduism: A Short History, Klaus K. Klostermaier, ISBN 1–85168–213–9
Hindu Writings: A Short Introduction to the Major Sources, Klaus K. Klostermaier, ISBN 1–85168–230–9
Hinduism: A Short Introduction, Klaus K. Klostermaier, ISBN 1–85168–220–1
Islamic Philosophy, Theology and Mysticism: A Short Introduction, Majid Fakhry, ISBN 1–85168–252–X
Muhammad: A Short Biography, Martin Forward, ISBN 1–85168–131–0
Islam: A Short History, William Montgomery Watt, ISBN 1–85168–205–8
Jesus Christ: A Short Biography, Martin Forward, ISBN 1–85168–172–8
Christianity: A Short Introduction, Keith Ward, ISBN 1–85168–229–5
Judaism: A Short History, Lavinia and Dan Cohn-Sherbok, ISBN 1–85168–206–6
Judaism: A Short Introduction, Lavinia and Dan Cohn-Sherbok, ISBN 1–85168–207–4
Judaism: A Short Reader, Lavinia and Dan Cohn-Sherbok, ISBN 1–85168–112–4
A Short Introduction to the Old Testament Prophets, E. W. Heaton, ISBN 1–85168–114–0
Sufism: A Short Introduction, William C. Chittick, ISBN 1–85168–211–2
The Bahá'í Faith: A Short Introduction, Moojan Momen, ISBN 1–85168–209–0
The Bahá'í Faith: A Short History, Peter Smith, ISBN 1–85168–208–2
The Psychology of Religion: A Short Introduction, Kate M. Loewenthal, ISBN 1–85168–212–0
Confucianism: A Short Introduction, John and Evelyn Berthrong, ISBN 1–85168–236–8
Pluralism in the World Religions: A Short Introduction, Harold Coward, ISBN 1–85168–243–0
Global Philosophy of Religion: A Short Introduction, Joseph Runzo, ISBN 1–85168–235–X

RELATED TITLES PUBLISHED BY ONEWORLD:

The Fifth Dimension, John Hick, ISBN 1–85168–191–4
The Phenomenon of Religion, Moojan Momen, ISBN 1–85168–161–2
The Meaning of Life in the World Religions, Joseph Runzo and Nancy M. Martin (eds), ISBN 1–85168–200–7
Love, Sex, and Gender in the World Religions, Joseph Runzo and Nancy M. Martin (eds), ISBN 1–85168–223–6
God, Faith and the New Millennium, Keith Ward, ISBN 1–85168–155–8

Scripture in the World Religions

A SHORT INTRODUCTION

Harold Coward

ONEWORLD
OXFORD

SCRIPTURE IN THE WORLD RELIGIONS: A SHORT INTRODUCTION

Oneworld Publications
(Sales and Editorial)
185 Banbury Road
Oxford OX2 7AR
England
http://www.oneworld-publications.com

Oneworld Publications
(US Office)
160 N. Washington St.
4th floor, Boston
MA 02114
USA

A CIP record for this title is available
from the British Library

ISBN 1–85168–244–9

Cover design by Design Deluxe, Bath
Printed and bound in Great Britain by Creative Print and Design

For Hazel

CONTENTS

PREFACE

Growing up in a Protestant Christian family in Canada gave me a deep appreciation for scripture. Indeed, hearing the parables of Jesus at my mother's knee, when I was too young to even go to school, formed the foundation of my religious life. These parables, along with the other stories and teachings of the Bible, remain the fundamental grounding of my life to this day. In university my scholarly curiosity naturally turned to wanting to understand how the words of scripture could have such a powerful and transforming effect on one's life. At first I studied within my own Christian tradition. But it was when my study led me beyond the Jewish and Christian sources to an examination of Hindu texts that I finally began to understand the spiritual power of the word. My teacher of Hinduism, Professor T. R. V. Murti of Banaras Hindu University in India, introduced me to a new way of studying scripture.

In the traditional teacher-student relationship of India, study proceeds in a quite different fashion than the classroom approach of the modern university. Of course, I did attend Professor Murti's classes at the University, but the "real study" of the scriptural text occurred when I would go to his home three afternoons a week for traditional *guru*–student style study. We would study a text by reading it together line by line, not going on the next one until he was satisfied that I understood the first line. But "reading" is not really the right description of what was happening – it was more speaking and hearing. Professor Murti would chant the verse of Hindu scripture or commentary aloud in its original Sanskrit (he knew all these texts by heart, so used no books), then he would give me an English translation and finally an explanation of the meaning. I would ask questions if I did not understand, and sometimes he would question me to ensure I had understood. Only when he was satisfied that I had a full understanding would we move on to the next line of text. After studying together in this fashion for about three hours we would stop and he would make me tea. Over tea he would explain other aspects of the culture and tradition that provided the context for our textual study. The first book we read together was "the Yoga Sutras of Patañjali,"[1] the foundation text for the Hindu Yoga spiritual tradition dating from between 200 B.C.E. and 200 C.E. It took us about two years to get through the Yoga Sutras for often a line would refer to another scriptural tradition (e.g. the Buddhist) necessitating time out for Professor Murti to teach me the Buddhist position, for example, so that I could understand what was being said. I also had to learn Sanskrit, so that I could experience the text in its original sound and meaning before an English translation was attempted. It was through this method of study that I came to a new understanding of how Christian scripture worked in my own life.

One of the Yoga Sutras that particularly intrigued me was 11:44, "By study of the scriptures comes communion with the Lord": *svadhyaya*. To a Protestant boy this seemed to be a wonderful confirmation of the daily Bible study tradition in which I had been reared. But Vyasa's commentary, as elucidated by Murti, led to a severe challenging of that tradition and an opening up of the question of the power of *mantra* chanting. My Protestant practice of Bible study involved rising early in the morning and reading through the books of the Bible in a systematic way. I would do this at my desk with the commentaries spread out around me. After reading a verse I would consult the leading commentaries to determine the historical context, linguistic points and the intellectual meaning of the passage. While all of this was a thoroughly acceptable Enlightenment approach to the text, it was clearly far from Patañjali's concept of study or *svadhyaya*.

The idea of leaving behind a rational analytical approach in favor of a meditative immersion in the text was completely new to me. It did not go against the *sola scriptura* of my Protestant tradition – in fact, that aspect seemed reinforced. But the rational liberal Enlightenment method of Bible study, championed in my seminary training, was thoroughly challenged. Rather than intellectual analysis of the passage leading to a clear conceptual understanding, Patañjali's *svadhyaya* aimed at a stilling of the rational thinking activity of the mind so that the Bible verse itself became the sole occupant of one's consciousness. The power of the revealed word itself, freed of the obstacles of the thinking processes, was then able to transform one's whole being. My Protestant tradition believed strongly in the transforming power of Scripture, and I had occasionally experienced that power when the word of the Bible was powerfully spoken by a preacher like Martin Luther King. But in my private daily Bible study, I was blocking out much of that power by turning it into a rational, intellectual exercise. Exposure to the Hindu Yoga Sutras taught me that while reason has a useful role, it is a minor one, namely, the removal of obstacles to the direct immersion of the mind in the revealed world.[2] That is the purpose of *svadhyaya* – to chant and meditate on the chosen passage until one loses the subject-object separation with the word and it becomes the whole of one's conscious and unconscious experience. The test for mastery, says Patañjali, is that one's study will be blessed by a vision of the Lord. One's consciousness is so completely one with the word that it is the object of the scripture itself that is revealed (i.e., the Lord) rather than the object of the rational activity of the mind (i.e., conceptual thought about the Lord).

This discovery led me to a complete change in my approach to daily Bible study. I put away the commentaries from my desk and immersed myself only in the revealed word itself. My morning Bible study became less and less intellectual and more and more an opening of myself to the transforming power of the biblical word. Surprisingly, I found myself recovering an experience I had not had since when, as a young child, my mother would tell me the parables of Jesus. The hearing of those words of Jesus by my clear and open young mind, as yet uncluttered by rational thought, made a deep and lasting impression. The foundation of my faith was established. My new approach to Bible study opened the way to a recovery of the kind of direct and transforming experience of the word that I had had at my mother's knee. It did not mean that I gave up my intellectual study of the word – only that the rational/analytical approach to the word to which I devoted myself during my working hours as a scholar was balanced by a non-rational devotional experience of the word in my early morning *svadhyaya* study. The over-balance on the rational side was corrected and I was reconnected with the deep transforming power present in the direct devotional experience of the word. I felt my faith to be more nourished, my life to be more vital and my intellectual academic study, in turn, became more fruitful. The intellectual and personal experience of my Christian religion had been returned to its formative basis in my childhood hearing of the parables of Jesus by my encounter with Patañjali's Yoga Sutras.

Yet another aspect of the Hindu approach fascinated me – its emphasis upon the oral over the written word. Unlike my modern Western training in scientific biblical criticism, the Hindu tradition sees the written text as corrected by the carefully transmitted oral word. This stress on the oral word led me to re-examine the history of the Christian experience of the word to see if there had been a similar period of dependence upon the oral over the written. Jesus himself left no writings. Our knowledge of his words and works comes from his immediate followers or apostles and their disciples. At first this information circulated orally. Later it was written down and some of it became canonized. However, for the early Christians, it was the oral experience of scripture that had the power to transform persons. The importance of oral rhetoric in Greek culture came together with the oral practices of the Jewish rabbis to provide a strong oral context. Jesus, and some Jewish rabbis of his day, did not write but depended on oral teaching to communicate their messages.[3] Jesus' teaching and much of the early Christian mission was by word of mouth, in Aramaic and Greek, the common languages of the day; sermons were neither written in advance nor copied down by the hearers. They listened and remembered. As was the case with the great Jewish rabbis and their academies, the cultural traditions of the day were more oral than written – although there was certainly writing going on. Jesus and his disciples followed this pattern. The oral nature of their teaching was not due to illiteracy, but was consciously chosen by the rabbis because of its greater power for reaching and transforming the people of the day.[4]

Jesus' words were not studied or written out in advance but spoken *ex tempore* in a specific situation. His utterance is dynamic and immediate, spoken in live face-to-face communication. The great biblical scholar Amos Wilder comments, "the Gospel meant freedom of speech . . . One did not hoard its formulas, since when the occasion arose the Spirit would teach one what to say . . ."[5] This special "for the present" quality of Jesus' words comes through in other New Testament authors even when they did write or dictate. Paul's letters, for example, were written to be read aloud in oral performance to the congregations to which they were addressed. Like the other writers of the New Testament, Peter, James and Jude, Paul felt that in his letters it was the Holy Spirit speaking through him rather than his own voice. Paul's personality as an author is both humbled and exalted as he feels the Spirit of Christ speak through his words. Here one is reminded of the Vedic *ṛṣis* who emptied themselves of *karma* (mental distractions) so that the eternal word (*vāk*) could speak through them.

Although both the Gospels and letters were widely circulated in the early Christian churches, the power came when they were spoken aloud in congregational worship. In a sense they functioned much like the score does in a musical performance. It is the heard music, not the written score, that is the real thing. Similarly, it is the spoken word in scripture reading, sermon or the individual telling of the parable to another (as my mother did to me) that has transforming power. Unlike the merely written text, the oral speaking of the Scripture enters the hearts of individuals and joins speakers and hearers together into a fellowship of the word – a *logos* of giving and receiving (Philippians 4:15; Galatians 6:6). The obstacle to faith is a defective sense of hearing. It is through true hearing and oral confession that salvation is realized. A hearing resulting in a spoken confession is Paul's view of the appropriate response to the gospel (Romans 10:9). All of this is very close to the Hindu view that the obstacle to release (*mokṣa*) is the mind's *karma* which is removed by the devotional hearing of the spoken scripture. Indeed, it was Hindu understanding of this process that sensitized me to the power of the spoken word in early Christian experience. Looking over Christian history one sees that this continues to be true through Augustine, Luther and the Puritans right up to the present day. All emphasize that God's word as written scripture is dead, only when it is spoken can it be heard. As Luther put it, when we read and write books, we have not fulfilled our responsibility as Christians. The church is a "mouth-house, no pen-house"[6] and today Luther would surely add, "or computer house." In modern times, scholars such as Walter Ong and Paul Ricoeur have emphasized the importance of the preaching of the Scripture. Ricoeur describes preaching as "the permanent reinterpretation of the text which is regarded as grounding the community."[7] Ong observes that in Protestantism, God is powerful through the spoken word which may be heard in sermons or in prayer or in the imagination of the devotee reading the Bible in print.[8] We are reminded of Paul's understanding of revelation. Paul does not say that the gospel is about revelation; rather, that when the gospel is preached, revelation happens.[9] From my own experience I would add that when Scripture is combined with music and sung in anthem or hymn, a most powerful oral-aural experience of the word can occur.

My study of Hinduism and its understanding of the nature of the power of the oral word resensitized me to the importance of spoken Scripture within the Christian tradition. Having grown up within Protestant Christianity, this led to a strong rerooting of my own religious experience within the living presence of the spoken word. However, Hinduism also opened my eyes to the spiritual merit of a Roman Catholic practice which I as a Protestant had always judged to be nothing more than superstitious ritual. I refer to the chanting of the rosary. As a university student I used to listen to a radio station that played good classical music but once a day broadcast a chanting of the rosary. This used to annoy me and I would dismiss it as a Roman Catholic superstition. In India I was surrounded by ritual chanting. At first I viewed it as I had the Roman Catholic rosary chanting – an empty superstition. But as I studied Bhartṛhari's philosophy of language, I came to understand for the first time the spiritual power present in devotional chant. Bhartṛhari's analysis of language as functioning on the three levels of uttered sound (*vaikharī*), inner thought (*madhyamā*) and the supersensuous seeing (*paśyantī*) of the meaning-whole (*sphoṭa*) provided a theoretical basis for understanding ritual chanting as having spiritual power.[10] Instead of empty repetition, each sounding of the chant or *mantra* is inherently meaningful in that each sound attempts to reveal the whole *sphoṭa*. Repetition of the uttered sounds of the *mantra*, especially if spoken clearly and correctly, will each time evoke afresh the *sphoṭa* until the obscuring ignorance is purged and the meaning-whole of the *mantra* is seen. If the scriptural word has power, which I as a Protestant had always believed, then the chanting of a *mantra* or rosary, far from being a superstitious ritual, was actually a powerful technique for focussing the mind on the word so that its spiritual power could work within one's consciousness.

Patañjali makes the psychological process at work even more explicit. Through the practice of fixed concentration (*samādhi*) consciousness is purified of karmic obstructions and the supersensuous reality "seen." The chanting of the *mantra* is a form of fixed concentration which keeps it front and centre in one's mind to the exclusion of everything else one might perceive or think. Through the chanting the devotee becomes one with the *mantra*, be it OM, the rosary or the Jesus prayer. It is as though one's whole world becomes only the *mantra* and for the period of the chanting nothing else exists. The power of such *mantra* concentration is to induce a perfectly clear identity with the signified deity (be it Īśvara, Mary or Jesus) as given detailed psychological explanation in Yoga Sutra 1:42. With continued *mantra* concentration all traces of uttered sounds and conceptual meaning are purged until only direct pure perception of the deity or spiritual truth remains. The result is that one not only intimately knows the truth but it becomes the motive of all of one's actions (*Īśvaraprandidhānam* as Patañjali calls it in Yoga Sutra 11:45).

For me personally, the study of Hinduism has been both a confirming and deepening experience. It has confirmed my Protestant Christian experience of the power of the scriptural word but broadened my awareness of how that power functions in processes such as devotional chanting. Study of the Yoga Sutras has led me to discover traditions of daily spiritual discipline within Christianity, of which I was previously unaware. My daily Bible study has been changed from a rational to a devotional exercise and I have been resensitized to the roots of my spiritual foundation in the hearing of the parables of Jesus as a young child. A balance between an intellectual and a devotional experience of the word has been established in my life.

After completing my Ph.D. research with Professor Murti in India, my scholarly curiosity led me to begin a study of how scripture functions in religions other than Hinduism and Christianity, namely, Judaism, Islam, Sikhism and Buddhism. In all these traditions I found roles for both the oral and the written experience of scripture, with the emphasis between the two differing from religion to religion.

In our modern Western way of thinking, "scripture" as a written book is very familiar to us. Today most of us in the West simply take for granted that "scripture" means "holy writ," "holy writing," or "sacred book." Our focus both as lay people and as scholars is on the written or printed character of the holy text. Little attention has been given to its function as spoken and heard sacred word. Reasons for this emphasis upon the written rather than the oral word are not hard to find. In our recent past, at least, the Jewish and Christian traditions have emphasized that study of the written text for both scholarly and devotional purposes. Indeed the very words "scripture" (from the Latin *scriptura*, "a writing") and "bible" (from the Latin *biblia*, "a collection of writings" or "book") have led us to think of divine revelation as a written or printed object. This conception of scripture as written word is bolstered in our culture by the great importance that we attach to the written or printed word. In so many areas of life today, we say that unless you have something in writing, it is not to be trusted. This valuation of the written over the oral-aural experience of language is, however, characteristic of only the most recent period of Western cultural history. Even today it is not typical of the way the experience of the sacred word functions in most of the world religions examined in this book.

As we shall see, a recovery of the oral experience of scripture would seem to be crucial if it is to function as a transforming power in people's lives. More than that, however, the scholarly study of scriptures of the various religions will remain seriously limited and one-sided if it does not become more sensitive to the fundamental oral character of scriptures such as the Veda, the Qur'an, and even the Gospels. This book is directed toward that goal. Its analysis shows that "scripture" has been understood by more people in most times and places (other than in our own modern period) as including both the oral and the written word, and that of the two it is the oral word with its relational context that has the greater power to transform lives.

The book proceeds by looking at each religion in turn under the headings of: oral text, written text, exegesis, devotional experience of the word, and the relationship to other scriptures. Throughout, the terms "scripture" and "text" are used in a generic sense as including both the oral and the written sacred word. The book concludes with a reflection on the nature and function of oral and written scripture in past religious experience, and future requirements for worship, education, and private devotion.

Thanks are due to Gerry Dyer, Jennifer Bailey, Pati Poulton and Vicki Simmons for their long hours spent in preparing the manuscript. Drafts of individual chapters have been read by many colleagues, and I have benefited from their corrections and suggestions for revision. Special thanks are due to Werener H. Kelber for his critical reading of the complete manuscript and his encouragement for its publication. I wish to thank Novin Doostdar and the staff of Oneworld Publications for encouraging me to publish a revised edition of this book which was first published in 1988. For this revised edition, each chapter has been checked by leading scripture specialists of each religion. In all chapters only minor changes were deemed necessary and these have been made. A new Preface has been written.

While I have to thank my Hindu teacher, Professor T. R. V. Murti[11], for reawakening me to the power of the spoken word and of language in general, my greatest debt is owed to my mother who sowed the seed of scripture within me in my childhood, and it is to her that this book is dedicated.

Harold Coward
Director, Centre for Studies in Religion and Society
University of Victoria
Victoria, B.C. Canada

NOTES

1. *The Yoga System of Patañjali*, trans. J. H. Woods (Delhi: Motilal Banarsidass, 1966).
2. For a helpful discussion of the respective functions of reason and revelation in Hindu thought, see T. R. V. Murti's article "Revelation and Reason" in *Studies in Indian Thought*, edited by Harold Coward (New Delhi: Motilal Banarsidass, 1983), pp. 57–71.
3. Henry J. Cadbury, "The New Testament and the Early Christian Literature," *The Interpreter's Bible* (Nashville: Abingdon, 1951), vol. 7, p. 32.
4. See e.g. Jacob Neusner's analysis of the power and practice of the oral Torah in *The Memorized Torah: The Mnemonic System of the Mishnah* (Chicago: Scholars Press, 1985).
5. Amos N. Wilder, *Early Christian Rhetoric: The Language of the Gospel* (Cambridge, Mass.: Harvard University Press, 1978), p. 13.
6. Martin Luther, "Works," as quoted by Willem Jan Koorman, *Luther and the Bible* (Philadelphia: Muhlenberg Press, 1961), p. 201.

7. Paul Ricoeur, "The 'Sacred' Text and the Community," in *The Critical Study of Sacred Texts*, ed. Wendy Doniger O'Flaharty. (Berkeley: Berkeley Religious Studies Series, 1979), pp. 274–75.
8. Walter Ong, *The Presence of the Word* (New Haven: Yale University Press, 1967), p. 282.
9. Leander E. Keck, "Toward a Theology of Rhetoric/Preaching" in *Practical Theology*, Don S. Browning (ed.) (New York: Harper & Row, 1983), p. 135.
10. For a complete presentation of Bhartṛhari's position, see Harold Coward and K. Kunjunni Raja, *The Philosophy of the Grammarians* (Princeton: Princeton University Press, 1990).
11. For a study of the life and scholarly contribution of Professor Murti, see Harold Coward, *T. R. V. Murti* (Delhi: Manohar, 2000).

1

SCRIPTURE IN JUDAISM

Scripture begins and ends the day of a pious Jew:

> Hear, O Israel: The Lord our God, the Lord is One.
>
> You shall love the Lord your God with all your heart, with all your soul, with all your might.
>
> These words which I command you this day shall be in your heart. You shall teach them diligently to your children. You shall talk about them at home and abroad, night and day.
>
> You shall bind them as a sign upon your hand; they shall be as frontlets between your eyes, and you shall inscribe them upon the doorposts of your homes and upon your gates [Deuteronomy 6:4-9].

This scripture prayer is called the Shema from its opening word (*shema*, "hear"). The phrase "Hear (*shema*), O Israel" calls Jews to live out the day "in scripture": proclaiming their Lord YHWH as the one God, and responding to God's love for them with the loving obedience of their whole being (heart, soul, and strength). As verse 3 indicates, this loving response to God should arise from keeping his words in one's heart, and from talking about them from morning until evening both inside and outside the home. Thus the words of scripture are to permeate every sphere of life. By thinking on God's words and meditating about them, obedience to God is not a matter of formal legalism, but a response based on understanding. *Torah*, the Jewish term for scripture, although usually translated as "law," really means "teaching" or "instruction."[1] As the passage from Deuteronomy says, God's teaching must be understood not just intellectually (in the head) but also practiced (in the heart) and implemented (with all one's strength). Having understood God's words for themselves, parents were responsible for teaching them diligently to their children. For Judaism the essence of the relationship between God and his people is that a person's eyes are open to Torah and that one's heart is open to the commandments.[2]

Verse 4 of the prayer gives further emphasis to the complete living of one's life in Torah. Scriptural verses were to be bound as a sign upon one's hand, as frontlets on the forehead, and written upon the gates and doorposts of one's house. The placing of these symbols constantly in front of one, and the chanting of the *shema* morning and evening, forcefully drives home the message that life is to be lived in Torah. The very word *torah* came to serve as a symbol for all of Judaism.[3] When a rabbi spoke of Torah, he used the word to refer to a complete worldview with its distinctive way of life. Torah, the book of scripture, is also something one does.

Jewish tradition teaches that at Mount Sinai God handed down the Torah, which until then had existed only in heaven. The Torah that Moses received was in two parts: the written part, the Pentateuch, and the oral part, which was passed on by word of mouth until it was systematized by the rabbis as the Mishnah (ca. 200 C.E.). Interpretation of the Mishnah resulted in the development of two Talmuds—the Talmud of the Land of Israel (ca. 400 C.E.) and the Talmud of Babylonia (ca. 600 C.E.).[4] Since then interpretation of both the written and the oral (including the Mishnah and the two Talmuds) Torahs has continued right up to the present day. Indeed the total body of scripture and interpretation has become so vast that computers are now being pressed into service in the study of Torah.[5] This entire corpus of materials is also referred to as "Torah."

In our study of the nature and function of scripture in Judaism, we shall employ the following headings: Moses and the Written Torah; The Rabbis and the Oral Torah; Exegesis; The Study of the Torah; and Torah in Relation to Other Scriptures. Throughout, both the traditional viewpoint and the theories of modern scholars will be noted. Our major focus, however, will be on the role Torah has played in the lives of traditional Jews.

MOSES AND THE WRITTEN TORAH (*TORAH SHE-BI KHETAV*)

Traditional Judaism regards Moses as "our rabbi," and as such an image of the ideal Jew. Moses received the Torah, the gift of God to Israel; conformation to the Torah leads one into God's way.[6] Moses is portrayed as a servant who is entrusted by God with all his house. The relationship between Moses and God was not one of servility, but of trust and free exchange between Lord and servant. It is distinguished from the kind of relationship God had with prophets as follows:

> Hear my words: If there is a prophet among you, I the Lord make myself known to him in a vision, I speak to him in a dream. Not so with my servant Moses; he is entrusted with all my house. With him I speak mouth to mouth, clearly and not in dark speech; and he beholds the form of the Lord [Numbers 12:6-8].

As a result of his meeting with God on Mount Sinai, Moses is seen to be in a unique relationship with God, one that is not open to his contemporaries or his successors.[7] "There has not arisen a prophet since in Israel like Moses, whom the Lord knew face to face" (Deuteronomy 34:10). Yet even in this very special relationship, Moses' request to be shown the Lord's glory is denied. God, however, does reveal the divine name to Moses and declares God's freedom and the mystery of this name: "I will be gracious to whom I will be gracious, and will show mercy on whom I will show mercy" (Exodus 33:19). Moses' meeting with God on Mount Sinai results in the proclamation of a covenant that Moses enters into with God on behalf of the people of Israel. This covenant between God and the people is described in the Pentateuch. The Pentateuch contains the teachings that, as their part of the agreement, the Jewish people must obey to maintain their special covenant relationship with God. Thus Moses on Sinai is told by God to go down the mountain and tell the people of Israel:

> You have seen what I did to the Egyptians, and how I bore you on eagles' wings and brought you to myself. Now therefore, if you will obey my voice and keep my covenant, you shall be my own possession among all peoples; for all the earth is mine, and you shall be to me a kingdom of priests and a holy nation [Exodus 19:4-6].

What is involved is much more than just a legal agreement. God, the creator of the universe, chooses Israel to be his people and fulfill his special purpose for them among all the peoples of the earth. Moses, at Sinai, proclaims YHWH, as the God of uncontainable energy, to be a jealous God. It is this combination of power and redemption, so clearly set forth by Moses, that the prophets restate in later centuries. It is also rehearsed daily by each Jew in the Shema: with the opening prayer before the Shema celebrating God as creator of the world, and the closing prayer after the Shema, which speaks of the forgiveness and redemption necessary from God. It is this theme of God not as creator or revealer, but God as redeemer that concludes the twice daily saying of the Shema.[8] Even in his very special relationship with God, Moses' own life is marked by the kind of human frailty that makes him, like all other people, subject to punishment for disobedience.

In Hellenistic Judaism, Moses is praised as the father of learning and skills. Truth in Greek philosophy is seen as coming from the Mosaic fountainhead. For example, Philo, an Alexandrian Jew of the first century C.E., sees Moses as the ideal person, reconciler and mediator between God and humanity, and revealer of the changeless law that existed with God before the creation of the world. In this tradition Moses tends to become superhuman, a divine man.[9]

By contrast, Palestinian Judaism stays closer to the biblical sources and portrays Moses as the "servant of God set apart by marks of patience and humility."[10] Although Moses is seen as the fountainhead of prophecy,[11] the Hebrew Bible is seen to have a threefold division of Torah, prophets, and writings, with a relative degree of holiness in each of them.[12] The prophetic books, along with the writings, are seen as the transmitters of a continuous tradition that begins with the five books of Moses (the Pentateuch). The unity, which begins with Moses and runs throughout these writings, is also extended to the oral law and the whole (both written and oral) referred to as Torah. Thus tradition understands the twofold scripture: both parts are transmitted from Moses to the scribes who pass them on in an unbroken succession to later generations.

The books of the Hebrew Bible are divided into three groups: (a) the Pentateuch consisting of the five books of Moses (Genesis, Exodus, Leviticus, Numbers, Deuteronomy) often simply called "the Torah"; (b) the prophets subdivided into the former prophets (Joshua, Judges, Samuel, Kings) and the latter prophets (Isaiah, Jeremiah, Ezekiel, and the twelve minor prophets); and (c) the writings: Psalms, Proverbs, Job, and the five scrolls (Song of Solomon, Ruth, Lamentations, Ecclesiastes, Esther), Daniel, Ezra-Nehemiah and Chronicles. Scholars are uncertain as to exactly when this collection with its threefold division was completed.[13] Tradition reports that Ezra returned to Jerusalem from exile in Babylon (ca. 400 B.C.E.) bringing with him a copy of the Torah received by Moses from the mouth of God.[14] According to Nehemiah 8 the whole community came together to listen while Ezra read the Torah to them. Since the Torah was in Hebrew, it was orally translated into Aramaic, the language of the people (Nehemiah 8:7-8) as it was read by Ezra. Ezra and the leaders of his day are said to have formed the Great Synagogue, and to them is ascribed the completion of the collection of the law, the prophets, and the writings into what is now called the Hebrew Bible. For modern scholars, the first firm evidence comes from Joshua ben Sira (Ben Sirach), the author of Ecclesiasticus (ca. 180 B.C.E.) who in his praise of the great men of Israel (chapters 44-49) reflects the collecting of books into three sections as described above.[15] The ordering, however, was not fixed and may have been determined by the size of the books that could be fitted together onto a scroll. Ancient scrolls could not accommodate very much. The canon was established in Talmudic times (by the third century C.E.) with only minor adjustments of order occurring later.

Traditional Jewish literature from the early rabbinic period, the first six centuries C.E., gives no direct description of how the books of the Hebrew Bible were collected into the canon. A passage in the Babylonian Talmud comes close to offering such a description but contents itself with ascribing authorship and ignoring the process of collection.[16] From the rabbinic point of view it seems that the crucial requirement for a book to be in the written canon was that it was written down by a prophet, namely, someone under the control of God's Spirit (*ruach*), or to have been inspired by the Holy Spirit. Thus Job is credited to Moses and Ruth to Samuel. Ezra is almost always known as "Ezra the scribe." There seems to have been a clear distinction between the prophets and the writings (e.g., Proverbs) with the latter judged divinely inspired but qualitatively different from the prophetic inspiration of the former. The criterion of prophetic inspiration was also used to close off the canon. As one rabbinic source puts it, "When Haggai, Zechariah, and Malachi died, the Holy Spirit left Israel" (Tosefta Sotah 13:2). The age of the prophets was over and the age of the rabbis had come. Books written later such as Ben Sirach's Ecclesiasticus or other of the Apocrypha books could not be included because the period of inspired prophets had come to an end. To be included books also had to be written in Hebrew or Aramaic.

In traditional Hebrew psychology the experience of prophecy or inspiration occurred when God's Spirit (*ruach*) took possession of a person's human spirit (*nephesh*).[17] The superior power of God's *ruach* over human *nephesh* would allow this to happen even when the human concerned wanted no part of it—as was the case with Jeremiah. Jeremiah pleads with God that he is only a youth and does not know how to speak. But Jeremiah is told that God had chosen him to be a prophet even before he was born and that " 'whatever I command you you shall speak. . . .' Then the Lord put forth his hand and touched my mouth; and the Lord said to me, 'Behold I have put my words in your mouth' " (Jeremiah 1:7-9).

The Bible is authoritative in Judaism because it is the written record of the words that God has put in the mouths of his prophets. Such words from God were experienced as timeless—the chronological concern that dominates much modern scholarship was simply not important. From the perspective of God's timeless words spoken through his prophets, the words of successive prophets could easily be gathered up and put into the mouth of an outstanding prophet (e.g., Moses). They could also be put into the hands of someone specially suited to sustain the revelation being given (e.g., a rabbi). Thus there could be the tradition of an oral Torah, actually the product of generations of interpretation through a long succession of rabbis, yet equally ascribed to Moses together with the ultimately closed written Torah.[18] Likely the rabbis understood themselves to be bringing out from the written Torah that which had always been there in seed form—to add to the nucleus of oral material that had developed prior to the completion of the written Torah. But all of this, both oral and written, was seen as arising from Moses' original experience of God's *ruach*. God's Spirit, given through Moses, rested on those who succeeded him and operated through them. This sense of the continuity of the one original revelation is strongly presented in the important passage of Deuteronomy 18:15, where Moses says, "The Lord your God shall raise up for you a prophet like me, from your midst, from your brothers; you shall listen to him." Peter Craigie notes that the singular "a prophet" is a collective form indicating a succession of prophets—thus, God would raise up a succession of prophets to come who would resemble Moses in their function and authority.[19] However, Jewish tradition would emphasize the uniqueness of the prophecy of Moses.

Authority, for the written Torah, meant the authority given by God's spirit in commissioning someone to speak his word—the role Moses filled in a supreme way. A modern scholar goes on to suggest:

> The intervening generations and the long process of accretion from them dropped out of sight, and the result of it all was thrown back to him in whom the process had begun. . . .

> The same psychology may be seen in the emphasis on the Torah as something given once and for all in its entirety, regardless of the process, so making more natural the ascription to Moses. [20]

From the traditional perspective of early rabbinic Judaism the notion of a progressive revelation was rejected: the revelation to Moses was complete and final. Due to the disobedience and dullness of the people, God had occasion to speak again through later prophets so as to try to get the people to listen. But these later prophets neither added anything new nor took anything away from what Moses had said. They repeat, reinforce, amplify, and explain the law, and thus are on a second level of authority. The prophets and writings simply explain the Pentateuch.[21]

Taking this traditional perspective a step further, the scriptures as the written record of God's voice are, throughout Torah, his revelation. They are all Torah, not in the sense that the authority of the Pentateuch is extended to the latter books, but because in them all, God has revealed himself—his character, his ways, and what he requires of his people in their relations to him and to their fellows. This is the content and meaning of every word of scripture, sometimes easily understandable even to the shallow reader, sometimes open only to those who know how to penetrate to the deeper sense lying below the surface of every word and letter. To discover and teach to the people these deeper meanings present in every word of scripture is the role of the scripture scholar in Judaism. This approach has led to a style of interpretation that focuses on sentences, clauses, phrases, and even single words or letters independent of context or historical situation. Yet all of this could be justified if indeed the writings were the literal record of God's voice. The eternal and universal quality of God's words renders them impervious to mundane human influences.

As the record of God's voice the scriptures were holy and required careful handling in their copying, storage, and speaking. In Judaism the scribe was a professional expert in the writing of Torah scrolls.[22] According to tradition, one should not dwell in a town where there is no scribe. In writing a Torah scroll the scribe must devote the utmost care to the task. He must specially prepare himself by taking a ritual bath so that he will write the names of the Lord with proper devotion and purity. The scribe writing a Torah scroll must not rely on memory but write from a model copy, the *Tikkun Soferim*. It contains the traditional text, specific rules regarding decorative flourishes, spacing regulations, and rules for writing Torah scrolls in which each column begins with the Hebrew letter *vav*. Illustrations are permitted only in the scroll of Esther, but sometimes the name of God has been gilded (although not technically allowable).[23] The writing of the Torah scroll can require a full year of work from an accomplished scribe.

Once completed, the parchment and ink are carefully maintained. As the ink tends to chip with time, the Torah scroll must be periodically examined by a professional scribe who touches up the text and refurbishes the parchment. An imperfect scroll is disqualified from use in the worship ritual. The Torah scroll itself is treated with great respect and love. As part of the worship ritual, its mantle is kissed by the congregation. As a holy article it is carefully kept from unclean places and guarded against falling to the ground. Torah scrolls are stored in an ark, which may be quite decorative. The accidental dropping of a Torah scroll is regarded as a communal disaster requiring the giving of charity and fasting. Biblical manuscripts written for use in phylacteries, and scrolls from the prophets and the writings have a lower status but are given displays of reverence similar to those accorded a Torah scroll. Printed texts are less holy than written scrolls, but still command special treatment. A Hebrew Bible is never to be placed on the floor and must always go on top of other books such as a Talmudic text.[24]

The practice of reading the Torah in public is very old. The earliest reference comes in Deuteronomy 31:10-13 where Moses commands that every seven years all men, women, and children are to gather for public reading of the Torah scroll. The purpose was both educational and for worship. As verse 12 puts it, "in order that they may hear and in order that they may learn, and they shall fear the Lord your God and they shall be careful to do all the words of this law." The second reference is found at Ezra's reading of the Torah to all the people from early morning until noon (Nehemiah 8:1-8). Regular public reading of the Torah in the synagogue has apparently continued since the third century B.C.E.[25]

Philo and Josephus refer to public Torah readings as an ancient practice and the New Testament reports, "For Moses of old time hath in every city them that preach him, being read in the synagogue every sabbath day" (Acts 15:21). The Mishnah indicates that by the end of the second century C.E. there were regular Torah readings on Mondays, on Thursdays, on Sabbaths, with special readings prescribed for festivals and fast days. The Babylonian Talmud gives evidence of a fixed cycle of consecutive readings that finished the Torah in one year, while in Palestine the cycle of readings took three and one-half years to complete the whole Torah. In the early period it was customary to translate the Hebrew into the vernacular language as it was being read. This *targum*, or translation, was done by a special synagogue official. Eventually, however, the practice of translation into the common language was discontinued and everyone was expected to be able to follow the ancient Hebrew. Both the Mishnah and the New Testament refer to the practice of completing the Torah reading with the reading of a passage from a prophetic book. The particular prophetic passage is chosen so as to follow on from the theme of the day's Torah reading. In the synagogue service the readings from the scriptures were accompanied by a homily, if a competent person were present. The Shema is recited as the Torah is removed, and the recitation is preceded and followed by benedictions.[26] The Shema, scriptures, sermon, prayers and benediction were given in Hebrew. The sermons traditionally contained a great deal of quotation from the law, the prophets, and the writings.

As the most holy object for the Jew, the Torah scroll and its reading is hedged about by traditions. Before and after the reading the Torah scroll is taken from the ark and carried in procession around the synagogue. The congregation rises and kisses the scroll as it passes. The reader must prepare carefully by rehearsing the portion to be read. This is especially important because the words of the scroll are unpointed, that is, mostly consonants, with very few indications of vowels and no punctuation. The original Torah scrolls were likewise unpointed, did not specify many of the vowels, and had no word divisions. This means that the reader must know the text by heart or have an excellent knowledge of Hebrew grammar so as to be able to divide into words and to insert the correct vowels as required. The reader is to stand erect and enunciate the words clearly but not excessively. If a word is read incorrectly so that the meaning is changed, it must be repeated correctly. According to tradition the Torah can be read only if ten adult males (a *minyan*) are present. On the Sabbath a minimum of seven persons are to be called up from the congregation to read from the scroll, reading not less than three verses each. In traditional synagogues to this day only adult males are called to read. The seven adult males only symbolically read the scroll—the expert reader reads on their behalf. They say the blessings before and after their section and follow in an undertone. In Reform and some Conservative congregations, however, women are now being called to read the Torah. Some portions of the Torah are more valued than others, for example, the concluding portions of the Pentateuch books, the Song of Moses (Exodus 15:1-21), and the Ten Commandments (Exodus 20:1-14 and Deuteronomy 5:6-18). Persons of special learning or piety are called to read these sections and the congregation stands during the readings. The portions Exodus 32:1-33:6, Leviticus 26:14-43, Numbers 11, and Deuteronomy 28:15-68 are read softly because they deal with Israel's backsliding.[27]

While the words of the Torah have always been held to be important, the addition of music to the speaking of the scripture aided memorization and gave the words added power. The singing or cantillation of the Torah appears to have developed in a systematic way from the sixth century onward. "Having begun with the simple indication of the traditional places of the cadences, they ultimately arrived at a 'learned art' of Bible chant, prescribing how the reader was to organize his recitation."[28] The aim was to use the music to highlight the meaning of the words by making the chanted Bible verse into a continuous chain of musical motives. "Since the single motives are often linked by a short bridge of linear recitation, this kind of chant may also be likened to a string of beads."[29] Through the centuries, different communities developed different styles of scripture cantillation so that Jewish reading practices of today form a living museum of chanting styles. Over the years Jewish practice has been influenced by the customs of other traditions, for example, Christian Gregorian chant.[30] The added power of the sung or chanted scripture is caught in the following quotation describing a worship service in a junior college:

> "When the rabbi began to sing the blessings, every one of the girls began to weep. . . ." The words were important, but when the singing began,

> the Jewish girls began to weep. The music touched deep hidden chords within their being—memories, hopes, dreams—the heavenly echo within our earthly clod.[31]

Parchment scrolls containing scripture are not limited to public readings; they have private uses as well. Phylacteries containing such texts are worn on the head and weaker arm as part of the morning prayers. At every entrance to a room in a Jewish home (with the exception of bathrooms) a *mezuzah* or small scroll containing Deuteronomy 6:4-9 and 11:13-21 placed in a decorative container is attached to the doorpost. In addition to these private ritual activities, the daily study of scripture has traditionally been a most important part of Jewish life. Such study according to the rabbinic ideal was a part of daily family life as well as a planned activity within the Jewish community. Study included not only Bible but rabbinic texts as well.

In Rabbinic Judaism, to enable the individual to engage in both private study and public reading of the Torah, special schooling was necessary in which the learning of the Hebrew language was emphasised. Thus each community maintained a school in addition to a synagogue. In its fullest development the school was divided into an elementary school (*Bet Sefer*) which focused on teaching the reading and writing of ancient Hebrew, the language of the Bible, and an advanced school (*Bet Midrash*) in which both the written and oral Torahs were taught. A graduate from such a school was expected to be able to read from all three parts of the Hebrew Bible (Pentateuch, prophets, writings) and therefore prepared to give public readings in the synagogue service. Traditionally only boys received this education. A full education required not only the learning of the Hebrew language and the ability to read scripture (which dealt only with the literal sense) but also the ability to interpret the scripture through the guidance of the oral Torah. This higher religious education had for its subject matter tradition in the widest sense of the term. In the classical period the two branches of advanced education included: *Halakah*, the precisely formulated precepts of the oral law; and *haggadah*, the nonjuristic teaching—religious, moral, and historical. These in turn involved two methods: midrash (scriptural exegesis) and mishnah (the teaching of traditions unconnected to a scriptural text). Mastery of all of this demanded intelligence and hard work. Moore notes, "The method of the schools developed not only exact and retentive memory and great mental acuteness, but an exhaustive and ever-ready knowledge of every phrase and word of scripture."[32] The classical medieval pattern had a boy (girls traditionally did not engage in Torah study) begin elementary or Bible school at age five, go on to advanced school at age ten (Mishnah first and then Talmud at fifteen), and marry at eighteen. Even though not fully realized by all, this education allowed many men to join in the discussions that took place in the school every sabbath afternoon and to fulfill the role of teachers within their own families. Moore concludes, "The high intellectual and religious value thus set on education was indelibly impressed on the mind, and one may say on the character of the Jew, and the institutions created for it have perpetuated themselves to the present day."[33]

In the modern period, and especially in diaspora situations in which Jews are a minority group within a majority culture, this classical pattern of schooling has been seriously challenged. Responses to this challenge have varied widely from the engaging of private tutors (*melammedim*) to the operation of exclusive private schools or special sections in established schools and universities. In North America, for example, the most common solution was the operation of special schools (Talmud Torahs) after public school hours. In such schools the children learn Hebrew, the Bible, liturgy, religious practices and traditions, and Jewish history. There are also Jewish day ("parochial") schools, which integrate the public and Jewish curricula within the traditional public school timetable.[34]

THE RABBIS AND THE ORAL TORAH

Already we have come to sense that in Judaism "Torah" has an ever expanding meaning. At its narrowest the Torah refers to the five books of Moses, the Pentateuch: Genesis, Exodus, Leviticus, Numbers, and Deuteronomy. Torah in this sense contains doctrines, laws, narratives, the fundamental written teachings of Judaism. It is this Torah scroll that calls forth the greatest sense of holiness in the synagogue service (the standing and touching by the congregation). Second, the Torah comes to include all of the Hebrew Bible, the prophets and the writings along with the Pentateuch. This corresponds to what Protestant Christians call "the Old Testament." Third, "Torah" expands to include study of the Hebrew Bible *and* the traditions of Israel as they have accumulated over many centuries. In this last expansion, leadership has been provided by the rabbis. Although some rabbis were Pharisees, the connection between the two groups is not clear. During the period 200 B.C.E.-100 C.E. the Pharisees contended with the Sadducees for dominance. One of the main points of contention was over the meaning of "Torah." According to rabbinic literature the Sadducees restricted Torah to the Pentateuch and its literal interpretation; however, the Pharisees contended that alongside the written Torah there existed an oral Torah that, like the written Torah, had been given to the people by Moses at Sinai. Soon after the destruction of the Temple in Jerusalem (70 C.E.) the Sadducees virtually disappeared, leaving the Pharisees to become the dominant force in Judaism. The formulations of their heirs, the rabbis, became and remained normative for Judaism right up to the present day.

According to the rabbis the oral Torah is both the authoritative interpretation of the written Torah and a separate Mosaic tradition. The complete Torah, then, is composed of two parts given by Moses at Sinai, one written and the other oral.[35] There is a close bond between the two parts, neither of which can exist without the other. "The Oral Law depends upon the Written Law, but at the same time, say the rabbis, it is clear that there can be no real existence for the Written Law without the Oral."[36] Arguments for this contention are offered as follows. The oral is needed to interpret the written. Much that is in the written is obscure and requires explanation. Even that which seems plain is not, for the written Torah appears to contain internal contradictions or problems that require clarification. For example, the prohibition against doing work on the Sabbath in the written Torah does not specify the nature of the work. Nor are the punishments related to the breaking of such a law clearly spelled out. For all of these reasons it was necessary that God give the oral Torah to Moses as the means by which the written law could be interpreted and applied to daily life. Through the oral Torah the unchanging written Torah could be adapted to changing circumstances. Thus tradition sees an intimate reflexive relationship between the two Torahs. The oral Torah is seen to have its basis in, and derive its validity from, explicit verses in the written Torah. At the same time, however, the written Torah itself obtains its full validity and authority for practical application in daily life from the oral Torah. In specific and temporary situations the oral Torah may even need to set aside a stated requirement of the written law. Just as in certain situations a physician may need to amputate a hand or leg in order to preserve life, so also in certain situations the oral law may rule that some requirement of the written Torah be temporarily transgressed in order that the whole Torah be preserved.[37]

The rabbis imply that the nature of the oral Torah is paradoxical in that although it was given by God to Moses at Sinai, it is not fixed but is alive and constantly evolving. This is why it could not be written down. The oral Torah was received by Moses and transmitted orally to Joshua and the sages or teachers following him right down to the great rabbis, Akiba, Hillel, and Shammai. In this oral transmission, the oral Torah is understood as both fixed and evolving from generation to generation. It is fixed in the sense that the essence of whatever comes to be revealed by later generations of rabbis was already present implicitly or in seed form in the oral law given by God to Moses. Consequently, from the point of view of its functional essence, the whole of the oral law was given to Moses at Sinai. Jewish tradition sums up this viewpoint with the following story about Moses:

> When he [Moses] ascended to Heaven and the Holy One, blessed be He, showed him R. Akiba sitting and expounding, Moses did not understand what he was saying, but nevertheless "his mind was set at ease" when he heard that, in reply to a question of his disciples: "Master, how do you know this?" R. Akiba answered: "It is a Halakha of Moses given at Sinai."[38]

Eventually through the discussions and teachings of the leading rabbis such as Akiba and Meir, the oral Torah evolved into a more systematic form until the final edition was completed as the Mishnah by Judah the Patriarch ca. 200 C.E.

The Mishnah takes the form of tersely formulated majority opinions, occasionally reporting the contrary opinion of certain significant scholars. The Mishnah is formed of six divisions divided into tractates. In terms of their relationship to the written Torah, the material in the Mishnah may be grouped into three categories: (a) tractates that systematically develop what is said in written Torah, amplifying and completing these ideas; (b) tractates that take up the facts of written Torah, but work on them to produce surprising conclusions; and (c) tractates that either take up problems never suggested by written Torah or use insignificant details to develop full blown and often surprising theories (e.g., the comparing of a text and utensil in discussion of the theory of uncleanness).[39] Thus some tractates of the Mishnah closely parallel written Torah, some simply use scripture as an occasion for their own theorizing, and some fall in between. The rabbis of the Mishnah conceded to written Torah the highest authority. In attempting to deal with their own world the rabbis brought to the scriptures the questions generated by their own times. In their interpretations they developed their own ideas as to what was important in scripture. Their approach might be characterized as: "All of scripture is authoritative, but only some scriptures are relevant."[40] The result of their analysis was a systematic statement about the meaning of scripture appropriate to their time. Neusner notes that their approach was not unlike that of modern biblical scholars:

> When the framers of the Mishnah spoke about the Priestly passages of the Mosaic law codes, with deep insight they perceived profound layers of meaning embedded within those codes. What they have done with the Priestly Code (P), moreover, they have also done, though I think less coherently, with the bulk of the Deuteronomic laws and with some of the Covenant Code. But their exegetical triumph—exegetical, not merely eisegetical—lies in their handling of the complex corpus of materials of P. Theirs is a powerful statement *on* the meaning of Scripture, not merely a restatement of its meaning.[41]

What the rabbis of the Mishnah were doing was not out of character with the activity of other groups during the same period (200 B.C.E. - 200 C.E.). The decentralization of the Jews brought on by the Exile produced many diverse postexilic communities. Although they all laid claim to the same scriptural authority, they differed radically as to its meaning and application in daily life. The challenge of how to bring the ancient laws and prophecies into relation with their current and diverse experiences of life was the crisis facing the Judaism of the day. Different groups responded differently, and their different interpretations of scripture became the basis of group boundaries as well as the content of new religious behaviors, ideas, and hopes.[42] For example, an initiate into the Essene (Dead Sea) community was taught that the Essenes had the true meaning of scripture. Their claim was that their founder-teacher had been given divine guidance into the interpretation of the laws of Moses. As a result two Torahs were identified: the exoteric Torah revealed to all Israel at Sinai, and an esoteric Torah, known only to the Dead Sea community and providing the basis of the rules for their daily life. In the Alexandrian Jewish community another method—that of allegory—was adopted. Faced with a clash between

Hebrew and Greek values, biblical allegory allowed Alexandrian Jews like Philo to interpret one worldview in the terms of another. Torah is identified with Sophia, or Divine Wisdom, and the Stoic truths are discovered as the scripture's inner essence. For Philo, Abraham and Sarah become figures of ethical and spiritual values, and ritual and legal requirements are read as guides to meditation and inner piety. In Philo's hands the written Torah becomes nothing less than a spiritual-philosophical document, "an expression of divine wisdom given to humankind to guide its perfectibility."[43] Yet another group, the Sadducees, wanted to hold to the Priestly interpretation of the written Torah in the context of Temple ritual.

It was in this larger context that the rabbis, who may have had some relationship with the Pharisees, put forward a remarkable claim in regard to the oral tradition eventually collected in the Mishnah—namely, that it had been divinely given to Moses at Sinai, alongside the written Torah, and that it had been preserved through an unbroken chain of oral transmission until it was finally redacted by Judah the Patriarch ca. 200 C.E. This approach allows if not for a "progressive revelation" at least for "progressive interpretation of the revelation." The interpretations of the rabbis were claimed to have been given already at Sinai. "When God spoke 'all these words' (Exodus 20:1) at Sinai, said R. Elazar ben Azariah, he spoke the exoteric Torah and the various—even contradictory—words of human exegesis. Thus oral Torah is a progressive unfolding of the mysterious plenitude of the original divine revelation."[44] One traditional source even went so far as to proclaim, "The Holy One, Blessed is He, speaks Torah out of the mouths of all rabbis."[45] One question that might be asked of the Pharisaic/rabbinic tradition is this: "If the oral Torah has been successfully transmitted from teacher to student down through the centuries, why was it necessary for Judah the Patriarch to write it down and in so doing remove it from the oral tradition with all its advantages for future evolution? An answer is offered by Rosenbaum as follows:

> . . . the origin of the oral law can be traced at least to the Zugot, possibly to the Great Assembly and Ezra, and by tradition, to Moses himself. From the time of Hillel and Shammai onward, large collections of *halakah* [oral laws] were assembled and transmitted orally from teacher to student to avoid any challenge to the Written Law. However, between 66 and 135 C.E. three Jewish revolts erupted against the Romans, two of them in the land of Israel itself. This resulted in the brutal suppression of Jewish religious rights and scholarly leadership. For this reason Rabbi Judah the Patriarch reduced to writing the fundamental Oral Law ca. 200 C.E.[46]

Following the systematizing and writing down of the Mishnah, rabbinical academies in Babylonia and the land of Israel produced commentaries on the Mishnah resulting finally (between ca. 400-600 C.E.) in the formulation of the two Talmuds. These will be discussed in the next section on exegesis.

The claim that the material composing the Mishnah had been orally learned and transmitted for centuries from teacher to student was recently supported by Jacob Neusner in his book *The Memorized Torah*.[47] Specifically, Neusner examines the form in which the material of the Mishnah is organized and concludes that the way in which the material is grouped and presented supports the oral-transmission claim. In the course of his analysis, however, Neusner suggests that memorization is not just a neutral technique but indeed allows for the "grasping of consciousness at a deep level." Since this suggestion supports a thesis that will be developed later in this book, namely, that memorized scripture has a much greater power to transform consciousness than written scripture, we shall look at Neusner's study in some detail.

Neusner notes that the Mishnah frames its ideas in syllogistic patterns. "The smallest whole units of discourse (cognitive units), defined as groups of sentences that make a point completely and entirely on their own, become intelligible on three bases: logical, topical and rhetorical."[48] In his book Neusner claims to prove that it is the confluence of logic, topic, and rhetoric that generates at the deepest structure of the Mishnah's language a set of mnemonic patterns that make possible the easy memorization of the text of the Mishnah. Memorization is a crucial point for our discussion of oral Torah. To aid in memorization the rabbis arranged the material on a topic in groups of three or five, or multiples of three or five. The same topic would be presented, say, three times in three different examples, each of which would be introduced by a common sequence of words. When the topic changes, the formal pattern also changes. The repeating and changing language patterns of the Mishnah text enabled the professional tradition-memorizers, *Tannaim* ("people who repeat"), to learn and recall large amounts of material. Neusner claims to be able to pick out the subunits of discourse in the tractates by studying the changing language patterns that mark off distinctive topics.[49] The smallest syllogistic pattern in the Mishnah follows the formula of "If such and such is the case, then so and so is the rule"—a propositional statement which finds resolution in a rule or an answer. Although in themselves such mnemonic devices do not demonstrate that Mishnah materials come from what was originally an oral tradition (things could have been first written and then memorized), other evidence along with internal evidence does support the claim. Indeed the evidence suggests that even after it was formulated and written down by Patriarch Judah, the Mishnah continued to function as an oral text.

In the entire Talmudic literature we do not find that *a book* of the Mishnah was ever consulted in case of controversies over a particular reading. Rabbis did possess written *halakot*, or oral law statements and comments, but they were private notes without legal authority. The Mishnah was "published," consulted, and passed on in a different way:

> A regular oral . . . edition of the Mishnah was in existence, a fixed text recited by the Tannaim of the college. The Tanna (repeater, reciter)

> committed to memory the text of certain portions of the Mishnah, which he subsequently recited in the college in the presence of the great masters of the law. When the Mishnah was committed to memory and the Tannaim recited it in the college it was thereby published. . . .[50]

The authority of the college reciter (*Tanna*) was that of a "published book."

According to Saul Lieberman, at the time of Akiba the body of the Mishnah was made up only of the opinions of the representatives of the schools of Shammai and Hillel and their predecessors. But Akiba organized matters, sifting through the whole oral collection and crystallizing it into a definite shape—the new Mishnah. Akiba then orally taught the new Mishnah to the first *Tanna*, then to the second *Tanna* and so on until all knew it by heart. They then all repeated it in the college in the presence of Akiba, who supervised the recitation and corrected any errors. Neusner observes that analysis of the internal structure of the Mishnah supports the theory advanced by Lieberman.[51] Accepting this reconstruction of the rabbinic practice of Akiba, we can see that the oral transmission of a text was no primitive or chance affair, but was done in a sophisticated academic manner with careful checks to ensure validity was being maintained.

Neusner's analysis of the internal structure of the Mishnah not only supports Lieberman but adds additional information as to the nature of the memorization process. The materials are organized in such a way that grammatical and syntactical distinctions accompany the movement from one thematic, conceptual, or other intermediate division of a tractate to the next. Further, the organizer of the materials grouped it into sequences of threes or fives.[52] The result of all of this is a distinctively shaped language which speaks in rhymes and balanced, matched declarative sentences, imposing on the conceptual, factual prose of law a peculiar kind of poetry.[53]

Language, as Neusner correctly observes, not only contains culture but also expresses a worldview and ethos. By putting the Mishnaic materials into language suited for memorization, the last generation of Mishnaic rabbis may well have been indicating that these are the things which we know for certain and should be memorized and taken to heart. Such memorized material has a special status. It exists in consciousness at a deeper level than the written Torah (except when the written Torah is also memorized), or other commentaries like the Tosefta, which can be consulted. The memorized oral Torah of the Mishnah is the "Torah of the heart." This special knowledge is set apart from other worldly knowledge. It is not useful for communicating with others and the everyday world.

> Rather, it distinguishes its users from that ordinary world, and sets apart one aspect of their interrelationships, the one defined in the Mishnah, from such other aspects as do not require speech in a few patterns and a kind of poetry. . . . So far as the Mishnah was meant to be memorized by a particular group of people for a distinctive purpose, it is language

which includes few and excludes many, unites those who use it and sets them apart from others who do not."[54]

Even the nature of the mnemonic pattern used is not neutral but conveys a message about reality to those who memorize it. It is a sense for the deep, inner logic of word-patterns, of grammar and syntax, rather than for external similarities, that governs the Mishnaic mnemonic. It identifies the relationship, rather than the thing or person, which is related as primary. Neusner observes:

> The thing in itself is less than the thing in cathexis with other things, so too the person. The repetition of form creates form. But what is repeated here is not form, but a formulary pattern, a pattern effected through persistent grammatical or syntactical relationships and affecting an infinite range of diverse objects and topics. Form and structure emerge not from concrete, formal things but from abstract and unstated, ubiquitous and powerful relationships.[55]

The point Neusner is making is a subtle but important one. The patterns employed for memorization, not only help one to memorize, but also evoke a sense of reality which embodies the teaching of the oral Torah. The medium of memorization powerfully evokes the message. In repeating the Mishnah aloud the Tannaim heard not only the abstract relationships expressed in the rules being recited, but also deeper principles. What was memorized,

> was a fundamental notion, expressed in diverse examples but in recurrent rhetorical-syntactical patterns. Accordingly, what they could and did hear was what lay far beneath the surface of the rule: both the unstated principle and the unsounded pattern. . . . The Mishnah talks of this-worldly things, but these things stand for and evoke another world entirely.[56]

Just as in the Covenant of the written law, "relationship with God" is the underlying principle of reality behind what is said in the Mishnah. The genius of the Mishnah is its transformation of common secular language into sacred speech. In Neusner's view it is the imposition of fixed patterns of syntax, which transforms talk about common things into sacred language. The Mishnah becomes a vehicle of sanctification, a transformer of human consciousness. Part of the reason the Mishnah can do this is that it presupposes the existence of Scripture. It would be difficult to make sense of the details of any tractate without knowledge of the written Torah. These resonances from scripture help to give transformative power to the words of the Mishnah.

The sanctifying power of the Mishnah also depends on the listener's ability to put many things together and to draw important conclusions. It is the mind of a hearer, which already knows Scripture and is intensely concentrated, that makes sense of the otherwise superficial incompleteness and disorder of the Mishnaic sentences. "Hearing discrete rules, applicable to cases related in theme and form, but not in detail and concrete actualities, the hearer puts together two things. First is the repetition of grammatical usages. Second is the repetition of the same principle, the presence of which is implied by the repetition of syntactical patterns in diverse cases."[57] All of this requires an active intellect, scriptural sophistication, and profound sensitivity on the part of the hearer. In this sense the Mishnah serves both as a book of laws and as a book for learners—a school book that not only teaches its hearers to obey laws but leads them to participate in a deeper intuition of the truth of reality. As is the case in all such intuitions, scientific and religious, there is a need for rational analysis to follow. Thus the Mishnah takes for granted that exegesis of its fixed text will be undertaken by the hearers. The Mishnah requires commentary and anticipates that its audience is capable of undertaking such work.[58] It is no surprise, then, to find the Mishnah evoking the commentaries of the Talmuds within Judaism. Such commentaries attempt to understand rationally the transcendent purpose and revelation of the Mishnah.

Neusner suggests that the transcendent purpose of the Mishnah is to have language replace the Temple cult. If the performance of rituals within the Temple exposes the lines of God's revealed reality, then thinking about these rituals outside the Temple, even without the possibility of performing them, has the same result. In the crisis of the destruction of the Temple, the rabbis through their specific use of language in the oral Torah, provided a means for internalizing the priestly ritual of Judaism. Instead of Temple sacrifice, study, learning, and exposition became the basic activity by which one was sanctified. ". . . It is by the formalization of speech, its limitation to a few patterns, and its perfection through the creation of patterns of relationships in particular, that the old nexus of Heaven and earth, the cult, now is to be replicated in the new and complementary nexus, cultic speech about things."[59]

Memorization and repetition of the Mishnah is also fundamental to its sanctifying power. Whereas writing and reading are routine, says Neusner, memorization is special. When one knows the Mishnah and its scriptural resonances by heart, something happens that does not happen when one just reads it in a book or scroll. It is that when one walks in the street, when one sits at home, when one sleeps, and when one awakes, one carries it in one's deepest consciousness.[60] It enables the Jew to make the Shema present at the deepest level so that he or she lives in Torah!

Although he fully accepts and values the oral nature of the Mishnah, Neusner, as a modern scholar, challenges the traditional view that the oral law was given at Sinai. In Neusner's view the two-Torah idea is a myth created by rabbinic Judaism after the Mishnah had been put together.[61] After analyzing the Mishnah, Neusner finds that it refers back to no source of truth other than the written Torah, that it lays no claim to come from Sinai; that it does not invoke the names of prophets, and that it does not call itself a book of Torah or revelation.[62] Shortly after its completion the Mishnah gained an exalted political status as the constitution of the Jewish government of the land of Israel. This raised questions about the status of Mishnah law in relation to the law of the Torah. The need to answer these questions, says Neusner, resulted in the formation of the myth of the two Torahs. Already in the Mishnah tractate Abot, it is said that Moses received Torah at Sinai and handed it on to Joshua and onward, ending up reciting the names of authorities of the Mishnah such as Hillel and Shammai. In this way the connection of the Mishnah to Sinai is suggested in Abot.[63] Later, some two hundred years beyond the closure of the Mishnah, the need to explain the standing and origin of the Mishnah led some to posit two things: (a) God's revelation of the Torah at Sinai encompassed the Mishnah as well as the written scripture; and (b) the Mishnah was handed down through oral formulation and oral transmission from Sinai to the framers of the Mishnah. These two convictions, claims Neusner, emerge from the references of both Talmuds to a dual Torah—one part in writing, the other oral and now the Mishnah.[64]

Neusner makes clear in his analysis that Abot (ca. 250 C.E.) did not know of a dual Torah,[65] nor did the Tosefta (collected ca. 400 C.E.).[66] It is when we come to the Talmud of the Land of Israel (ca. 400 C.E.) that the Mishnah is first seen to be treated as Torah, and the myth is stated in penultimate form.[67] In this Talmud, says Neusner, the word "Torah" has ceased to refer to a specific thing. Its meaning is enlarged to include the scripture, the Mishnah, or even the act of study itself as a way to salvation. To the rabbis of this Talmud, "the principal salvific deed was to 'study Torah,' by which they meant memorizing Torah-sayings by constant repetition, and, as the Talmud itself amply testifies (for some sages), profound analytic enquiry into the meaning of those sayings."[68] Also new is the fact that this kind of Torah study is judged to have power. And if the words and their study have power, then this power is shared by the rabbi or sage, the teacher of these words. So the word "Torah" also comes to stand for the rabbi or sage who is identified with its power.[69] Neusner even goes so far as to speak of the sage as "Torah incarnate."[70] Thus Neusner sees the rabbis, in their need to account for the Mishnah, as expanding the meaning of "Torah" from its original reference to the written Torah scroll to include the tractates of the oral Mishnah and finally to embrace the rabbi or sage and the act of study as a means of power and salvation.

Not all scholars agree with Neusner's theory. For example, Daniel Jeremy Silver states that the tradition of an all-encompassing Torah is ancient and was not an invention of the Pharisaic rabbis.[71] What the rabbis did was to conceptualize and systematize an oral practice and a broad notion of Torah as the way of life that had been growing down through the years. Traditional scholars would of course reject Neusner's "Myth theory" on the basis that God really gave the two Torahs to Moses at Sinai. Whether there were two Torahs from the beginning or, if not, when the oral Torah notion first came into prominence is obviously an old dispute within the Jewish tradition. Urbach reports:

> At first there were no disagreements in Israel. One Torah went forth from the Chamber of Hewn Stone to all Israel, but when the Sanhedrin was abolished and the number of the disciples of Shammai and Hillel that did not wait sufficiently upon the scholars increased, the disputes in Israel multiplied (*Tosefta Sanhedrin* i, 1) "and two Torahs were formed" (*Tosefta Sota* xiv, 9). This dictum is preceded there by a parallel saying "When the proud of heart increased, the disputes multiplied in Israel and became two Torahs."[72]

EXEGESIS

While the scripture proper of Judaism is taken as including the two Torahs, the written and the oral, the term "exegesis" includes a vast range of materials from the Abot and Tosefta to the two Talmuds and the Haggadah. Indeed, "exegesis" in Judaism might well be extended even further. As Michael Fishbane puts it:

> Judaism is an exegetical religious culture par excellence, and the Hebrew scriptures is its foundational document and principal text. For more than two millennia, it has been reinterpreted for simple meaning, for spiritual moral insight, and for legal applicability. Whether one turns to early halakhic (legal) or aggadic (moral) texts to medieval homilies or arcane poetry, to philosophical theologies or mystical theosophies, to moral tractates or late legal codifications—the matter is the same: Biblical exegesis serves either as the explicit structural feature of the composition, or as the implicit religious foundation of the very possibility of composition.[73]

Judaism places scripture at the very center of its religious and cultural life. Scripture gave structure and authority to the theological speculations, the moral values, and the folk customs of the people. Up until 200 C.E. the focus of exegesis tended to be on the written Torah, appropriating the work associated with Ezra and his followers, traditionally called the Great Synagogue. During the period 200-500 C.E., however, a shift began to occur. While Midrash continues to be composed on the written Torah (e.g., the great commentaries *Genesis Rabba* and *Leviticus Rabba*), the biblically based halakic commentaries Mekilta, Sifra, Sifre give way to the authority of the Mishnah. Although scripture continues to be cited in the Talmuds, the chief exegetical focus in the Talmuds is the elucidation of the Mishnah. The result is a shift in emphasis away from the written Torah to the oral Torah as codified in the Mishnah as the focal point for Jewish study. Let us briefly trace the history of the exegesis of both Talmud and scripture right up to the present day.

There are two Talmuds, one from the land of Israel, one from Babylonia. The earlier one, the Talmud of the land of Israel (the Jerusalem Talmud) was written about 400 C.E. and offers a line-by-line exegesis of the Mishnah, often citing for the purposes of elucidation the Tosefta as well. In addition to focusing on the specific ideas in the Mishnah text, the Talmud goes on to a systematic and wide-ranging expansion of the ideas abstracted from the basic text. The Talmudic discussion often involves discussion of problems of biblical exegesis, theology, and principles of law.[74] Neusner suggests that the main difference in the Jerusalem Talmud from Abot and the Tosefta is the independent frame of mind of the Talmud. Whereas both Abot and the Tosefta remain closely tied to the Mishnah in their style of writing, the Talmud keeps a distance from the Mishnah. Individual Mishnaic sentences are picked up one by one and reworked in accordance with the Talmud's own interest. Rather than using the rhetoric and language of the Mishnah (Mishnaic Hebrew), the Talmud is written in a kind of scholastic Aramaic.[75] Talmudic commentaries on all Mishnaic tractates have not survived antiquity, and it remains unclear precisely what explains this. In commenting, the Jerusalem Talmud draws heavily on materials from the Tosefta.

The Jerusalem Talmud fully accepts the two Torahs (one written and one oral) perspective and ascribes the authorship of both to God through Moses. This Talmud presents us with a succinct and exhaustive description of what the Torah way of life demands—namely, "perpetual concentration on teachings of the Torah and their performance, to the exclusion of other thoughts and deeds."[76] It is not just the intellectual repeating of the words of Torah but the humble acting in accordance with them that is required. Validation that a person is a true scholar of and living in accord with Torah was said to consist in the ability to perform miracles. As the person became more holy, through Torah study and practice, so the person's supernatural powers increased. But the goal of Torah study, according to the Talmud, is not just intellectual knowledge of the revelation or miraculous powers, but salvation. The traditional claim that Israel would be saved by obedience to the Torah (as found in the Hebrew Bible) is expanded and interpreted in the Talmud. The stories repeated in the Jersualem Talmud treat the word "Torah" (whether written scroll, oral Mishnah, or the act of study) as the source and guarantor of salvation. For the Talmudic rabbis the principal salvific deed was to "study Torah," by which they meant memorizing and constantly repeating Torah sayings, as well as inquiring into the deep meaning of those sayings.[77] Such Torah study transforms and saves a person. Through the interpretation of the Talmud, says Neusner, the term "Torah" no longer merely specifies a specific scroll but now expands to include the oral Mishnah, the process of study itself, and is perhaps supremely symbolized in the rabbi or teacher (sage) of Torah himself.

> The sage was holy because he knew Torah. That meant that, in his act of learning Torah, his work of memorizing and repeating sayings, and his dialectical arguments on the amplification and analysis of what he learned, the sage took over the work of Moses in receiving and interpreting the will of God. This made the sage equivalent to the prophet, indeed, superior to him. . . .

> What has happened here is that the sage finds his way into the center of the Torah, so that a single symbol—the Torah—now stands for the sage and his power, as much as for the Torah and its power.[78]

The significant contribution of the Jerusalem Talmud was to highlight the incarnation of the Torah in the sage. But this sage was not otherworldly. What made the sage distinctive was his combination of this-worldly authority and power (as clerk of the court) with his otherworldly influence. Consistent with Israel's past history, the Talmud kept a tight union between salvation and law, the supernatural power of the sage and his lawgiving authority. As a kind of "living Torah," the very deeds of the sage, as much as his words, served to reveal Torah law.[79] An example of the way in which all of this is interpreted from scripture is found in the following exegesis of Exodus 24:12 (quoted by R. Levi bar Hamma in the name of R. Simeon b. Laqish):

> What is it that is written: . . . *and I will give thee tables of stone and a law and commandments which I have written that thou mayest teach them? Tables* are the ten commandments, a *law* is the Pentateuch, commandments are the Mishnah, *which I have written* is the Prophets and the Hagiographa, *that thou mayest teach them* is the Talmud. This teaches that all were given to Moses on Sinai.[80]

The specific method adopted by the sages in fulfilling their teaching of salvation may be seen in their approach to the interpretation of scripture. They took for granted that the world they knew in the fourth century C.E. had flourished a thousand years earlier. As Neusner puts it, they simply projected their own worldview back onto the biblical stories and figures they were interpreting. "Biblical and talmudic authorities lived on a single plane of being, in a single age of shared discourse; the Mishnah and associated documents amply restated propositions held for all time and proved in scripture too."[81]

The other major center of rabbinical study was located in Babylonia. There, too, a major commentary on the Mishnah was developed and completed ca. 500 C.E., about one hundred years after the Talmud of the land of Israel. The Babylonian Talmud is more developed and comprehensive than the Jerusalem Talmud. In addition the textual condition of the Babylonian Talmud was preserved more satisfactorily. Thus it gradually became dominant in the teaching of Jewish law and theology. The contents of the Babylonian Talmud also helped to ensure its central position. It tended to include anything presented in other documents. Thus the Talmud of Babylonia serves as a kind of *summa* and encyclopedia of Torah. It depends heavily on what circulated earlier as well as preserving many other things. Neusner summarizes the modes of discourse of the Babylonian Talmud as four: "(1) exegesis of Mishnah and Tosefta, (2) abstract discourse on law in general, (3) exegesis of Scripture and (4) abstract discourse on mythic or theological themes of Scripture in general."[82] The

Babylonian Talmud brings together the various types of discourse on the Mishnah and on scripture, and forms them into a single composition.

The Babylonian Talmud embraces the expanded meanings of the word "Torah" already noted in the Jerusalem Talmud, but perhaps gives more emphasis to the national dimension of the salvation to be realized through Torah study. For example, in the Babylonian Talmud we find God saying, "If a man occupies himself with the study of the Torah, works of charity, and prays with the community, I account it to him as if he had redeemed me and my children from among the nations of the world."[83] Also in the Babylonian Talmud, the study of the Torah takes the place of offering sacrifices in the Temple. If a person studies Torah, it is as if he has rebuilt the Temple—the central focus of Jewish national spirituality.[84] In this sense a connection was made with the important concept of the Messiah. One key task of the Messiah was described as the rebuilding of the Temple and the renewal of sacrifices. By studying the Torah, the disciple took part in the messianic process. The action of study bore the promise of rebuilding the Temple and bringing the Messiah. His act of learning was to be compared to an act of sacrifice in the cult, a foretaste of the messianic time to come. In terms of the implications of Torah study for Israel as a nation, the Babylonian Talmud in a long and important statement at the beginning of the tractate Abodah Zarah explains that such study defines who is Israel and who is not. God is pictured with a Torah scroll in his arms calling the nations before him one after the other. As each comes forward, God asks: "Wherewith have you occupied yourselves?" Rome, as the most important, comes forward first, confessing to having spent its time building baths and markets, and accumulating much gold—all for the sake of Israel so that they might have the leisure to study Torah. But Rome is condemned as foolish for having chased after its own desires rather than studying Torah. Persia then steps forward and confesses to having spent time in building bridges, waging wars, and capturing cities, again, all for the sake of Israel that they might study Torah. Like the Romans the Persians, too, are condemned as having been foolish not to study Torah. Then all the other nations are called up, but protest by saying they did not accept Torah and therefore should not be held responsible. To deflect attention from themselves, they ask God if Israel, who accepted the Torah, has lived up to it. God responds by producing evidence that Israel has observed the Torah. The nations then plead with God, "Offer us the Torah and we shall obey it." God's response is that they, like Israel, have had the Torah but have not lived up to it.[85] So Torah serves to distinguish between Israel and the empires of Rome and Persia as well as among all nations. Only because of Israel's Torah study does Israel enjoy God's favor. If this passage of the Babylonian Talmud is taken seriously it suggests that the keeping and studying of the Torah is not only crucial for salvation of the individual, but also for the role and purpose of Israel as a nation among nations.

Before leaving this classical period of Jewish scriptural interpretation, a word must be said about midrashim, or the compilations of exegesis of scriptural verses that were put together during this same period. These compilations are of three kinds: (a) those dealing in a verse-by-verse exposition of the Pentateuch; (b) two collections also dealing with the Pentateuch but developed in a more discursive way on a thematic basis and which expand upon Exodus and Leviticus; and (c) thematic theological or philosophical studies where the explanation of individual verses, phrases, or words is subordinated to the exposition of a basic theme. These midrashim, or parts of them, are often included in the collections that make up the two Talmuds. Neusner suggests that analysis of the midrashim produces evidence of two groups: (a) a group that cites the same ideas and authorities as those found in the Midrash; and (b) a group that contains ideas similar to those found in the two Talmuds.[86]

After the final editing of the Babylonian Talmud, the responsibility of Torah interpretation passed to the heads of the Babylonian academies who were called *gaon* (excellency). The same patterns involving the exegesis of written and oral Torah at various depths of symbolization and seriousness continued up to the ninth century C.E. culminating in the commentary by R. Saadia Gaon, who focused on the plain sense of the biblical text. Throughout the classical period there is evidence of an at-once playful and serious interpretative imagination. In addition to the philosophical and theological concerns, matters of grammar, custom, and moral behavior are discussed. But in doing the exegesis, the assumption is made that somehow all of this Torah—written, oral, midrashim, and so forth—is a unity, a Gestalt. "The exegete is permitted and encouraged to move back and forth across its surface, connecting texts, and reconnecting them, harmonizing the contradictory and bringing the seemingly discordant into patterns of new and surprising concordance."[87] By the eleventh century the Babylonian academies had faded and the center of Jewish learning shifted to North Africa and Western Europe, marking the start of the medieval period.

At the beginning of the medieval period two types of scholars arose: commentators (*meforeshim*) and decision-makers (*poseqim*). The best-known commentator is Rabbi Shelomo Yitzhaki (Rashi, 1040-1105) of Champagne, France. In addition to a major biblical commentary, he wrote a massive commentary on almost all of the Babylonian Talmud. The first of the major decision-makers of Jewish law was Rabbi Isaac of Fez (Alfasi, 1013-73) of Spain. He produced a codification that closely followed the law passages of the Babylonian Talmud.[88]

In medieval Spain the challenge of Neoplatonic and Aristotelian philosophy produced another development—philosophical exegesis. As Philo had been lost to Jewish thought, the introduction of Greek philosophy seemed revolutionary. Through such interpretation, the Torah was now seen as being capable of guiding one to the rational contemplative love of God. The full expression of this development is found in the writing of Moses Maimonides (1135-1204). His *Guide of the Perplexed* reexamines the language of the Torah in an attempt to reconcile it with philosophical truth. Using exegetical techniques borrowed from the Islamic commentators, Maimonides distinguishes between two levels of language and meaning by using metaphorical interpretation (*ta'wīl*). Rather than taking the plain sense of the text, Maimonides put more emphasis on its inner meaning. Although the masses could concentrate on the surface images of the text and not be led away from moral truth, one who was philosophically sensitive could perceive the inner meaning of the text, which reveals a deeper experience of truth in all its reality. The surface meaning of the text gives way to the inner as one grows in wisdom.[89] An understanding of philosophical truths helps one to see past the surface to the deeper spiritual meaning of the text. Thus philosophy and Torah are brought together and shown to be complementary. Maimonides also wrote a major law code, Mishnah Torah, in which he attempted to transcend the need to refer back to the Talmud and other legal sources.[90]

The philosophical/mystical tendency was pushed even further in thirteenth-century Spain by the *Zohar*, the source of medieval Spanish Kabbala. Instead of just two levels of interpretation, the *Zohar* focuses on the fourth level of inner meaning—the luminous truths of *sod*. This fourth level is seen as hidden within the shell of outer meanings, like the seeds of a pomegranate, and beckons the sensitive soul even through the plain sense of the outer meaning. To those who can respond, exegesis of the inner fourth level becomes a deep mystical experience of the various emanations of God. The Torah as a condensation of God is said to pulse with the rhythms of the divine potencies that structure the cosmos. Exegesis is a subtle decoding of these Torah rhythms so that the inner mystic truth can be seen and the devotee ascend into the recesses of the Godhead. The Torah is a kind of linguistic concordance bridging the realms of the human and the divine. Exegesis of Torah provides an opening to Divine Reality.[91]

The consolidation of law codes continued in Spain, France, and Germany and reached a new plateau with the works of Joseph Karo (1488-1575). Karo took the codes of earlier authors such as Alfasi and Maimonides and especially the code called the *Tur* of Jacob B. Asher and combined them methodically into his own commentary the *Bet Yosef*. In it Karo explores each law from its place in the Talmud and up through the latter sources. After completing this monumental great code, Karo wrote a short synopsis of it, which he called *Shulkhan Arukh*, or the "Set Table." This uncluttered digest of Jewish law together with the *Mappah*, or "Table Cloth," a series of glosses describing Eastern European (i.e., Ashkenazic) divergencies written by the Polish scholar R. Moses Isserles (1530-72), became the basic code of Jewish law and remains so for traditional Jewry to the present day.[92]

Another vehicle for the application of Jewish law to changing conditions has been the responsa literature. "Responsa" are answers to questions asked by scholars and lay people alike. Responsa have grown to comprise thousands of decisions, which are only now being made fully accessible by computer projects sponsored through Yeshiva University and Bar-Ilan University in cooperation with the Institute for Computers in Jewish Life in Chicago.[93] Reponsa literature provides a means for the continual updating of the law so that modern answers to new and sometimes old questions are constantly being made available. For example, the success of space explorations has prompted questions as to how an inhabitant of the moon will observe the Sabbath, which normally begins on earth at sunset on Friday.

Modern Judaism is split by divisions into the Neo-Orthodox, Conservative, Reform, and Reconstructionist movements. Within each of these movements both biblical and legal commentaries have been written and sanctified by the rabbis of the movement. For example, the Reform movement has published responsa, many of which have been composed by a leading Reform scholar, Rabbi Solomon Freehof.[94] The Reconstructionist movement grew out of the philosophy espoused by Rabbi Mordecai Kaplan (1881-1983). For the committed Reconstructionist, Kaplan's writings possess a real centrality.[95] However, most Orthodox Jews have rejected the compositions of the Conservative, Reform, and Reconstructionist movements even when produced by scholars with strong international reputations. The basic cause of this rejection is related to the attitude most Reform and Reconstructionist scholars and many Conservative writers take toward the Torah—specifically their denial that Moses received the written as well as the oral Torah at Sinai. This denial of what is a fundamental belief for Orthodoxy disqualifies a person as an author of holy literature regardless of his or her credentials.[96]

The root problem is a clash in method and presuppositions between traditional and modern scholarship. In modern exegesis the religious context of traditional Judaism has been replaced by the secular and humanistic presuppositions of post-Enlightenment scholarship. Now historical and literary critical analyses of the sort employed by Jacob Neusner dominate modern scholarship. Instead of a confidence in the two Torahs, oral and written, as having been revealed by God to Moses at Sinai, Neusner offers literary critical evidence for his "Myth of the Two Torahs" theory. Rather than being seen as revealed by God, Neusner shows the oral Torah to be a myth created by the rabbinic community to explain the authority and status of the Mishnah. For many modern Jews, the questions raised by critical exegesis of the kind exemplified by Neusner are: "What happens when the transforming and sanctifying power of the myth is called into question by modern scholarship?" "What will replace this central role of the Torah in the lives of individual Jews and the people as a whole?" "When the Torah is but one of many books, will Jews be able to find in it wisdom and a source of spiritual memory sufficient to nourish a community of faith?" These questions brought by modernity to the experience of scripture challenge the exegesis of all religions, but perhaps none so strongly as Jewish exegesis. A positive and hopeful response to such questions is offered by the modern European Jewish thinker, Franz Rosenzweig. He formulated the following exegetical option for modern Jews:

> Modern man is neither a believer nor an unbeliever. He believes and he doubts. . . . Whoever lives this way can approach the Bible only with a readiness to believe or not believe, but not with a circumscribed belief

> that he will find confirmed in it. . . . For such a man the days of his own life illumine the Scriptures, and in their quality of humanness permit him to recognize what is more than human. . . . This humanness may anywhere become so translucid under the beam of a day of one's life that it stands suddenly written in his innermost heart. . . . Not everything in the Scriptures belongs to him—neither today nor ever. But he belongs to everything in them, and it is only this readiness of his which, when it is directed towards Scriptures, constitutes belief.[97]

THE STUDY OF THE TORAH

The study of the Torah (*talmud torah*) as a supreme religious duty is one of the key ideas of rabbinic Judaism. The Mishnah, after describing such duties as honoring parents and performing acts of charity, concludes that the study of the Torah is "equal to them all."[98] The commentary Abot (6:4) contains the following advice on the ideal of Torah study: "This is the way of the Torah: a morsel of bread with salt to eat, water by the measure to drink: thou shalt sleep on the ground, and live a life of hardship, whilst thou toilest in the Torah. If thou doest thus, happy shalt thou be—in this world, and it shall be well with thee—in the world to come." The traditional link between study and the next world is seen in the practice of a scholar's notes on Torah studies being kept in a special drawer for burial with the person and the person's tattered holy books. This custom emphasizes the ongoing chain of learning to be found in each generation. Jewish law in fact states that it is a religious obligation (*mitzvah*) for every Jew to write a Torah scroll or to participate in such a project. The sixteenth-century commentary of Joseph Karo adds that, in addition to the Pentateuch, one must also write out the Mishnah and its commentaries.[99] Even today it is not unusual to find Orthodox Jews who as an avocation are devoting much of their life to writing a Torah commentary.

The ideal of Torah study had a twofold aim. First, it was believed to lead to a spiritual life, since without knowledge of what the Torah requires, compliance is not possible. Second, Torah study itself was a religious duty of the highest order. As to which of the two, study or practice, was greater, tradition records the response of Rabbi Akiba, "Study is greater for it leads to practice."[100] Yet study without the intention of carrying out the teachings is seen as having no value. The prerequisite requirements for study are listed in Abot 6:6.

> . . . by the hearing of the ear, by the discernment of the heart, by awe, by reverence, by humility, by cheerfulness; by attendance on sages, by consorting with fellow students . . . by knowledge of Scripture and Mishnah; by moderation in business, in worldly occupation, pleasure, sleep, conversation and jesting; by long suffering, by a good heart, by faith in the Sages, by submission to sorrows; . . . by being one that asks and makes answer, that harkens and adds thereto; that learns in order to teach and learns in order to practice; that makes his teacher wiser;

that retells exactly what he has heard, and reports a thing in the name of him that said it.[101]

The requirements for students were thus both of intellect and of character. In addition to factual knowledge, the student had to demonstrate skills in debating. The debaters were described as warriors battling for the Torah.

Although the ideal above was framed for the full-time scholars, study was also a binding requirement on every Jew. Maimonides spells out the requirement as including the young, the old, the weak, the poor, the beggar, and "even one with a wife and children to support is obliged to set aside a period for Torah study by day and by night, as it is said, 'Thou shalt meditate therein day and night.' "[102]

Since the Torah is holy, the approach to it is carefully regulated.[103] Three benedictions are to be recited before studying the Torah. A fixed time is to be set aside each day for Torah study, preferably in the company of others. Each community is expected to have a house of study (*bet ha-midrash*) whose sanctity is greater than that of the synagogue. The rabbis believed in the spiritual value of verbal expression and therefore taught that study should not be just a mental study but that the text should be chanted aloud. As to age requirements, study of the written Torah is to begin at age five, the Mishnah at ten years, the fulfillment of the commandments at thirteen, and the study of Talmud at fifteen (Abot 5:21). In adulthood, a man should devote his time one-third to scripture, one-third to Mishnah, and one-third to Talmud. In the traditional approach, serious Torah study by girls or women does not seem to have been encouraged, although from time to time there were educated Jewish women (e.g., a rabbi's daughters). One of the innovations of Reform Judaism is to open Torah study to females. From the late nineteenth and early twentieth centuries on, the Orthodox started cultivating women's education also. In the medieval period, especially in Europe, most of the efforts were directed to study of the Babylonian Talmud under the assumption that what it contained concerning Mishnah and scripture was most salient and authoritative. The philosophical teachers (e.g., Maimonides) and the Kabbalists downplayed attention to the law codes in favor of more time being spent on philosophical and mystical meditation. Following in the Kabbalistic tradition the Hasidic movement of the eighteenth century challenged the ideal of Torah study as the supreme religious duty. While prayer had traditionally been taken as inferior to study, it was frequently elevated by the Hasidim above study.

In Western Europe from the beginning of the nineteenth century more and more time had to be allocated to secular studies. Also, even that portion still devoted to Torah study began to be influenced by "scientific scholarship." Historical-critical studies of the background and authorship of texts made it difficult to maintain a faith perspective toward the Torah. While the "scientific approach" has shed new light on many aspects of the Torah, it has helped to produce two different worlds of Torah study: the world of the yeshiva (Jewish seminary) which is skeptical, indifferent, or even hostile to critical scholarship, and the world of modern secular study with little interest in study as a religious act. To date there has been little interchange between these two worlds.[104]

One modern scholar, Jacob Neusner, has recently questioned the ability of today's yeshivas to produce any serious Torah study.[105] While agreeing with the traditional Jewish claim that when you study certain books you are changed and made holy, Neusner contends (based on a study by Samuel Heilman) that what happens in today's yeshivas and synagogues bears little resemblance to Talmud Torah as practiced by the great masters and their students in the past. What is missing in today's yeshivas, says Neusner, is criticism, freedom of imagination and inquiry, and devotion to learning as a quest for enlightenment or understanding. Instead the modern yeshivas teach students to repeat in a ritual way what they are told by their teachers, with little or no understanding of the text being studied. In addition much time is wasted in free-associating, in expressing how people feel. It all adds up, says Neusner, to be little more than an "empty ritual."[106] True Torah study even in its traditional requirements involved: (a) acquisition of facts—of texts and their contents accurately interpreted by repetition and memorization; and (b) critical reflection on the meaning of the text which involved a committing of the heart, the imagination, and the emotion to the study. Some of this, argues Neusner, is done today more effectively in the secular academy than in the yeshivas. Neusner finds a certain parallel between the approach to learning offered in the secular university at its best, and the approach of the great classical Jewish academies. In modern university study of the Torah, students are required not just to master facts but to be able to assess critically these facts and arrive at new knowledge. The aim is not merely to repeat knowledge but to renew learning—"to rediscover the logic, the principles of order and structure, that dictate knowledge. For that purpose merely repeating what we know is not enough. Every good course promises to look for the new, leads students into the unknowns."[107] All of these qualities of learning, Neusner finds to be characteristic of study in the Talmuds—stress on the flow of argument and use of the critical intellect along with a voyage into the new and the unknown because no one masters the whole of Torah ("everyone undertakes an unending voyage through the worlds of the Torah"[108]). More than merely erudite repetition of what everybody knows is required.

However, only the Jewish community can pass judgement on the merits of Neusner's criticism of yeshivas. And even if the secular university may in some ways free Torah study from "empty ritualism," it cannot supply the faith community, which shares the presuppositions of Torah as God's revelation to Israel. Thus there is a need for a renewal of the yeshivas just as there is a need for the renewal of the seminaries of most religions. Still suffering from the deadening impact of the so-called scientific age upon their medieval patterns of spirituality, traditional institutions in their study of scripture need to find ways of bringing together the two worlds of modern knowledge and traditional study. The Hartman Institute in Jerusalem is one attempt to foster this kind of understanding. Given its past history of successfully meeting challenges such as that of Greek philosophy, Talmud Torah should be capable of coping with this new test.

TORAH IN RELATION TO OTHER SCRIPTURES

Judaism arose out of the pluralistic context of the Ancient Near East. The Torah recounts how Israel came to be separated out from the vast array of different religions that characterized that area. The origin of the Jews is traced to Abraham who left Mesopotamia and migrated to Canaan. The religious significance of Abraham's journey is that in leaving Mesopotamia he also left the gods of this world, idols and nature deities, to serve the Lord, creator of heaven and earth. According to Jewish thinking the Abraham event marked the appearance not only of a new people but also of a new religious idea—one God, the creator, separate from and transcendent over all creation.[109]

The Torah records that the early experience of the Jewish people with the God of Abraham took the form of a covenant relationship. Scholars suggest that this covenant relationship may well have been set in the form of the vassal treaties that were common at that time. For example, in reporting the liberation of the Hebrews from bondage in Egypt, the book of Deuteronomy understands the Jews now to be in bondage to God through the covenant entered into by Moses. Instead of being held in a worldly vassaldom as they were in Egypt, the Jews are now committed to a relationship of service and obedience to God. "Like the other small nations that surrounded her, Israel was to be a vassal state, but not to Egypt or to the Hittites; she owed her allegiance to God alone."[110] It is this notion of being committed to God that is fundamental to the Torah and to the way the relationship of other peoples to God is understood. Just as God has entered into a special covenant relationship with the Jews, so also there is no reason why God could not enter into other relationships with other peoples. Thus, from the Jewish biblical perspective, the various religions and their scriptures may be seen as the expressions of the relationships obtained between other peoples and God. While for the Jews it is the Torah that is true and authoritative, for another peoples (e.g., Christians or Muslims) it will be their particular relationship with God expressed in their scriptures that will be true and authoritative for them. Indeed in the most ancient covenant relationship, described in Genesis 9:8-17, God enters into a covenant with Noah, his family, and with every living person and animal. In the Noachiam covenant we see a simple but powerful statement of God's love for all people. A later resonance of this theme in "The Song of Moses" is recorded in Deuteronomy 32:8:

> When the Most High gave the nations an inheritance,
> When he separated the sons of mankind,
> He fixed the boundaries of the peoples
> According to the number of the sons of God.[111]

Israel is one among the many nations, each of which received its inheritance and had its boundaries fixed by God. Commenting on the last line, Craigie notes that the exact sense of the phrase "according to the number of the sons of God" is difficult to determine but seems to refer to a divine council of "angels" or "sons of God," with one for each nation or people.[112] In the Masoretic text, however, the last line of the verse reads "the children of Israel" and not "the sons of God." This, of course, provides the basis for a much narrower interpretation.

The personal nature of the covenant relationship between God and his people is emphasized in the Torah. The old Israelites experienced the Divine as a very personal God who presided over their destiny. "God was not just there and acting; he was turned towards man, asking for him and calling for his co-operative response."[113] God's calling his people was experienced as God's word spoken through Moses and the prophets. In the Torah, God calls his people, and all they have to do is listen and obey. This conception of the one Lord to whom they owed loyalty and obedience was the unifying power within Judaism. Instead of seeing a variety of gods performing particular functions (e.g., special gods for the different natural powers) or controlling specific geographical locations, or representing the metaphysical forces of good and evil, the Torah experiences the one God as the transcendent source and unity of all being.[114] Thus when the Babylonians defeated Israel, it was theologically interpreted not as a failure on the part of their God, Yahweh, but rather, that their God, the Lord of all, was using the Babylonians as his instrument to punish the Jews for their failure to keep their covenant agreement with God. When the defeated Israelites were carried off into Babylonian exile (587-538 B.C.E.), this was understood as God's punishment of Israel for its conscious neglect of the covenant.[115] This mode of reasoning is today still held by many Orthodox Jews and provides the basis of the way they view other religions and their scriptures.

The ending of the Babylonian exile and the return to Palestine marked a more exclusivistic approach to other peoples and religions. To a large extent this was the result of living among gentiles in a way that the pre-exilic Jews had not had to experience. Under the leadership of Ezra and Nehemiah, both of whom were intense, rigid individuals, a strong feeling of religious separation was nurtured.[116] This emphasis was probably needed at the time to help the demoralized struggling community of those who had returned to Palestine to re-establish their identity and rebuild Jerusalem. But the proscription against mixed marriages (Nehemiah 10) and the condemnation of other peoples laid the foundations for the more exclusivist attitude that tended to dominate in the postexilic period. There are other places in the Torah where there is condemnation of other religions and insistence that the Lord is the only true God, or that all other gods must bow before the Lord (Deuteronomy 5; Exodus 20). But even in the midst of the renewed exclusivism following the postexilic period, the books of Ruth and Jonah claim that the Lord's concern extends far beyond Israel's borders. In the life of a Moabite woman named Ruth and in the repentance of the foreign city Nineveh, the Lord's compassion for all people triumphs over narrow provincialism. Thus Israel was not to assume an exclusive claim on God, but to fulfill its covenant responsibility of being a light to the nations.

During the classical and medieval period, important Jewish thinkers directly addressed the question of the relationship between Judaism and the other religions. Philo viewed the various religions (including Greek philosophy) as different manifestations of the one divine *Logos* and identified the Torah in its eternity with that *Logos*. The Torah, as *Logos* existed before the world was created and provided the pattern for creation. All the scriptures of the world are but manifestations of the pre-existent *Logos*. Maimonides taught that of all religions, Judaism was the only faith revealed by God and was therefore true in every respect. His rejection of other religions such as Christianity was based on an interpretation of them as containing idolatrous forms (e.g., the worship of the saints)—and thus subject to the Mosaic proscription against idolatry. Nevertheless, Maimonides, in his *Guide of the Perplexed*, sees Christianity and Islam as having come into being by the will of God and being capable of leading humanity to the messianic age.

> But it is beyond the human mind to fathom the designs of the Creator, for our ways are not His ways, nor our thoughts His thoughts. All these matters, relating to Jesus of Nazareth and the Ishmaelite, who came after him [Mohammed], only served to clear the way for the King Messiah, to prepare the world for the worship of God with one voice [Zephaniah 3:9]. Thus the messianic hope, the Torah and the commandments have become familiar topics, topics of conversation even [among peoples] of the far away islands, and among many people uncircumcised in heart and flesh. These discussions, though filled with error, will prepare people for the time when the Messiah will come and correct their errors (Mishneh Torah: Judges-Kings Ch. 11).[117]

In the late medieval period the Kabbala became influential. The Kabbala's attitude, however, is not in the slightest degree positive toward other religions or their scriptures.

In one of the first significant Jewish works of the modern period, *Jerusalem*, Moses Mendelssohn (1729-86) set out to bridge the gap between the medieval Jewish ghetto and modern Europe.[118] He attempted to bring together the high recognition given reason by eighteenth-century Enlightenment philosophers, such as Immanuel Kant, and an unquestioning loyalty to the God of Sinai: In line with Kant, Mendelssohn argued that the truth of religion was not dependent upon supernatural revelation but was immanent in human reason and thus available to all. It was inconceivable to him to believe that God could have revealed the truth to only part of humanity leaving the rest without revelation and therefore without access to happiness. No one religion or scripture can be the sole instrument through which God has revealed his truth.

> According to the tenets of Judaism, all inhabitants of the earth have a claim to salvation, and the means to attain it are as widespread as mankind itself.
>
> Providence made wise men arise in every nation and bestowed upon them the gift to look with a clear eye into themselves as well as around themselves, to contemplate God's works, and to communicate their insights to others.[119]

Thus, for Mendelssohn, Judaism does not claim to possess the exclusive revelation of truth necessary for salvation. That is available to all people through reason. The unique revelation given to the Jews in the Mosaic law is a code of conduct that binds them to God and unites them as a people. The Torah is unique and valid for the Jewish people alone. Its purpose is to guide the Jew in moral and spiritual conduct and to make him or her ponder the nature and destiny of life. For Mendelssohn the God of reason and the God of Sinai were one and the same. All religions shared the same truth given by God through reason, but each religion had its own unique scripture to give meaning and guidance to practical life. To those who would argue that the practice of religion, as well as its truth, must be one and the same for all, Mendelssohn responds as follows: ". . . it is not necessary for the entire flock to graze on one pasture or to enter and leave the master's house through just one door. It would be neither in accord with the shepherd's wishes nor conducive to the growth of his flocks."[120] To require a union of religions into one is not tolerance but the very opposite. The exercise of reason and freedom of conscience requires pluralism in religious experience.[121]

In the modern period Jews have begun to associate with non-Jews more freely than ever before. Modern scholarship has made other scriptures easily available and the Jewish tradition of study has resulted in their being read by Jews. In addition the modern technological and demythologized world seems to have largely removed the threat and temptation of idolatry from Jewish consciousness. It seems as if the earlier Jewish attitude toward other religions was rooted not in exclusivism but, rather, in the fear of idolatry. According to Emil Fackenheim, a modern Jewish philosopher, now that this fear of idolatry no longer has a place in modern Jewish consciousness, the basis for the rejection of other religions seems also to be removed. Evidence for this is the modern Jewish willingness to participate in interreligious dialogue, and the widespread interest in interfaith cooperation. Fackenheim concludes that no modern Jew would regard another religion as idolatrous simply because images or statues are part of it—so long as the one imageless God is the intended object of worship.[122] If the modern Jew thinks of idolatry at all, it is in the form of the worship of sex, money or nationalism (especially as practiced by the Nazis [123]) instead of the God of the Bible.

While the viewpoint of the modern Jew opens the way for relations with Christianity, Islam and perhaps Hinduism, and Buddhism—especially Mahāyāna Buddhism—may prove to be in a separate category. The Buddhist scripture in which no "over and above" God is recognized, and the Mahāyāna awareness of the Divine in the secular may be judged by the Jewish philosopher as a modern idolatry. In Fackenheim's view, idolatry is still possible if the notion of the one transcendent God is desecrated.[124] Jewish thinkers do not seem to have thought this through in relation to Buddhism.

Some modern American Jewish thinkers have adopted a very open attitude by considering other scriptures to be various manifestations of God's word. As Abraham Heschel puts it,

> God's voice speaks in many languages, communicating itself in a diversity of intuitions. The word of God never comes to an end. No word is God's last word.[125]

Thus God is speaking to all of the traditions uniquely in their scriptures, and it is the ecumenical efforts of each tradition that will help the others to hear the unique word that God has spoken to it. Only if one listens to all the scriptures of all the religions will one hear all of God's word that has so far been spoken. Hearing God's word in other scriptures stimulates one to creative development within one's own religion. In this way religious differences provide the challenge to keep religions alive and fresh. But such a stimulating variety is possible only when religions share a common universe of discourse, and thus the necessity of a pluralistic perspective. Diversity among scriptures is seen as a positive element creatively strengthening the total religious community in its opposition to surrounding forces of secular society. Unity among the religions is grounded in the individual believer's experience of the depth-dimension, the direct meeting with God through one's own scriptures. This is open to the experience of the believer in each of the traditions and thus provides the common ground for all of the religions.

With the American Jewish response we seem to have come full circle back to a logic not unlike that of Philo's *Logos* model. The ancient rabbis also had a universalistic view of the Torah. They taught that the message of the Torah is for all people. Before giving the Torah to Israel, God offered it to the other nations, but they refused it. When he did give the Torah to Israel, he revealed it in the extraterritorial desert and simultaneously in seventy languages, so that people of all nations would have a right to it.[126]

2

SCRIPTURE IN CHRISTIANITY

Whereas for a Jew the fundamental aspiration is the scripture prayer, the Shema, for a Christian it is the confession of faith in the words "Jesus is Lord" (Romans 10:9). Although Christianity from the very beginning had a scripture, the Hebrew Scriptures, the faith of the earliest Christians was evoked by and focused on a person, Jesus of Nazareth. Jesus, in the earliest Christian communities, was known not in Bible texts but in missionary preaching, oral tradition, and charismatic experience. The Hebrew scriptures were used only in a secondary way—to confirm and defend the Christian experience of God through Jesus Christ.[1] While for Judaism (post 70 C.E.) it was the oral Torah that provided the criteria for interpreting the Hebrew Bible, in Christianity it was the teachings of Jesus and the testimony of his apostles that provided the criteria for interpretation. Both religions started from the same basic Bible, the written Torah, but each used different oral means of interpretations to develop the truth of the Hebrew Bible.[2] Whereas Judaism gave highest place to the Pentateuch, the books of Moses, in Christianity there was a definite preference for the prophets and Psalms. When the books of Moses were used by Christians it was not their prescriptive and practical import (their Jewish value) that was emphasized, but their historical narrative, which was seen as prefiguring the arrival of Jesus. Thus while Jews ordered the Bible in terms of Torah, first, and prophecy, second, Christians reversed the order and saw the whole as preparing the way for Jesus. In their use of the Hebrew Bible, Christians preferred some books (e.g., Genesis, Exodus, Isaiah, Jeremiah, Zechariah, Malachi, the Psalms) and ignored others. By such means Christians used the Jewish scriptures but for their own purposes, giving them a different meaning. "The perspective which furnished this meaning was not the scriptures themselves, but the confession of Jesus as Messiah: the scriptures were seen to prefigure him, and he was seen to fulfill them."[3] It is in this context in the late second century C.E., that the Hebrew Bible comes to be called the Old Testament (the old covenant with God) as opposed to the New Testament (the new covenant with God in Jesus Christ).

In the early Christian community a principal use of scripture was in the service of worship. This practice was taken over with the Hebrew Bible from the synagogues of the day. Every Sabbath, in the Jewish synagogues it was customary for portions of the law (Pentateuch) and the prophets to be read to the people and then interpreted. Originally, in Christian worship, only the scriptures of Judaism were read, since no distinctive Christian scriptures had yet developed. Gradually, however, Christian writings such as Gospels and Letters gained acceptance and were read alongside the Jewish scriptures in congregational worship. This practice, that was in full use in the second century C.E., gradually gave authority to the Christian writings that were read, and was one factor leading to their later acceptance into the canon of the New Testament.

The New Testament is made up of twenty-seven books, which constitute the second of the two portions into which the Bible is divided by Christians. The relation between the Old and the New Testaments is understood on the basis of a passage from the prophet Jeremiah, chapter 31:31-34. The Christian interpretation of the passage is that Jeremiah predicted that the covenant relationship of God with his people, instituted through Moses on Mount Sinai, would be replaced or renewed in the future by a more intimate and personal covenant. The apostle Paul (2 Corinthians 3:6–15) regarded Jesus as fulfilling Jeremiah's prediction and instituting a new covenant with God—thus "the New Testament." For Christians then, the Holy Bible includes both the Old and the New Testaments. The twenty-seven books of the New Testament were written down within a period of about one hundred years. Four major types of books were eventually included in the New Testament canon: (1) Gospels, of which there are four, so named because they tell the "good news" of Jesus Christ including his birth, baptism, ministry, death, and resurrection; (2) church history in the Acts of the Apostles, an account of the spread of the Christian faith during the first thirty years or so after the death and resurrection of Jesus Christ; (3) twenty books in the form of letters (twenty-one if one includes Hebrews, which is actually a homily); and (4) the last book, which is an apocalypse or a revelation of God's will for the future.[4]

Jesus himself left no writings. Our knowledge of his words and works comes from his immediate followers or apostles and their disciples. At first, this information circulated orally. Later it was written down, and finally some of it became canonized. Let us begin by examining Jesus and the oral tradition. Then we shall trace the formation of the written New Testament and its exegesis. We shall then look at the functions of scripture in Christian life, and finally we shall turn our attention to New Testament in relation to other scriptures.

JESUS AND THE ORAL TRADITION

Many years ago the great biblical scholar C. H. Dodd said that the Bible as the written word is the perfect medium by which we reach and experience the personalities of the Bible.[5] More recently, however, scholars have pointed to the oral nature of the early Christian scriptures as the source of their power for the transforming of persons. The importance of oral rhetoric in the Greek culture came together with the oral practices being developed by the rabbis to provide a strong oral context. Jesus, and some Jewish rabbis of his day, did not write but depended on oral teaching to communicate their messages.[6] Jesus' teaching and much of the early Christian mission was by word of mouth in Aramaic and Greek, the common languages of the day. Sermons were neither written in advance nor copied down by the hearers. They listened and remembered. As was the case with the great Jewish rabbis and their academies, the cultural traditions of the day were more oral than written—although there was certainly writing going on. Jesus and his disciples followed this pattern. The oral nature of their teaching was not due to illiteracy, but was consciously chosen by the rabbis because of its greater power for reaching and transforming the people of the day.[7] "Jesus and his disciples could write as well as read (John 8:6,8; Acts 15:23). Indeed it is quite probable that in the bilingual country of Palestine they could use two languages, Greek and Aramaic, just as could Paul, who wrote in the former language but could speak in either (Acts 21:37; 22:2)."[8] Although Jesus' teaching was first given in Aramaic, no early Christian writings in Aramaic have come down to us, and we have no certain knowledge that any such writings ever existed. As we shall see, when the teachings of Jesus did get written down, they had already been translated from Aramaic into Greek.[9]

Amos Wilder in his study of the language of the Gospel observes that the power of the Bible is in its spoken word.[10] And the nature of the spoken word of Jesus is that it is not studied or written out in advance, but spoken *extempore* in a specific situation.

> This utterance is dynamic, actual, immediate, reckless of posterity; not coded for catechists or repeaters. . . . We find ourselves at first and for rather a long time in the presence of oral and live face-to-face communication. The Gospel meant freedom of speech in this deeper sense. One did not hoard its formulas, since when occasion arose the Spirit would teach one what to say and how to witness and what defence to make. . . . The speech of the Gospel was thus fresh and its forms fluid and novel.[11]

These qualities, says Wilder, distinguish Christian speaking from the beginning and are still found to be present when it is obliged to take on written form. To our knowledge, Jesus left no writing behind. "Jesus was a voice, not a penman, a herald not a scribe. . . . That Jesus confined himself to the spoken and precarious word is of a piece with his renunciation of all cultural bonds such as home and trade and property."[12] For Jesus and his generation, history and continuity culminated in the end time, the eschaton, which was momentarily expected. Jesus' word was for the present, for the eleventh hour. Jesus, as a prophet, brought the word of God "into the present with inexorable sharpness and actuality. Only the living voice can serve such an occasion."[13] This special "for the present" quality of Jesus' words comes through in the other New Testament authors even when they did write or dictate. In New Testament writings, the voice of the writer is often the voice of a speaker.

In this, the New Testament is following the lead given by the Old Testament, or Hebrew Bible. There, as Robert Culley has shown, much of the material begins as oral performance (e.g., Genesis 24:10-33 and 1 Samuel 23:14-24:23), which then is written down. Even though changes occur as the oral tradition becomes written, still many written biblical texts reflect the oral style very strongly.[14] Also in the Old Testament, as in the New, there is often a period of oral transmission "in which there is no original text but only a series of performances, all of which are valid because they are realizations of a traditional pattern or bundle of elements."[15] In this way the oral transmission of scripture preserves tradition while allowing for freshness and creativity. We may recall similar arguments being offered by Neusner in his assessment as to the need for, and strength of, the oral Torah in Judaism.[16]

According to Roger Lapointe another implication of the analysis of the relationships of the oral to the written is that in the texts that were originally oral, the "biblical inspiration cannot be limited to scribes who held the pen at a particular moment and in a particular place, thereby to write the original text of the Holy Scriptures. Such scribes never existed."[17] The inspiration that existed was shared by all those involved in the oral and written process: the original speaker, the repeaters, their listeners and those who finally wrote down the words, and those who interpreted the written texts.

To return to Jesus, there is evidence that his own words and deeds were carried in memory and retold. But in what fashion did this oral transmission take place? Some scholars hold that Jesus taught in a formal way following the patterns used by the rabbis and described here in chapter 1.[18] Others, such as Wilder, argue for a radical difference between Jesus and the Jewish teachers. Jesus was not schooling his followers in a learned mode that could be passed on to future generations. Rather, he spoke to the immediate crisis of the day in a free and spontaneous style. As Wilder puts it:

> The incomparable felicity and patterning of his sayings is indeed evident, but this formal perfection is not a matter of mnemonics; it is the countersign of the most effective communication of the moment. Naturally his words and parables were remembered and retold, often with great accuracy, so lucid and inevitable was his phrasing. But here as always the new speech of the Gospel was not a matter of words on a tablet but a word in the heart, not a copybook for recitation but winged words for life.[19]

Of course the *extempore* character of Jesus' words did not continue indefinitely. The free oral dialogue of Jesus and his disciples was memorized, repeated, and eventually written down and published. But, maintains Wilder, even the published words of the New Testament are characterized by a dramatic element that evokes afresh the face-to-face encounter. The writing is meant to be read aloud and dramatically experienced. And, as commonly in the ancient world, most would know a written work only through hearing it read aloud. As Martin Luther put it much later, the New Testament "proclamation should take place by word of mouth, publicly in an animated tone, and should bring that forward into speech and hearing which before was hidden in the letters and apparent concealment. . . . Christ himself did not write his own teaching as Moses did his, but gave it forth by word of mouth and commanded that it should be done orally."[20] The preaching of Jesus and his disciples, says C. H. Dodd, was radically different from the teaching of the day. Whereas teaching *(didaché)* was reasoned and often formulaic instruction, preaching *(kergyma)* was inspired public proclamation—the lifting up of one's voice as a town crier or herald who draws attention to something important to be said.[21] This inspired oral preaching had much in common with Greek rhetoric, which also understood itself to be divinely inspired. Both stressed oral spontaneity and immediacy over the careful reading aloud of a written text.

Before looking at the different forms taken by the oral tradition of the New Testament, let us examine the kind of language employed. Jesus and his followers did not use a sacred or learned language; they used the languages and idioms of the wider world of their day. Jesus spoke in Aramaic, and Paul and the later evangelists spoke and wrote in the Greek *koine* of the Roman world. Christian speaking and writing did have charismatic power, but not through the use of esoteric language. Christians used the common language of their day and made it the medium of revelation. Nor did Jesus or Paul uncritically embrace the ecstatic language, the *glossolalia* or speaking in tongues, which was popular at the time. Even though many of Jesus' sayings reflect a charismatic mood and suggest visionary experience, he used common speech and did not go beyond it. Paul explicitly faced the alternative of ecstatic speech and downplayed it (1 Corinthians 14:1–25). This mode of ecstatic speech, in which believers are so carried out of themselves as to feel impelled to transcend ordinary human language, is carefully controlled in the New Testament. To be able to hear and understand the revelation of Jesus Christ was the important thing. Thus the early Christians had no hesitation in translating the words of Jesus into Greek, Latin, Syriac, Coptic, or the language of whatever people was being evangelized. The early church transmitted the words and deeds of Jesus not in a mechanical way, "but by a combination of his words and imagery with new variations and new resources of all kinds."[22] Thus there was no set holy language, but there was indeed a rhetoric of faith, the language of the Spirit, which through the words of Jesus pressed itself outward in the media of the various common forms of speech. Pentecost symbolically represents the fact that there is no peculiarly Christian tongue.

A second characteristic of much of the language of the New Testament is its brevity when compared with the scriptures of other religions. Wilder sees in this conciseness a testimony to a purification of language. Jesus warns against heaping up "empty phrases as the Gentiles" (Matthew 6:7) or uttering idle oaths and protestations (Matthew 5:34–37). The sayings of Jesus, Wilder claims, are free from the taints of falsehood, emptiness, and hollowness. In contrast with the fullness of much of the Old Testament, Jesus spoke in short aphorisms, oracles, and tightly knit parables—but also in silences. Even the writings of Paul and his other followers are not full but economical, urgent and faithful to the command of Jesus. This economy of speech, and the various forms it took, is partly a result of the context of the early Christian church—a new and, to begin with, small but intense fellowship of the spirit. The dynamism of these New Testament utterances is evident both in private meetings in upper rooms, and in public missionary activities. Wilder suggests the analogy of the special groups that produced the North American Negro spirituals and slave songs. As was the case for the early Christians, black slave communities of North America took the materials of their day, the general hymnology of the period along with the rhythms and chants of Africa, and in their small intimate groups created the new form of the religious song, the spiritual. Wilder notes:

> Their oral, anonymous and unliterary character offers a significant parallel to primitive Christian utterance. . . . The texts of the slave songs not only varied from region to region, but from decade to decade. In fact, the successive versions of a given slave song reflected the actual changed circumstances of the Negroes, just as we can recognize adaptations and overlays in early Christian traditions.[23]

The three forms of recorded speech found in the New Testament are gospel, letter, and apocalypse, or vision of the end time. We shall look at the oral character of each of these in turn.

The Gospels

The gospel is the result of the contributions of many unknown transmitters of oral traditions for a period of over thirty years from the time of Jesus to the composition of the Gospel of Mark. This Gospel originally circulated in the church anonymously but in the second century it was ascribed to John Mark, a companion of Paul in Acts (Acts 12:12,25; 15:37,39). It may have been composed in Rome and then rapidly circulated quite widely.[24] Mark's Gospel is not like the ancient biography or tragedy, which is focused on an appeal to sentiment and filled with biographical detail. Rather, "Mark represents a divine transaction whose import involves heaven and earth, and even the scenes of the Passion are recounted with a corresponding austerity.[25] The early Christian congregations did not hear the gospel as a record of the past but as a ritual reenactment of God's action in the world. In the midst of the early Christian community, the listeners to the retelling of the gospel found themselves caught up in the middle of a world-changing transaction of conflict, death, and glory. It was a new communication of meaning by which people could live.

The author of the Gospel of Mark collected and connected into a written narrative many bits and pieces of oral tradition. The most extensive unit of this oral material was probably a passion story, an account of the arrest, trial, and crucifixion of Jesus. This story may have been produced by the Christian community in Jerusalem to show that Jesus was the Messiah and that his death had fulfilled and been in accordance with the scripture of the Old Testament, or Hebrew Bible—to help Jews believe in a crucified and risen Messiah. Also included were oral collections of miracle and healing stories showing Jesus to have divine power, a collection of the parables of Jesus, an account of the founding of the Lord's Supper, a group of controversy stories concerning forgiveness or sins, eating with tax collectors and sinners, fasting and the like, and a cycle of stories describing the feeding of the five thousand, a crossing of the lake, and controversy with the Pharisees.[26] Using these variations of oral materials that were circulating in the church of his day, Mark created a connected narrative of the life and ministry of Jesus for evangelistic purposes. Since the later Gospels of Matthew and Luke rely heavily on Mark, it is clear that these oral materials put together by Mark form the basic core of the synoptic Gospels in the New Testament.

The oral nature of these materials used by Mark has been the focus of special study by Werner Kelber.[27] Kelber finds that the oral form of storytelling dominates the oral collections used by Mark. This does not, of course, exclude written traditions. The bulk of Mark's Gospel is made up of stories of four kinds: healings, exorcisms, ethical teaching stories, and parabolic stories. Each of the ten healing stories[28] exhibits a common story sequence and forms a coherent unit. Each story, though remarkably uniform in style, is amazingly unique, picturesque, and colorful. This creative variety within a uniformity of genre is a characteristic of the flexibility of the oral tale, which must be repeated with interest if it is to survive. As Albert Lord has shown, that variability within repeated formats is an important characteristic of oral transmission.[29] In oral performance the story is like a musical instrument that is capable of producing an infinite variety of sounds depending on the skills of the player and the reception by the audience:

> The narrator plays the role of the musician who achieves effects by variation and phrasing: he renders emphatic one part while deemphasizing others. No single rendition is exactly like any previous or subsequent one. Every performance is "true," but no performance is the original or permanent one. In sum, it is the plurality, uniformity, and variability of the healing stories that attests to their oral production and quality of performance.[30]

To help with the memorization, each story recounts a single plot with no more than two principal characters making a joint appearance. Oral performers prefer personalized stories: yet at the same time none of the characters is developed into an individual personality. In Mark's Gospel, the persons to be healed are virtually exchangeable; the important thing to be preserved was the functioning of Jesus as a performer of powerful deeds. In these stories it is this single but extraordinary aspect of Jesus that is magnified to make his a figure worth remembering. While Jesus is seen as a heroic figure with a status beyond that of mere mortals, he still stays close to ordinary human frailty and mortality. This simplified and heroized Jesus, who acts outside the common order but retains earthly touches, exhibits both the hallmarks of oral rhetoric and the manifestation of an oral Christology.[31]

The exorcism stories in Mark's Gospel (the exorcism at the synagogue of Capernaum, 1:21–28; the Gerasene demoniac, 5:1–20; and the epileptic boy, 9:14–29) are labeled by Kelber as "Polarization Stories"—polarization because they dramatize the opposition between Jesus and the forces of evil. Their oral characteristics are seen in the three-part pattern: (a) of confrontation between Jesus and a demon; (b) expulsion of the evil spirit; and (c) acclamation of Jesus' power and authority. While each of the exorcism stories is seen to follow this uniform pattern, there is great freedom left for variation in the oral narration. What is essentially the same story can be told in many different ways, but with a compulsion to return to expected endings much in the way a jazz solo often ends with a return to the melody line. Exorcisms are thus constructed on the same oral principle of variation within a set pattern that characterized heroic healing stories. In these stories the challenge for the storyteller is not primarily to engage in deep theological reflection on the nature of Jesus and the essence of redemption or to restore his historical actuality as in a modern historical biography. Rather, the task of the oral storyteller is to make Jesus live in the imagination of the audience. Narrated actions, especially those involving a struggle between good and evil, are an effective way of accomplishing this goal. As the opposite to Jesus, evil is not an "it" but a "thou," an evil one, endowed with speech and intelligence that functions to highlight the redemptive quality of Jesus (see Mark 5:1–20; 9:14–29).[32]

Mark's didactic or ethical teaching stories include examples such as table fellowship with sinners (2:15–17), the issue of fasting (2:18-19), plucking grain on the sabbath (2:23–28), the issue of divorce (10:2-9), the issue of possessions (10:17–22), and payment of taxes (12:13–17). The oral pattern in these stories involves two rounds of conversation: (a) a provocative question is asked and Jesus asks a counterquestion, (b) a response is given by the questioner(s) that opens the way for Jesus' answer in the form of a memorable saying. The story generally opens with a controversial issue or situation in which the entrapment of Jesus is often suggested. The questioners, as opponents of Jesus, create a dramatic situation that hits home with the listener and will be easily remembered. The questioners usually defend or propose the opposite of the final message to be remembered and thus in a *via negativa* fashion prepare the way for the final ethical teaching. The listener is drawn into the controversies through the oral technique of the polarization of the issues and individuals.

After the debate has climaxed, the listener is left with a memorable teaching that will provide the basis for the social ethic of the Christian community, for example, sayings such as "The sabbath was made for man, not man for the sabbath" (2:27) and values such as friendliness with outcasts (2:17), prohibition of fasting (2:19), ban on divorce (10:9), and renunciation of possessions (10:21). Such ethical teachings are not given in a list like the Ten Commandments to be memorized, but are presented in the form of a speech that combines a story with a statement. Not only does the story context serve as an aid to memory, but it makes the teaching "come alive" in the mind of the listener as the story is told. In simple but powerfully suggestive lines the story is told (e.g., "One sabbath he [Jesus] was going through the grainfields; and as they made their way his disciples began to pluck ears of grain") sparking visual images in the hearer. This embedding of the abstract ethical teaching in the story context makes remembering and recall easy as well as powerfully promoting a living experience in which the teaching is reflectively applied to one's own life. In the oral tradition it is the method of applied ethical teaching that is followed.[33]

Mark's Gospel records six specific parables: the sower (4:3-8), the reaper (4:26–29), the mustard seed (4:30–32), the wicked tenants (12:1–11), the fig tree (13:28), and the doorkeeper (13:34). But almost throughout, Jesus as an oral performer speaks in a parabolic style. Unlike the healing, exorcism, and ethical teaching stories, the parables of Jesus do not follow a set oral pattern. Jeremias suggests that the great variety and latitude of parabolic stories may be traced to their linguistic prototype, the Hebrew *mashal* and the Aramaic *mathla*, which embrace a great variety of oral forms.[34] Any attempt to force the parables of Jesus into the categories of Greek rhetoric is to be rejected. Jeremias welcomes the determination of C. H. Dodd to interpret the parables by placing them in the setting of Jesus' life.[35] The oral quality of the parables is seen in Jesus' speaking to people of flesh and blood in real-life settings with marked effect upon his listeners. The power of the parables is their ability to describe everyday life in such a way as to be clearly "true to life." Yet at the same time other elements are employed to make them memorable. In some, for example, the sower, mnemonic patterning in the form of series of threes (three failures and three successes) is employed. Contrast between the smallness of the seed and the end result is employed to make the mustard seed story orally impressionable on the hearers' minds. Sometimes the very ordinariness of life is put under strain as, for example, when the parable of the sower leads one to believe that failure is inevitable, only to have the tables turned in the last part. In the parable of the mustard seed also there is a paradoxical emphasis on the seed's beginning and ending without regard for the period of middle growth. The use of paradox in the parables often serves to deliver an "imaginative shock" to the minds of the hearers, as, for example, in Jesus' putting together of the two words "good" and "Samaritan." As Crossan has demonstrated in his analysis of the parable, the consciousness of the first-century Jewish hearers is confidently expecting to be told that the Samaritan gives no help to the wounded man and is shocked when that "deep structure" of their expectation is contradicted.[36] In attempting to get at this same aspect of the parable, Paul Ricoeur has used the term "extravagance." Parabolic extravagance exaggerates, introduces paradox and hyperbole, and strains the hearers' sense of realism. Thus a parable of Jesus, after starting with the plain and ordinary, has power to evoke the extraordinary. This is the "extravagance" of Jesus' parables, as Ricoeur puts it, which has the power to interrupt the peaceful course of action and transform the poetics of the parables into the poetics of faith.[37] This unexpected interruption of the expected flow of one's consciousness not only shocks one out of one's stereotypes and provokes new ways of thinking, but also provides by its very "oddness" a "memory peg" on which "to hang" the story.

Underlying all of the foregoing, however, is the fundamental metaphorical quality of Jesus' parables. His parables point beyond themselves. They invite the hearers into the story and take them, by surprise, to a special awareness (a revelation) that lies hidden beyond the story. Thus the closing admonition of many parables, "He who has ears to hear, let him hear." As metaphors, parables suggest but withhold meaning. This open-endedness makes parables particularly dependent on the oral context. The parable, when told, engages the hearer to complete the process begun by the story. This does not happen effectively when the parable is frozen into a written text and read in the abstract. Instead,

> Speaker and hearers are . . . wholly indispensable to a successful delivery of parabolic speech. Because parabolic language is not self-explanatory but intent on transcending what it says literally, it needs all the help it can get to carry out this delicate transaction. The sounding of words, the gestures of the speaker, facial contact between speaker and hearers, as well as an environment shared by the speaker and hearers alike are all crucial aids in conveying the meaning without saying it.[38]

The reader of parabolic texts lacks the physical and social interaction of the living oral context and thus may be unable to enter into the meaning of the parable. Unless the reader can empathize with the implied oral context, the written parable will remain largely lifeless and perhaps even alienating. In the modern context the power of the parable may show itself only in the situation that is sufficiently sensitive to the words to bring them to life in the speaking and hearing of worship or teaching. The language of the parables is much like that of an American Indian who said to a white man, "You know our language is not at all like yours. In our language, we talk about something and never even mention it. But everybody knows what is meant. We understand from the context."[39] Those who understand the meaning of the parables become insiders and their newly shared knowledge brings them close together in an intimate communion (Mark 4:10–12).

In the oral tradition, then, the parable is seen to be an open-ended speech act that is dependent on the oral context of speakers and hearers. In addition, parabolic speech is seen to lack both *an original form* and *an original meaning*. Every time a parable is told or retold, it is a new event. No single telling of a parable is quite like any other, and different social contexts will produce different hearings, different interpretations. Each new oral context provides the opportunity for a fresh experience of the revelation to which the parable points. In this sense, as long as the oral context of the parable is maintained the story never loses its power to grasp and change the psyches of hearers in unexpected and new ways. It is only when the parable is written down and distanced from the oral setting that its power and freshness dissipate. Even the literary practice of imposing on the parables convenient titles, like the "Parable of the Sower" already begins to foreclose on other possible hearings such as the "Parable of the Seed."[40] In the oral context it is this open-ended metaphoric quality that makes parables so attractive for remembering and retelling. Although they appear to be deceptively simple, parables continue to engage the minds of new generations of hearers because of their concealing and revealing natures. They bear repeating because they are never fully told or heard. Parables, therefore, may be described as unfinished oral stories that stimulate a process of interpretation that is never entirely brought to completion. "Whether parables shock hearers out of conventionality or gesture them toward something else, their secret strategy is in all instances seduction by the ordinary with a view toward the extraordinary."[41]

Aside from the important recognition of the oral nature of these different kinds of stories, Kelber further demonstrates that the connecting devices that link these stories together in Mark are also oral in nature. These devices line up the stories like successive beads on a string and lead the hearer on at a breathless pace. Actions and words juxtapose one another so the "words carry the force of action and actions speak as loud as words."[42] Mark also makes use of a standard oral technique of talking in terms of threes: three times Jesus predicts his death and resurrection, three times he asks the disciples to wake him at Gethsemane, three times he enters Jerusalem, three times Peter denies him. There is also the repetition of materials in ways that would be inappropriate in a written text. Whereas in a written text one can easily flip back a few pages to refer to something read earlier, in an oral context, however, there is only one hearing, so repetition functions parallel to the eye's privilege to revisit words on a page. "The reiteration of words, clauses, and themes allows the hearer to return to and link up with what was said before."[43] Mark is full of such repetition. Often the second presentation not only recalls the first but at the same time is made to serve the dramatic purpose of carrying the story forward.

If the oral tradition was the means used in the early church for keeping the memory of Jesus alive, what implication is there in this conclusion for the kind and quantity of material that was remembered? Kelber answers by noting that if the oral medium is entrusted with the preservation of information, it will control the data to be selected, the values to be preserved, and therefore the kind of Jesus to be transmitted. Unlike the modern mind's quest for the truth of the historical Jesus, the oral tradition of the day selected his words and deeds on the basis of their ability to be remembered and repeated with evangelistic power. Thus, his words and deeds are transposed into stories that are brief, concise, and easily remembered. The spoken word must be economical, patterned for remembering and not overburdened with philosophy or theology.

> The Jesus who is gathered into patterned episodes is a simplified, heroized, and visually impressive figure whose teachings emanate from controversies and who acts in a world divided into hostile camps. Oral usability prompts linguistic conduct that prefers type over character, action over tranquility, extravagance over ordinariness, confrontation over harmony, and formularity over fortuity.[44]

Unlike the modern mind, oral tradition frequently does not value preservation of the personal or historical elements of a person's biography. In the oral tradition, stories and sayings are validated not by virtue of their historical reliability, but on the authority of the speaker and in the existential reception of the hearers. From the totality of Jesus' life, the oral tradition made its selection based on the principles of mnemonic transmission and immediate relevancy. The transformation of people's lives in an oral tradition was the immediate goal. This, however, would not exclude the transmission of historical truth as a secondary function.

In Kelber's view one limitation of the oral tradition is that it does not seek to systematize its stories and sayings into the telling of a single comprehensive story of Jesus' life. Rather, orally transmitted material tends to gather to itself by association with similar oral stories or sayings already present in memory. The result, as Ong has suggested, is likely to be the stringing together of series of sayings or stories on the basis of formal association.[45] Thus the oral tradition is itself unlikely to draw all the sayings and stories of Jesus into a single, consecutive biography of the sort we find in the Gospel of Mark. Kelber's thesis is that the unique contribution of the author of Mark's Gospel comes in the organization of these orally transmitted stories and sayings into a written and carefully planned narrative of Jesus' life. Although the written version of Mark's Gospel was very likely meant to be read aloud in an oral context, the very act of writing, itself, did introduce changes into what seems to have been to that point a fairly unbroken oral tradition. These implications will be examined in the next section of this chapter entitled "The Written New Testament."

Mark is only one of the four Gospels found in the New Testament. We have focused on it for two reasons. It was likely the earliest Gospel to be written and used by the writers of two of the other Gospels in their writing. It also seems to show most clearly the oral tradition upon which the written Gospels are based. In addition to the oral sources preserved in Mark's Gospel, the writers of Matthew and Luke used another, possibly oral collection of the sayings of Jesus, which scholars have named "Q" (for *quelle*, meaning "source"). The author of Matthew followed Mark's format but wove into it other aspects of the church's concerns. Matthew is a well-planned manual of instruction and discipline for a thriving church institution. In Matthew there is a definite sense of the working out of God's cosmic plan as seen in the birth, life, death, and resurrection of Jesus. The author of the Gospel of Luke and the book of Acts does something quite different from either Mark or Matthew. For him there is a real period of elapsed time between the death and resurrection of Jesus and the giving of the Holy Spirit to his followers. Luke-Acts is therefore a kind of retrospective history of the acts of salvation in two parts. The different points of view from which Matthew and Luke-Acts were written show how the same oral sources can be shaped in different ways when woven into a written record. The Gospel of John seems to be of a different kind altogether. It is more like a meditation on the incarnation of God as the Divine Word in Jesus Christ and of his visit from heaven to earth. The narrative pattern established by Mark's Gospel or otherwise known to John imposed itself so that a unique heavenly discourse is presented in gospel form, "that is, interwoven with a recital of symbolic deeds and dialogues of the historical Christ."[46] The result is a kind of sacred drama.

The Letters

In the New Testament we find both actual letters and discourses composed in letter form. The New Testament letter offers a good example of how Christianity took over an established literary form of the period and reshaped it in creative ways. The church used the letter as a personal and intimate mode when oral communication became impossible. But the letter was much more than just a kind of direct correspondence between two people.

> To present an exhortation like the Epistle to the Hebrews in the form of a letter, or to write a doxology over the Christian salvation like the Epistle to the Ephesians, was to lend to these an intimate family character, especially when such make-believe letters could include cherished echoes of some great martyr apostle like Peter or Paul.[47]

With the exception of the genuine letters of Paul, the letters of the New Testament follow the practice of the day and are anonymous or pseudonymous—that is, given out to be the work of some great figure in the past, for example, Paul, Peter, James, or Jude. In such cases the likely intent of the real author was not to deceive or to gain fame by having the writing ascribed to someone else. "The unknown writer felt that he was a voice of the shared tradition and revelation, that all truth and leading was of a piece and derived from Christ and his chosen vessels."[48] In early Christian scripture it was understood to be the Holy Spirit that was speaking rather than an individual human author. This is often found to be the case even in the letters of Paul that he himself dictates. The personality of Paul as author is both humbled and exalted as he feels the Spirit of Christ speak through his words.

As was the case for the Gospels, especially Mark, this speaking of Christ's Spirit through Paul's letters is judged to be most real when it is predominantly oral in nature. Paul's approach throughout is characteristic of the oral tradition. Paul's focus is on the speaking and hearing, not the seeing of the written word.[49] Many of his letters are like those of a traveler who, because he cannot be with you now, writes in a very personal way as if he were there and speaking with you face to face. This oral approach to witnessing for the gospel is very much in line with the oral nature of the Gospel of Mark. Paul's whole thinking is oral and auditory in nature. He receives a "call" from God. For him life is allied to the oral word, while death is at times identified with the written word, that is, the law.[50] In his letters the *logos*, the word of God, is usually identified with the preached word of the gospel (Philippians 1:14). The gospel when spoken and heard has a powerful effect upon the believer (1 Thessalonians 2:13). And it is through the spoken word that the Holy Spirit manifests itself (1 Corinthians 2:4,13). For Paul there is an identity between the spoken word (or the letter read aloud) and the power of the Spirit to transform lives. It is through the power of the spoken word that the Spirit enters the human heart, which for Paul (and the Hebrews) is the seat of will, intentionality, emotions, and affections (1 Thessalonians 2:4,17). Thus we hear not just with our ears, but with our whole personality (mind, body, and soul). In Paul's thought the heart, which is the center of the personality and the oral word, is placed over against the outward word written with ink. In writing to the Corinthians, Paul puts it this way:

> You yourselves are our letter of recommendation, written on your hearts, to be known and read by all men; and you show that you are a letter from Christ delivered by us, written not with ink, but with the Spirit of the living God, not on tablets of stone but on tablets of human hearts.
>
> . . . our sufficiency is from God, who has qualified us to be ministers of a new covenant, not in a written code but in the Spirit; for the written code kills, but the Spirit gives life [2 Corinthians 3:2-3,5b-6].

Unlike the merely written text, the oral speaking of the gospel enters the hearts of individuals and joins speakers and hearers together into a fellowship of the word—a *logos* of giving and receiving (Philippians 4:15; Galatians 6:6). The preaching of the written Gospel is thus a key way in which the word of God may transform the hearts of individuals and create communities of Christian fellowship. Faith comes from hearing the spoken word, not seeing the written word. The obstacle to faith is a defective sense of hearing. It is through true hearing and oral confession that salvation is realized: "If you confess with your lips that Jesus is Lord and believe in your heart that God raised him from the dead, you will be saved" (Romans 10:9). Hearing and faith resulting in spoken confession is Paul's view of the appropriate response to the spoken gospel.

If Paul is so committed to the spoken gospel of the death and resurrection of Jesus, then why does he write letters? Aside from the fact that Paul was often away on his missionary travels and therefore had to write as a second best to being there, Richard Ward has suggested that Paul's use of letters may have at least partly been prompted to compensate for his weakness in oral performance.[51] With such a high value given to the oral word, any weakness in oratorical skills could serve to discredit both the speaker and the message. The Greek culture valued oral speech and produced highly trained orators. Apparently some of these were causing splits to develop in the Corinthian Church. Paul's letters could compete with these other orators successfully in that while they were written, they would have been read aloud by an elder or envoy more skilled at oral performance than was Paul. Thus the full weight and power of Paul's letters may well have been experienced not in silent reading but in public narration before the assembled congregation. The success of Paul's preaching against the splits that had developed in the Corinthian Church was perhaps due, not just to Paul's written text but also to its powerful oral performance.

In addition to Paul's own theological reasons for preferring the oral to the written (reasons not out of context with those given by the rabbis for the necessity of the oral Torah; see chap. 1), the Greek culture, in which Paul was preaching, for its own reasons gave the spoken word special status. The key to knowledge and power for the Greeks was the ability to speak well. More than that, the Greeks judged there was something divine in the feat of shining forth in a gathering by means of the spoken word.[52] If we can go by 2 Corinthians 10:10, it appears that Paul's approach was successful, for his opponents are reported as saying: "His letters are weighty and strong, but his bodily presence is weak, and his speech of no account." It seems likely that Paul wrote letters, but, for physical and theological reasons, wrote them to be spoken by the best orator he could enlist. Although written, the real life of his letters in the early church may well have been in their oral performance.

In his analysis of Paul's theology, Kelber offers a convincing analysis of how it has been an error of much Christian thought to link Paul's criticism of the Jewish law (Torah) with legal authority and salvation by works. According to Kelber the dialectic in Paul's theology is that of the oral versus the written implementation of the word of God. It is the written objectification of God's word in the law of Moses that kills the power of the Spirit to transform the heart. "In this situation the apostle refrained from consciously exploiting the religious and linguistic potential of the written medium, but embraced oral hermeneutics as a matter of theological principle."[53] Space does not permit a detailed presentation of Kelber's fascinating development of this thesis.

What is true of Paul's letters would also appear to hold for the other New Testament epistles. Although conceived in written form, their authors wrote them to be spoken in oral performance in the various Christian churches of the day.

The Revelation, or Apocalypse

The book of Revelation is a fitting conclusion to the New Testament, for its final chapters depict the culmination toward which the biblical message of redemption is seen as pointing. Like the Gospels, the letters, and other writings in the ancient world, Revelation appears to have been written to be orally performed rather than silently read. David Barr has argued that the original audience heard it as an aural experience.[54] Indeed Revelation 1:3 says, "Blessed is he who reads aloud the words of prophecy, and blessed are those who hear." Barr analyzes the signs of orality evident in the structuring of the Apocalypse that make it suitable for hearing aloud and remembering: the contents is presented in lists of sevens, threes, and twos (e.g., seven letters, seven seals, seven trumpets); the technique of remembering by place and image (e.g., a place such as a church is memorized into which a number of images can be fitted like a series of "pigeon-holes"); three scrolls each of which corresponds to a discrete action (the scroll of the churches shows the action on Patmos—Christ dictating seven letters to seven churches [2–3], the sealed scroll shows the action in heaven—worship, judgment, and salvation [4–11]; and the little scroll shows the action on earth—cosmic warfare in which the Dragon attacks the Woman but is overcome by the Divine Warrior).

Aside from its structuring in the foregoing ways for oral hearing and remembering, Barr finds that an oral setting is presumed for the presentation of the Apocalypse. A reciter stands before the congregation in the place of John, who, as the text tells us, is confined to the island of Patmos (1:3). As a prophet, John claims to have encountered the risen Christ, heard him speak, and now to be forwarding Christ's words to the believing communities in the form of the Apocalypse. The imagery of the texts indicates that John has the risen Christ dictate letters to the seven churches. The public reader then is heard, breaking into the narrative and speaking in the voice of Jesus. For example, in the final scene we suddenly hear: "I, Jesus, sent my messenger to bear witness to you these things concerning the churches. I am the root and offspring of David, the bright morning star"(Revelation 22:16).

With this kind of dramatic action, says Barr, "we are justified in concluding that the oral performance of the Apocalypse served to make Jesus present."[55] Through the public liturgical context, the Apocalypse serves as an oral mechanism to make Jesus present to the people. Barr suggests that the book was read completely through in a service that likely included a celebration of the Lord's Supper. By making the Apocalypse an enacted event in the congregation, says Barr, it has the oral dramatic power to transport us into a new world in which God triumphs over evil through the death of Jesus and the suffering of his followers. If, as is often suggested, the book is dated around 90 C.E.—a time when there was considerable persecution of the Christians—it is likely that the enacted message had a powerful effect upon its hearers.

In the paragraphs above we have seen that much of the contents of the New Testament is fundamentally oral in nature. Jesus does not write or dictate. His acts and teachings are passed on by word of mouth within the context of the worshiping communities of the early church. At some point thirty or forty years after Jesus' death, these various oral (and some written) collections of Jesus' acts and teachings are put together into a systematic life story for evangelistic purposes, perhaps first by the author of Mark and then, following that lead, by the authors of Matthew, Luke-Acts, and John. Although now in written form, these Gospels still seem to have functioned orally in the life and worship of the people. So also for the letters and the Apocalypse; although they are written, the writing is done with an eye to speaking, and the whole text was likely used as the script for oral performances in the congregations.

There seems no clear answer as to why the transition from the oral to the written basis of the word took place. The deaths of some of the original apostles, such as Peter and Paul in the Roman persecutions, may have prompted the writing of Mark. The change in dominance from oral to written literature may, in part, have occurred because the culture felt itself to be threatened.[56] Or it may be, as Kelber suggests, that the oral tradition by its very nature did not allow for a synoptic and complete presentation of Jesus—thus the author of Mark imposed the form of writing and organizing the scattered oral reports of healings, exorcisms, teaching stories, and parables into a unified whole. The unified whole of the Gospel of Mark, claims Kelber, itself functions as a parable.

> Both gospel and oral parables transcend their respective narratives by pointing to the Kingdom of God. The evangelist enacts the parabolic dynamic of Jesus' language much as the Platonic dialogues represent the Socratic form of philosophical reasoning. The gospel as a written parable may thus be understood as Jesus' Word bequeathed to Mark.[57]

It may be that the success of Mark's first written "parable of Jesus" sparked the composition of the other Gospels. As to the letters, we have already indicated some of the possible reasons as to why Paul, although thoroughly committed to the oral, devoted himself to the writing of so many letters. However, even after all of what was to be the New Testament became written, the written still only functioned as a script for the oral performance. It seems to have been in the flow of the Spirit from preacher to hearer and back that the power of God's revelation was experienced.

As we progress into the second century, we find that there was a gradual attempt to dignify the common oral tradition of the Gospels. Justin Martyr, for example, commends them as the *memorabilia* of the apostles, the same title that Xenophon gave to his literary account of Socrates, and which was used for other biographical writings of the day.[58] The shift from approaching the New Testament writings as texts to be enacted orally to seeing them as various kinds of literary writing to be read silently has continued gradually right up to the present day. To a large extent the result may be seen as a loss of contact with the transforming power of the Spirit that was evidently strongly present in the oral experience of the written text.

THE WRITTEN NEW TESTAMENT

We have seen how Jesus and the early Christian churches accepted the written Hebrew Bible as sacred scripture. Jesus made clear that he had no intention of repudiating the Jewish scriptures: "Think not that I have come to abolish the law and the prophets; I have come not to abolish them but to fulfill them" (Matthew 5:17). Paul also accepts the Hebrew Bible as scripture (Romans 1:2). Although Jesus and his immediate disciples would have used the Hebrew text or the Aramaic targums, once the mission led by Paul moved into Greek territories, the Greek translation of the Bible, the Septuagint, was used.[59] Because of the dominance of Greek speakers in the early church, the Septuagint rapidly came to dominate. It contained some additional books not present in the Hebrew text—the books that make up our current-day Apocrypha.[60] Thus, from the start Christianity was a religion of the book, although to begin with, that book was limited to the Hebrew Bible, or Old Testament, mainly in its Greek translation as the Septuagint. The attitude taken by the early Christians to the written scripture was somewhat different from that of the Jews. Whereas the rabbinic-Pharisaic Jews judged that the inspiration necessary to produce written scripture had ceased in the time of Ezra, the Christians believed that a new age of inspired revelation had dawned in Jesus, and that through him God had given the gift of the Spirit to every believer at baptism. This Spirit was judged to be the same Spirit that had inspired the prophets of old to speak God's words, which were committed to writing. The early Christians also rejected the oral Torah of the rabbis as "making void the word of God" (Mark 7:13). They were convinced that a veil was drawn over the minds of the rabbis when they read the Scriptures, and that only when a person turned to Jesus was the veil removed (2 Corinthians 3:14–16). The supreme presence of the new breaking forth of God's Spirit was to be found in the words of Jesus. His remembered words were the final authority for the early Christians, and provided them with guidance and full revelation. As John's Gospel puts it, "No man ever spoke like this man" (John 7:46). When the Gospels were first written and circulated in the early church their initial status was not as "holy books" but, rather, as books containing the "holy words" of Jesus.[61] The scripture of the New Testament, the Gospels and letters, gradually shaped itself in the struggle of the Christian community to understand its own identity. The New Testament did not drop as a stone from heaven, but grew out of the life of the Christian community as it attempted to understand the role God expected it to play in his plan for the redemption of the world.[62] This process in which the Christian community gave shape to the scripture, and was then shaped by it, is seen in the formation of the New Testament canon.

The New Testament Canon

The process that led to the collection of written items from the oral tradition into one book and its designation as the canon was a gradual one. It began with the collection of the letters of Paul and reached its climax in 367 C.E. with Athanasius' letter giving a list of the "books that are canonized and handed down to us and believed to be divine."[63] The first collection of letters attributed to Paul probably included nine letters (1,2 Thessalonians; 1,2 Corinthians; Romans; Galatians; Philippians; Colossians; Philemon), with a tenth, Ephesians, as a covering letter to the whole collection. This collection seems to have been in circulation by the end of the first century, and to be at times referred to as "scripture" (see, e.g., 2 Peter 3:15–16).

There were a fairly large number of Gospels written in the early Christian church. Unlike the letters of Paul they do not appear to have circulated in collections. Each of them seems to have come from a particular community, and to be the work of that community as much as of the anonymous author.[64] Each also employed roughly the same accumulation of oral traditions about Jesus—traditions that had been given shape by a generation or more of oral transmission. The different ways in which these oral traditions were selected from this common store and used in the writing of each Gospel reflected the special needs and interests of that community. Some Gospels gave more attention than do Matthew, Mark, Luke, or John to apparently legendary material about the infancy of Jesus or his postresurrection teaching of the disciples. Many sayings and discourse Gospels discovered at Nag Hammadi are separate from the narrative Gospels of Matthew, Luke, and John, and yet they apparently sustained a lively branch of Christianity. Although all of these Gospels circulated widely throughout the early church, by the middle of the second century the four canonical Gospels gained supremacy over the others and began to be called "scripture" by church fathers such as Justin Martyr.[65] By the end of the second century the books of Matthew, Mark, Luke, and John were accepted as the Gospels everywhere except in Syria.[66] Even then, however, there appear to have been some Christians who attached greater weight to an oral chain of testimony that could be traced back through teachers to apostles to Jesus. In their view, authority still rested in the living transmission of the words of Jesus, not in any of the books containing his words.[67]

The period that saw the collecting of the letters of Paul and the four Gospels (about 70–150 C.E.) also saw the production of a large number of other Christian writings: histories or "acts," letters, homilies, apocalypses, and so forth. Some of these achieved favorable enough status to be included in the eventual canon: Acts; the three Pastoral letters (1, 2 Timothy; Titus); the letters of James, John, Peter, and Jude; Hebrews and Revelation.

A major push toward collecting all of these writings into a single authoritative book of scripture was provided by Marcion, who lived in the middle of the second century. Before Marcion, the tendency was to add new writings to the Hebrew Bible to make up the Christian scriptures. Marcion, due to his Gnostic attitudes, believed that the creator God of the Hebrew Bible was an inferior deity to the God revealed by Jesus and so rejected the Jewish scriptures in favor of a new Christian scripture. The book of scripture that he collected contained an edited version of the Gospel of Luke and the letters of Paul. Marcion was very successful and attracted a wide following in Rome. His action and popularity forced the other Christian churches to develop their own definition of Christian scripture. Against Marcion they retained the Hebrew Bible, or Old Testament, but they accepted Marcion's division of the Christian scriptures into "gospel" and "epistle." They added, however, the other Gospels and letters mentioned above that came to be included in the final canon. In response to the challenge of Marcion and of other Gnostic writings like the Gospel of Thomas, the major congregations (a) established the idea of a Christian collection of scripture separate from the Jewish Bible; (b) expanded the Christian canon over Marcion's edited collection, but excluded others like the Gnostic Gospel of Thomas; and (c) so emphasized apostolic authority that apostolic authorship was asserted for all books included in the Christian canon.[68]

The first writer to speak of the "New Testament" as distinct from the "Old Testament" was Tertullian, who wrote in Latin in the West, mainly in Carthage (ca. 160–220 C.E.). Origen, who traveled widely and wrote in Greek in the East, mainly Alexandria (ca. 185–254 C.E.) listed the generally acknowledged books (the four Gospels, Acts, 1 John, 1 Peter, and Revelation of John) and those disputed (James, Jude, 2 Peter, 2 and 3 John). The signal event in our knowledge of the formation of the canon, however, is the letter of Athanasius, bishop of Alexandria in the East, which circulated among the churches in his charge in 367 C.E. He described the canon as follows:

> Continuing, I must without hesitation mention the Scriptures of the New Testament; they are the following: the four Gospels according to Matthew, Mark, Luke and John, after them the Acts of the Apostles and the seven so-called catholic epistles of the apostles—namely, one of James, two of Peter, then three of John and after these one of Jude. In addition to this there are fourteen epistles of the apostle Paul written in the following order; the first to the Romans, then two to the Corinthians and then after these the one to the Galatians, following it the one to the Ephesians, thereafter the one to the Philippians and the one to the Colossians and two to the Thessalonians and the epistle to the Hebrews and then immediately two to Timothy, one to Titus and lastly the one to Philemon. Yet further the Revelation of John.[69]

In the latter half of the fourth century, Jerome made a revised Latin translation of the scriptures (the Vulgate) that became the standard in the West, and in so doing he followed the New Testament canon as set forth by Athanasius. This canon gradually became accepted everywhere except in Syria. There a harmony of the four Gospels was used (the Diatessaron) rather than four separate books. But at the beginning of the fifth century, Syria accepted the four Gospels as separate books and began to move closer to the other churches. Gradually the twenty-seven-book canon gained general acceptance, not by the formal pronouncement of an all-inclusive church council, but by common consent.[70]

Much later a discussion arose between Roman Catholics and Protestants over the status of the Apocrypha—those books included in the Septuagint, the Greek translation of the Hebrew Bible, but not included in the Hebrew canon as formulated by the rabbis at Jamnia (ca. 90 C.E.). Jerome, following the practice of the early church, had used the Septuagint as the text for his Old Testament translation into Latin and so had included the Apocryphal books. But Luther in his 1534 translation of the Bible included only the books of the Hebrew canon in his Old Testament. The Apocryphal books he placed in a separate section following the end of the Old Testament, under the heading "Apocrypha: these are books which are not held equal to the sacred Scriptures, and yet are useful and good for reading."[71] This is the reason that Protestant translations such as the Revised Standard Version and the New English Bible usually do not include the books of the Apocrypha in the Old Testament whereas Roman Catholic versions do. The Council of Trent in 1546 declared the entire Bible of the Old Testament and the New Testament, and of the same extent as the Vulgate, as canonical.

We have seen that the emergence of written scriptures and the formation of the New Testament canon occurred as a gradual transition from oral authorities to written authorities, and from functionally authoritative writings to formally authoritative writings. The consequences of the formation of this canon on the Christian experience of its scripture have been far-reaching. These writings were originally seen to be authoritative because of their connection with the apostles, who were regarded as eyewitnesses and thus in a position to attest to the revelation given in Jesus. But once these writings were canonized, it was an easy step to begin to view them not as testimonies to the revelation given in Jesus, but as being revelatory in and of themselves. Instead of being seen as the words of the apostles, the New Testament comes to be seen as the word of God mediated through the apostles. The authority of scripture is no longer basically rooted in the historical proximity of the apostles to Jesus, but equally in its own divine "inspiration."[72] The written form of the New Testament now claims the "inspired" status that in the early church was reserved for the oral experience of the word. It is in this shift of the ontological basis of the New Testament revelation from the oral to the written that the roots of Protestant literalism may be found. This shift was further aided by the impact of printing, which made it possible for each person to possess his or her own Bible and to study it privately and silently.

Materials and Methods of Writing

The first-century Christians made use of the commonly used writing material of their day, papyrus.[73] Papyrus was made from the pith of a plant grown in Egypt. The pith was sliced thin, and strips running one direction were glued to other strips running at right angles to the first strips to form a sheet. These sheets were glued to each other end to end to form a scroll on which the writing was done in successive columns. One scroll could accommodate a work of the size of the Gospel of Matthew.

The early Christians seem to have pioneered another kind of writing, which in some ways prefigures the modern book. Papyrus scroll ends were trimmed to the same size and folded in the middle inside each other like the pages of a book. This book, called a codex, could be made up in any size by the writer. By the fourth century, parchment materials were being used in the making of codex as well as scroll copies of the early Christian writings. Parchment was more durable than papyrus, and in codex form could have two, three, or four columns of narrow writing to the page. Except in very dry climates, the papyrus perished quickly. This has likely been the fate of the originals of the New Testament Gospels and the letters. Once they were recopied onto parchment they had a much better chance of survival. In the writing of books, whether on papyrus or parchment, pen and ink were used (2 John 12). The large number of times that books and scrolls had to be recopied to be preserved and circulated allowed many sorts of scribal errors (e.g., missing out words or lines, recopying lines, etc.) to be introduced into the text. Thus the earlier the text that can be found, the closer we can get to the original. The writing was done in different scripts in different periods, and these differences help in dating the copy. A running hand was employed in which the letters and even the words were joined together, which meant the reader had to separate the letters into words while reading. To do this easily and without error presupposed previous knowledge of the text. In this way the oral is seen to continue as a strong influence over the written. The text was usually read aloud by a skilled reader for the whole congregation (Revelation 1:3). But even when one read alone, such reading was done aloud (Acts 8:30). Writing was probably also done aloud rather than silently as we do today.[74]

English Versions of the Bible[75]

Prior to the sixteenth century, translations of the Bible into English were made from the Latin Vulgate rather than from the Hebrew (Old Testament) and Greek (New Testament) texts. The first English translations of the complete Bible were those of John Wyclif, made from the Latin Vulgate between 1380 and 1397. They were copied by hand and some one hundred and eighty manuscripts remain. This was a careful literal translation with the English words closely following those of the Latin. The sixteenth century saw eight English versions of the Bible completed, beginning with Tyndale's translation in 1526 and culminating in the King James Version published in 1611. Tyndale was the first English translation made directly from the Hebrew and Greek manuscripts. A translation by Miles Coverdale in 1535 was the first Bible to be printed in English. But it was the Geneva Bible of 1560 that was the first Bible to be printed and widely distributed through English homes. It was set in easy-to-read Roman type and in a convenient size, rather than the unwieldly folio format previously used. The Geneva Bible was used by Shakespeare and John Bunyan, and was the Bible the Puritans carried with them when they settled in America. Thus it has had a wide influence.

The King James Version (KJV), which is also known as the Authorized

Version (AV), was made in response to the command of King James I of England, "That a translation be made of the whole Bible, as consonant as can be to the original Hebrew and Greek; and this to be set out and printed without any marginal notes, and only to be used in all churches of England in time of divine service."[76] The stated purpose of the King James translation was that it was to be used in worship. This meant that it was a translation intended to be read aloud to the congregation in line with the oral practice of the early Christian use of Scripture. In this it succeeded brilliantly, and its fundamental oral quality has been preserved in varying degrees through the revisions of the KJV right up to the present day. It has also had a lasting impression on English literature and popular speech. The translators of the KJV were men experienced in the public reading of the scriptures in the context of public worship. Their choice of the final wording of a passage was determined by oral criteria—what would sound good when read aloud. The particular merit of the KJV is the music of its cadences, and in this sense, although written, it is an expression in English of the original oral New Testament. A major failure of the majority of the recent English translations is that they lack this crucial musical quality. Written to convey the exact meaning of the text or to attempt a paraphrase relevant for modern secular society, they lack the oral power that is the essence of the New Testament experience of God's word and the hallmark of the King James Version (and its revisions).

EXEGESIS

The writing down of the oral traditions and their subsequent canonization as the New Testament has given to later Christian thought a fundamentally exegetical character. The task of exegesis, or interpretation, was posed by the canonization of the New Testament for two reasons. The first was the diverse nature of the canon itself. As a collection of writings embodying a variety of circumstances and viewpoints, these internal inconsistencies had to be harmonized if the doctrine of divine inspiration was to be taken seriously. Internal differences also needed to be overcome in the interest of the coherence and authority of the New Testament as a whole. In addition there was the need to demonstrate the unity of the Old and New Testaments. Exegetical efforts were thus directed to showing that internal differences were only apparent and that with proper interpretation all parts of the New Testament were in essential agreement. The second reason for exegesis was that once the canon was closed, there was a need for interpretation to make the fixed revelation relevant to the changing conditions of subsequent centuries. While canonization limited and stabilized the resources for Christian teaching and worship, exegesis has had the task of enlarging the meaning of the New Testament texts so that they apply to the ever widening life of the Christian church.[77]

Christian exegesis has always had the practical objective of teaching its followers. Although the literal and historical sense of the text is valued, doctrinal instruction also requires the discovery of more profound spiritual and moral truths. Thus any single passage of scripture may be found to yield a variety of interpretations at various levels of spiritual depth. The legitimacy of such interpretations, so long as they fall generally within the boundaries of orthodox doctrine, is determined by their relevance and usefulness in their own settings.[78] There is, therefore, a rich diversity of methods of exegesis to be found in the history of the interpretation of the Christian scriptures. Although some of the approaches may seem fanciful to the modern mind, their power can be measured only by the degree to which they enabled the Bible to remain a strong force in the long life of the Christian church. Throughout, the openness and flexibility to encompass a variety of interpretations has been the strength of the Christian tradition. In this connection it must be noted that two modern approaches (historical-critical interpretation and fundamentalist interpretation), each of which claims to be the "true interpretation," go against the open and flexible approach that has enabled scripture to maintain its authority within the church in the past. The modern historical-critical method of biblical interpretation, which claims to attempt to recover the "original meaning" of the biblical texts and represents this meaning as the "true" interpretation, is far removed from the methods and aims of traditional Christian exegesis, as is the literal fundamentalist type of biblical interpretation, which also claims "the truth" for itself.[79] What follows is a brief survey of some of the different approaches taken to exegesis in the history of the Christian tradition.

Allegory: Origen and the Church Fathers

A basic question behind the various approaches to scriptural exegesis is "How many meanings may a given passage have?" An answer that was strongly to influence the first thousand years of Christian interpretation was provided by Origen of Alexandria in the second and third centuries. Origen was influenced by the Jewish interpreter Philo who had lived in Alexandria two centuries earlier. Like Philo, Origen wanted to go beyond the literal meaning of a passage to find a "deeper meaning." The technique used to find the "deeper meaning" was the art of allegory, namely, of finding that the words of a passage stood for another suggestively similar subject, for example, that the mention of an "angel" or "the Lord" in part of the Old Testament really refers to Jesus. Origen, in fact, proposed three meanings to be found in a passage: the literal meaning, which he called its "body"; the deeper allegorical meaning, which he called its "soul"; and the anagogical meaning (the eschatological or end goal), which he called its "spirit." These three different levels of meaning were recommended by Origen so that three kinds of people could benefit: the simple person by the "body" of the text, the one who has ascended some way by its "soul," and the perfected person by its "spirit."

Although the church later condemned the theological results of Origen's interpretations, his exegetical method was adopted. Origen's legacy to the church was (a) the assumption of at least a second meaning lying universally beneath the letter and to be found by allegory; (b) a great fund of clever allegory to many texts of both Testaments; and (c) a theory of the threefold meaning of scripture.[80] There was one protest from scholars at Antioch, who argued against the allegorist's finding of predictions of Christ almost throughout the Old Testament. Otherwise the dominant exegesis of both the Eastern and Western wings of the church uncritically followed Origen's approach. So for a thousand years the Christian exegete could offer several meanings for each passage of scripture. One mnemonic couplet of the period put it this way: "The letter teaches the events, allegory what you are to believe, the moral sense what you are to do, anagoge whither you are to strive."[81]

The Literal Sense: Jewish Influence, Andrew of St. Victor, and Nicholas of Lyra[82]

The impetus to move away from a basically allegorical approach to interpretation seems to have come to Christian scholars from Jewish sources in the eleventh century. At that time the great reformer of exegesis of both the Torah and the Talmud, Rabbi Solomon ben Isaac (Rashi), directs his attention to the literal meaning of the text. He does not completely reject allegorical interpretations but sifts them and keeps only those that seem compatible with the literal meaning. His goal was to explain scripture according to its simple meaning and beyond that to include only secondary interpretations that expound the words of the Bible appropriately. A Christian group that seems to have been influenced by the exegetical approach of Rashi and his students was the school of St. Victor. This group of St. Victor was a chapter of canons regular (not monks) of the rule of St. Augustine founded in Paris in 1110, only some eighty miles distant from where Rashi had died at Troyes. The canon conducted a theological school that was led by three teachers: Hugh, Richard, and Andrew. Hugh, the earliest of the three teachers, while not abandoning mystical meanings had a clear grasp and insistence upon the literal meaning as basic. In his writings he frequently offers the exegetical interpretation of "a Hebrew" whom he does not identify but is quite likely Rashi. One of Hugh's students, Andrew, gave full development to the exegetical approach of his teacher. Andrew apparently had regular meetings with Jewish scholars and knew enough Hebrew to read a text with the help of a rabbi.[83] Andrew's method is to give a twofold exegesis: (a) the Vulgate and its Christian explanation; and (b) the Hebrew text and its Jewish explanation. Since he takes the traditional Christian explanation to be well known, he takes special pains to present the Jewish interpretation, which emphasizes the literal meaning.[84] Andrew demands that his text should make plain sense and he often finds that the Jewish interpretation fills this requirement better than the traditional Christian approach. Andrew's detailed study of the Old Testament, with his passionate desire to get closer to the text and its meaning, opened the window to a renewal of biblical scholarship in his day. As to the deeper theological meaning of the text, that he was happy to leave to the speculations of the theologians. Beryl Smalley's analysis of Andrew's influence suggests that he played a vital part in setting new directions for biblical exegesis, especially in the thirteenth century.[85]

Nicholas of Lyra, a Franciscan professor at the University of Paris (died ca. 1349), certainly knew Andrew's work and quoted him. Nicholas has the distinction of being the author of the first Bible commentary ever printed (eighty-five books in five huge folio volumes). Throughout the first two centuries of printing, this commentary was reprinted in many countries, editions, and forms. The first fifty books go through the whole of the scripture giving a literal interpretation. The other thirty-five books cover the same ground with a mystical commentary. His statement of method in the second prologue to the first fifty books shows the influence of Rashi, Hugh, and Andrew:

> All (senses) presuppose the literal as a foundation . . .: thus a mystical exposition at variance with the literal sense is to be regarded as improper and tactless, or, other things being equal, as at least not very decent or tactful.[86]

Nicholas insisted upon the literal sense, but he did not stop there. The purpose of the first fifty books and their focus on the literal sense was to furnish a firm foundation for the following thirty-five books of mystical commentary. While still allowing for the traditional finding of levels of meaning, he shifts the emphasis strongly to the literal sense.

Also during the thirteenth century, Roger Bacon in England (at Oxford) was making an important impact on biblical exegesis. Bacon criticizes biblical scholars for neglecting scientific Bible study. He means by that their ignorance of the biblical languages, which invalidates their interpretation. Bacon supported the earlier arguments of St. Jerome and St. Augustine for studying scripture in the original. "He explains how knowledge of Hebrew and Chaldean is indispensable to an understanding of the idiom and rhythm, and hence the meaning of the Old Testament, and Greek to an understanding of the New."[87] He called for a complete revision of the Vulgate on the basis of original sources. Yet his principles of interpretation did not really differ from those of Hugo, Andrew, or Nicholas, except perhaps in a requirement for a more extensive preparation for Bible study. His method was the study of language to establish the text and the use of science to expound the literal sense as a firm foundation upon which to work out the higher spiritual meaning.[88] During this period in England and in Paris many scholars were busily working on the very basis Bacon sets forth.[89]

Luther, the Reformers, and the Sole Authority of Scripture[90]

Luther began by adopting the old tradition of interpretation through allegory. Later he came to value the commentary of Nicholas of Lyra, and its stress upon the literal sense of the text. Allegories are only to be used if the text itself exhibited them or they could be cited from the New Testament. Luther warns readers to search for the literal and not be led astray by the church fathers who forsake the literal and hunt for allegories. He ridicules the idea that scripture has several levels of meaning and directs his energy to reach one simple, germane literal meaning. Luther says, "For I consider the ascription of several senses to Scripture to be not merely dangerous and useless for teaching but even to cancel the authority of Scripture whose meaning ought always to be one and the same."[91] Allegories are allowed by Luther only as an ornament or amplification of the simple story or the naked text. However, in his own exegesis Luther used allegory in interpreting the Old Testament so as to make it dovetail with the literal meaning of the New Testament. He found not merely messianic allusions but explicit references to Jesus Christ in many Old Testament passages.

Luther believed that the natural person alone cannot understand the Bible. Such a person must first be taken possession of or transformed by the action of God's Holy Spirit. Only then can the text be understood. As Luther puts it:

> Nobody can speak correctly of a word or scripture or really understand it, if his soul has not had an inner experience like the one of which he reads, so that deep within himself he feels what his eyes read and he cries out, "Yes, truly, this is right." . . .
>
> It is the mysterious quality of scripture that it does not take on the likeness of him who studies it, but rather it transforms whoever loves it into its own likeness and bestows its virtues upon him.[92]

Taking this principle seriously, Luther sometimes acknowledges that he cannot interpret a text because he has not had the requisite spiritual experience—"One would have to have the spiritual experience of Bernard to be able to understand this word."[93] For Luther, then, exegesis required two things: (1) one must first understand the words in their simple and ordinary sense, and (2) one must receive the words with a right disposition and feel them in one's heart.

In Luther's approach there are certainly strong resonances with the original oral tradition of the early Christian church. Luther's stress on the right disposition of the hearer and the simple word meant that an ordinary layperson possessing these qualities might be better able to understand the Bible than a scholar or church official who lacked them. Of primary importance for Luther is not intellectual understanding or the finding of proof-texts with which to win scholastic theological debates. Rather, it is that the reader is taken captive by the text and his or her life transformed. In Luther's view God intends to meet all people in the Bible through the working of his Spirit. Thus all theological and church authorities must submit themselves to the voice of God in the scriptures. For Luther the Bible is not just a collection of supernatural truths to be believed and laws to be lived, but a living book in which God encounters the individual, speaks his judgment, offers his grace, and demands an answer.[94]

Whereas Luther saw in the Bible God's judging and forgiving encounter with the reverent reader, Calvin

> tended to see the Bible as an extended narrative account of a single connected history of God's covenant with his people, first on the basis of a promise, which evokes hope (the Old Testament), and then on the basis of the fulfillment of that promise, which evokes faith (the New Testament) centering on Jesus Christ, to whom hope looked forward and at whom faith looks back.[95]

Calvin's contention about the unity of the Bible's message carried two implications for exegesis. First, it gave the Reformers freedom to be critical of some books included in the canon. For example, both Luther and Calvin could not see Christ's Spirit as being present in the Revelation of John and so they tended to set it aside. Second, the stress on Christ as the subject of all inspired scripture allowed the Reformers to acknowledge "errors" in scripture. Calvin, for example, with his awareness of the scientific knowledge of his day, had no qualms in suggesting that Moses (whom he assumed to be the author of Genesis) is in error on certain aspects of astronomical accuracy.[96] "The Reformers stressed that in inspiring the authors of the biblical writings, God 'accommodated' himself, both to the limitations of our capacities to understand God and to the limits set by the writers' personalities and historical settings."[97] Thus the writers of the Bible could be in error on details, but they would never be mistaken in regard to the Bible's basic point—the good news of God's reconciling love in Christ.

In 1567, three years after Calvin's death, a book entitled *Key to the Scriptures* was published by Matthaeus Flacius Illyricus in which the principal teachings of the Reformers about scripture are summed up. Flacius laid down four rules:

1. Ascertain how the original readers of the biblical text understood individual words. And that demands a command of Hebrew and Greek. "Without that, O Reader, you are necessarily dependent on the judgment of others, or you must guess at the meaning!"
2. Ascertain how the readers understand the sense of the passage as a whole that is imparted by the words of the individual sentences. "Only so can one avoid getting a false meaning from badly constructed sentences."
3. Ascertain how the original readers understood the "spirit of him who speaks"—"the reason, the understanding, the judgment, and the purpose (or *scopus*) of the speaker."
4. Ascertain how the application of any given passage of Scripture is to be understood. "For Scripture divinely inspired is useful for teaching, for clarification, for correction, and for instruction in righteousness. . . . This understanding is assisted usually by assiduous and devout reading and especially by meditation."[98]

Ascertain how the original readers of the biblical texts understood individual words, and the sense of the passage as a whole—the first two rules of Flacius—sum up the grammatical-historical method in interpretation used by the Reformers. The original meaning of the text is not discovered by getting into the mind of the writer but by putting oneself in the position of the original readers or hearers. Rather than looking for allegorical or deeper levels of meaning, the medieval method, the Reformers felt that their method of exegesis uncovered the literal meaning. But "literal" here needs to be understood with care; for them it meant the "natural" sense of the passage. "So if stylistic and grammatical analysis show that a passage would have been seen as a moral parable or as an allegory by its original readers, then its literal sense would be its moral or allegorical sense."[99] This is a quite different understanding of "literal" from the way it is often used today—the unimaginative grammatical meaning of a text.

As we have seen, the Reformers' approach to the text required that one already be in the context of faith—be in the grasp of the Holy Spirit. Only then would one be in a position to understand the religious sense of the text. For them this religious sense was the literal sense and the historical sense of the text, since that is what the text had meant to the original hearers. The Reformers simply assumed the identity of these meanings. But the very method they developed, requiring first a focusing on the understanding of the individual words in the original languages, sowed the seeds for a split between this and the religious sense of the text to develop—especially when the eighteenth-century biblical scholars adopted the historian's methods to discover the Bible's historical or literal sense. Printing enabled all people to have their own copy and also to engage in this detailed study of individual words of the biblical text. But more of that later. For the Reformers the important point was that God loves and forgives by faith alone, and the good news that this is so comes through scripture alone *(sola scriptura)*. Indeed, for Luther, it comes only through scripture used orally, that is, actively engaged in preaching.[100]

The Roman Catholic Church: Tradition in Relation to Scripture

If a scripture passage can have a variety of meanings, as in the allegorical interpretation of the Middle Ages, then some other authority beside it or above it would seem to be necessary to guide faith, conduct, and even the process of exegesis itself. Such an authority was at hand in the notion of "tradition," which began to develop from the second century on.[101] Originally it meant the sum total of what had been passed on by the apostles, oral and written. But by the third and fourth centuries, tradition was understood as being separate from scripture. Tradition is understood as "the unwritten ongoing life of the church handed down in unbroken succession from the apostles—indeed, tradition *is* the church."[102] Even with his high view of scripture, Augustine says, "I would not believe the gospel if the authority of the Catholic Church did not impel me to do so.[103] Thus the Christian accepts the canon and interpretation of scripture only at the direction of the church, for it was the church after all that established, and maintains, the canon. This notion of tradition, later formulated as "what has been believed everywhere, always, by everybody,"[104] proved problematic because the early church fathers clearly did not *always* agree, nor did the later church councils, which sometimes reversed each other. After the Council of Trent, tradition defined as "the mind of the church" was consistently placed above scripture. But where is "the mind of the church" to be found? The answer received by Roman Catholics from the First Vatican Council in 1869 was, "in the Pope; since then it is he who, as the embodiment of the Catholic tradition, decides what scripture means."[105]

Part of this Roman Catholic stress on tradition controlling scripture comes as a reaction to the Protestant emphasis upon "scripture alone." Bruce Vawter points out that before the Reformation provoked the Catholic church into its emphasis on tradition over scripture, the church had maintained a strong biblical orientation.[106] A theologian of the Middle Ages was primarily a biblical scholar. Before writing theological treatises, one had to produce biblical commentaries judged to be worthy. Vawter even claims "that no Fathers of the church, no medieval theologians of the church, would have been uncomfortable with the formula of *sola scriptura*."[107] This, he says, is exactly what they thought they were doing when they interpreted scripture in terms of what centuries of tradition had taught them it meant. What they could not accept, however, "was that the proverbial ploughboy with the vernacular Bible in his hand was a match for the pope of Rome with all the councils of the church behind him."[108] Another Roman Catholic commentator, George Tavard, takes a similar line to Vawter. Tavard's analysis shows that throughout the earlier centuries of Christian thought, there is no duality experienced between scripture and tradition.[109] Rather, the underlying unity, or oneness, of scripture and tradition is assured. The church, created by the gospel and guided by the Holy Spirit, passes on the scripture of the gospel from bishop to bishop, teacher to teacher, and generation to generation. Tradition as the art of passing on the gospel is not distinct from the gospel. Rather, it is the power of the gospel itself, which inspires the devotion and loyalty of the people and churches responsible for its transmission. Gospel creates tradition, and tradition safeguards and serves the gospel. At bottom, though, the two are one: "There is a sense in which 'Scripture alone' is an authentic expression of Catholic Christianity, inasmuch as, the Scripture is, in the Church, the apostolic tradition and *vice versa*."[110] Tavard's analysis indicates that the spirit of the Council of Trent also supports a unity of scripture and tradition: "It [Trent] finally respects the classical view: Scripture contains all revealed doctrine, and the Church's faith, which includes apostolic traditions, interprets it."[111]

Catholic thinkers have used the notion of progressive revelation to work back to a unity of scripture and tradition. Jean Levie, for example, sees scripture as entrusted to the church because the church is the continuation of Christ down through the centuries.[112] In the church, the structure in which

Christ intended we should receive the scripture, his Spirit constantly works toward a better understanding of scripture and the truths it teaches. The exegesis by an individual of scriptural texts could not have produced the great teachings of the church councils (e.g., the Trinity and the Christological dogmas). Only by the action of the Holy Spirit in and through the life of the church could the exegesis of the scriptures produce such truths. Through the continued action of the Holy Spirit in the changing life of the church, a progressively deeper insight into scripture is obtained. It is only in this dynamic interchange between tradition and scripture that God's divine plan in its various stages of realization is made understandable to us.[113] Levie's analysis is suggestive of Tavard's concluding illustration: "The Book is the Word of God, and the City is the Church. The Book leads to the City. Yet the City is described in the Book. To prefer the one to the other amounts to renouncing both."[114]

After reviewing the most recent pronouncements of the Roman Catholic Church on scripture, Vawter concludes that in terms of its balance and openness, the church of the fathers or of the Middle Ages was in a better position.[115] The adversarial situation initiated by the Reformation cry of *sola scriptura* and aggravated by the claims to truth of modern biblical scholarship (see below) has left a rift between scripture and tradition that, although progress is being made, has yet to heal fully.

Scripture in Eastern Orthodox Christianity[116]

At its roots Eastern Orthodoxy identifies itself with Antioch as opposed to Alexandria in matters of biblical exegesis. We recall that Alexandria under the influence of Philo first, and Origen later, was the home of the allegorical approach to interpretation. The great fathers of Orthodoxy, men such as John Chrysostom, relied on the scholars of Antioch and their concentration upon the historical event as opposed to the allegorization and mystical speculation characteristic of Alexandria.

To begin with, the Antioch scholars used a different text of the Bible as the basis for their exegesis. Whereas the Alexandrian school used Origen's text, the Antioch school used a text called the "Lucian." Lucian had prepared this version by comparing the Greek Septuagint with the Hebrew text so as to produce a corrected version, which sometimes preferred the Hebrew reading, sometimes the Greek, and sometimes gave both. The Lucian text became very popular and was adopted as the standard text of the Greek-speaking church. Lucian's aim seems to have been to achieve intelligibility and smoothness by replacing nouns with proper names, by using his own words to clarify the sense of a passage, and by filling gaps in the narrative with his own material. While this may not have met the standards of critical correctness, Lucian's aim was that the scriptural narrative convey clearly what happened on a certain occasion. He wanted the text to give the details of a historical event to later generations. Origen, on the other hand, was more concerned to have the inspired minute details of the text correct, to be used as a jumping-off point for mystical speculation. The import of this philosophical difference is seen in the attack on Origen's commentary on the Witch of Endor passage (1 Samuel 28) by the Antioch scholar Eustathius.[117] Origen gave little attention to the historical situation, instead concentrating upon details of the wording that conveyed moral and spiritual teaching relevant to his third-century congregation. The words of the text were a code or riddle to be solved—a riddle through which Christ spoke to Origen's congregation. Eustathius challenges Origen's method of seeing every syllable of the text as being a vehicle of divine oracles. What happens, Eustathius asks, when the text contains the words of evil people, for example, a devil-inspired witch? Surely such words cannot be read as God's words to his people. A discrimination is therefore called for. Each passage has to be judged on the merits of the historical circumstances in which it occurs. Only the words of scriptural persons judged to be scriptural persons should be relied upon for guidance. Eustathius and the Antioch school saw the historical sense of the text—that is, the sense which the writer of the text intended—as having final importance. This was not a simple-minded literalism but an insistence that the ancient text be seen in its own terms. It may be thought of as presupposing "a sacramental view of historical events."[118]

The differences between these approaches is clearly seen in the matter of Old Testament prophecies concerning Jesus. Whereas the allegorizing approach could find foretellings of Jesus in almost any line of the Old Testament, the Antioch exegete would consider such a possibility only when the historical context of the passage clearly indicates that the writer is referring to things to come. Another scholar of Antioch, Theodoret, takes the approach of first placing the passage historically and then interpreting it with the aid of typology. Certain things may be seen to happen historically in the Old Testament, for example, God's care for Israel, as a type that is fulfilled in the New Testament, for example, God's care for all people in Christ. But the Antioch scholar Theodoret is very restrictive about the use of such typology. Even though based on firm historical foundations, Theodoret would allow typological exegesis only on rare occasions—just a few great peaks of Old Testament history could be seen as foreshadowing greater peaks in the Christian age to come, for example, the deliverance from Egyptian exile and from Babylonian captivity. Such observations were not allegorizing but were instances of *theoria*, or insight, which enabled the Christian to see what could not have been seen by people living under the old law, and to recognize God's divine action, which runs through both Testaments. The conclusion of Theodoret's exegetical method is that "typology based upon historical fact is permitted, allegory is not."[119]

By the time of the fifth century, the Antioch school shows less difference from Alexandria. The use of allegory has begun to creep in and the use of typology by writers such as Aprahat is so uncritical as to be described as "running riot." All that is needed for a typological link to be made is a similar historical event happening in both Testaments. But the clear tradition that the Greek church had received from the Antioch scholars was "the restrained use of biblical allegorizations, the fixing of attention upon things known and understood as means of apprehending the unknown."[120] In the fifth century Theodoret's work was translated into Syriac, making him a strong influence in the Syrian church. For Theodoret and the other Syrians who followed him, the key issue was God's action in the salvation of the human soul. "If that was the center where the real battle was fought, the Scriptures provided a map of the battlefield, a history of the battle up to the time of Christ, and a vision of the cosmic scale of the conflict to its ultimate and inevitable outcome."[121] To misread one's map by using bad methods of exegesis might well prevent one from joining in the final victory.

Some modern Orthodox scholars still champion the typological method of the Antioch school. This method is seen as being grounded on the activity of God's Spirit in shaping historical events.[122] It is proposed that there is an ontological relationship between the original occurrence in scripture (the type) and the second occurrence (the typified mystery), for example, the Exodus from Egypt is a prophetic image of our salvation accomplished by Christ's death and resurrection. Both events are seen to be acts by God of a saving type but occurring at different stages in the historical realization of God's grand plan. For the Orthodox exegete, then, typology is an integral part of God's plan and manifests itself in the gradual progression of sacred history toward its ultimate goal—the kingdom that is to come. It is based on the belief that God acts continually within history through the Holy Spirit to shape events toward his desired end. Thus historical events do not just belong to a "secular realm" in which God is absent or dead, but to God's divine pattern of action in the world. Typology, therefore, is more than just a method of human exegesis; it is a pattern of God's activity within history created by the Holy Spirit.[123]

Modern Biblical Criticism[124]

Following the Reformation, humanistic scholars were boldly examining the composition and authorship of various ancient documents. It did not take long for these methods to be applied to the Bible. Thomas Hobbes (1588–79) denied that the Bible itself is God's revelation, maintaining instead that it simply contains the words of persons who received this revelation. Baruch Spinoza (1632–77) argued for the right of reason to interpret scripture free of church authority. The rationalistic studies of both Hobbes and Spinoza concluded that Moses did not write all of the Pentateuch and dated some parts of the Old Testament to after the exile. In 1753 Jean Astruc used the different divine names of Yahweh and Elohim as a basis for theorizing that the Pentateuch is made up of separate underlying documents. Other scholars such as Johann Gottfried Herder (1782) drew attention to the amount and quality of the poetry in the Old Testament. All of this laid the groundwork for the publication by Johann Eichhorn in 1780 of the first "Introduction to the Old Testament" based on independent historical investigation.

The eighteenth century also saw the beginnings of New Testament criticism.

The Enlightenment philosophers were attacking the miracles as simply wondrous tales. Various rationalistic analyses suggested that faith was opposed to reason and that the disciples had fabricated much of the scriptural record of Jesus. At the turn of the century—in 1794—the great German philosopher Immanuel Kant published his *Religion within the Limits of Reason Alone*, in which he argued that reason itself can produce all the teachings contained in the revelation of Jesus.[125] Kant intended this to be a defense of scriptural revelation, which had been discredited by attacks on the miracles. Kant's rationalistic analysis of scripture was followed by similar studies by Hegel and Schleiermacher. These philosophical influences led to a long series of attempts at producing a rationalistic reconstruction of the "historical" Jesus. The most outstanding of these attempts was the *Leben Jesu* of David Friedrich Strauss (1835). In Strauss's treatment Jesus appeared as nothing more than a Jewish wise man. Although failing to reconstruct the historical Jesus, Strauss did point out principles by which traditions appearing in the Gospels had been preserved, thus paving the way for the formulation of the synoptic two-document theory by Holtzmann (1863) and Weiss (1882).

The "historical" Jesus produced by nineteenth-century scholarship was little more than the ideal moral man of modern liberalism in the guise of a Galilean peasant.[126] The contribution of the liberal biblical scholars of this period was in the negative form of a radical antithesis to the traditional view of Jesus taught by the church. It became the task of the twentieth-century scholars to find a middle position or balance between the faith view of the church and the radical critique of liberal historical scholarship. A trio of conservative biblical scholars working in Cambridge, England, at the turn of the century—B. F. Westcott, J. B. Lightfoot, and F. J. A. Hort—provided an alternative to the liberal scholars and thus prepared the way for a more balanced approach in the twentieth century. As the twentieth century began, the nineteenth-century tendencies toward excessively rationalistic and evolutionary interpretations were being corrected. New methods of interpretation were being developed. A group of German scholars associated with Hermann Gunkel began to apply themselves to comparative religions and form-critical methods with fruitful results for biblical interpretation. Gunkel stressed three methods of approach: (a) determination of the oral tradition lying behind the written documents, (b) comparison of biblical motifs with similar motifs in the religions of Egypt and Mesopotamia and (c) a literary analysis of the forms in which the various tales, laws, and poems of the scriptures appear. Gunkel employed these methods with great success in his commentary on the Psalms published in 1933. Three New Testament scholars who followed his lead and pioneered literary studies of the forms of the gospels were Martin Dibelius, K. L. Schmidt and Rudolf Bultmann.

Bultmann may be taken as a good example of a modern biblical exegete. He rejects both the liberals' equating of faith with a moral life (following Kant) and also the liberal quest for the historical Jesus. For Bultmann, faith is not understood in moral terms but as "authentic self-understanding"—the way the words of scripture relate to oneself. Interpretation involves, first, recognizing the words of scripture as the author's own expression of faith's self-understanding, and second, a restating of that faith experience in the existential terms that are born in one's own response to the gospel. Authenticity is present, says Bultmann, when one's response to the word is "marked by freedom from every preoccupation with proving oneself and by freedom to respond in service to the needs of one's neighbour."[127] Contemporary restatements of the text, says Bultmann, do not reconstruct the historical Jesus, but recover and reexpress in modern terms the faith experience of the early Christian communities. This approach challenged the assumption, which was widely held by historians, theologians and philosophers, that the literal or historical sense of a text is its referent. Instead, following the earlier lead of Schleiermacher, it is the religious sense that had been experienced by the original author or hearer, and is now relived with input from the life-experience of the modern interpreter—it is this new existential religious sense that is the referent of the text.

Another modern interpreter, Karl Barth, takes a different but complementary approach to that of Bultmann. Bultmann's interpretation results in a loss of the historical dimension of the text. Barth also goes beyond the original historical dimension of the text, but does so by focusing on the "Divine giver" rather than upon the receiver of the text, as does Bultmann. For Barth, since God, Christ, and all of revelation stand above history, there is really no problem in reconciling the experience of the first-century scripture writers and hearers with our experience today. Since the referent of the text is God (or Christ) who stands unchanging above all history, therefore there should be no tension between the first-century experience of the text and our own today, for they are both experiences of the same unchanging God in Christ. Barth sees himself as following the exegesis of reformers like Calvin, who

> having first established what stands in the text, sets himself to re-think the whole material and to wrestle with it till the walls which separate the sixteenth century from the first become transparent, i.e., till Paul *speaks* there and the man of the sixteenth century *hears* here, till the conversation between the document and the reader is totally concentrated on the subject matter, which *cannot* be a different one in the first and sixteenth century.[128]

Because it is God who speaks to us in the scripture from beyond time, his word is universally relevant for all ages. Thus no interpretive footwork of the sort employed by Bultmann is needed. Barth's solving of the relevance problem by making the referent of the text eternal and "other" is an effective theological move, but one that does not seem to take seriously the differences that do exist between the hearing of the text by an early Christian congregation and the hearing of the same text by a contemporary congregation.

In contrast to both Bultmann and Barth, a third modern scholar, Oscar Cullmann, focuses on the historical sense of time. Cullmann's argument is that it is the experience of time and history rather than an eternal (Barth) or existential (Bultmann) truth that provides the context within which the New Testament moves.[129] In Cullmann's view it is essential that this linear-historical dimension undergird any exegesis of the gospel to the present age.

Krister Stendahl suggests that the success of scholars in achieving good descriptive knowledge of the first-century Christians and their neighbors has made possible a new goal for exegesis, namely, the empathetic understanding of the first century and its theology without having to make use of categories from later times.[130] "Never before," writes Stendahl, "was there a frontal nonpragmatic, nonapologetic attempt to describe OT or NT faith and practice from within its original presuppositions, and with due attention to its own organizing principles, regardless of its possible ramifications for those who live by the Bible as the Word of God."[131] This descriptive approach ushers the modern thinker into the world of biblical thought and its own theology. Especially important is the realization that the questions being asked in New Testament theology are often different from the questions being asked today. Such new or changed questions, says Stendahl, can only produce confusion when a biblical text is taken as a direct answer to them. Systematic Christian theology has often changed the nature of the questions from the understanding of the historical action of God in the world to questions that by their very nature were above history and beyond change, for example, Paul Tillich's focusing of the theological question on "Being," a category for which there is little biblical support.

Stendahl's suggestion is that a theology for bridging between the descriptive historical frameworks of biblical thought and our own time can be found in the actual history of the church. Such a theology "would recognize that God is still the God who acts in history when he leads his people into new lands and new cultures and new areas of concern."[132] This theology would retain history as the key category and in ecclesiology would be found the overarching principles of exegesis and meaning. The historical action of the Holy Spirit in the church is the means by which the chasm between the centuries is bridged.

The major contribution of modern biblical criticism may be well stated by Krister Stendahl. It has made possible, says Stendahl, an alternative to the traditional method of exegesis as handed down in a chain reaction of a philosophical nature, "with Augustine correcting the earlier fathers, Thomas Aquinas correcting Augustine, Luther refuting Thomas, Schleiermacher touching up Luther and Barth and Tillich carrying the traditional discussion up to our own time."[133] The alternative, which has been made possible by the descriptive approach of modern biblical criticism, is the attempt to understand the original in its own terms. This alternative, though, has demanding prerequisites: that scholars undertaking exegesis learn the languages (*koine* Greek, Aramaic, and Hebrew) and work from original texts, and that the modern scholar (with his or her written orientation) be open to reliving the word in the oral dynamic through which it functioned in the early Christian centuries. If the descriptive approach has helped us to rediscover the action of the Spirit in the historical process, it is also opening the way to recognizing the action of the Spirit in the oral hearing of the word.[134]

Protestant Fundamentalism

The fundamentalist approach to the interpretation of the Bible is based on two principles: (a) a very strong emphasis on the inerrancy of the Bible, the absence from it of any sort of error; and (b) a strong hostility to the methods, results, and implications of the modern critical study of the Bible.[135] Of these two, the first, the idea of the inerrancy of the Bible, is the most important for fundamentalist exegesis. Contrary to popular belief, it is not the taking of the Bible literally that is basic to fundamentalists, but that it is interpreted so as to avoid any admission that it contains any kind of error.

> The dominant fundamentalist assertions about the Bible, namely that it is divinely inspired and infallible, do not mean that it must be taken literally; . . . what they mean . . . is that the Bible contains no error of any kind—not only theological error, but error in any sort of historical, geographical or scientific fact, is completely absent from the Bible.[136]

In order to avoid finding error in the Bible, fundamentalists move freely back and forth between literal and nonliteral interpretations. For example, some fundamentalist interpretations of the Genesis passage that the world was created in six days frequently suggest that each day represents not a twenty-four-hour period, but a geological age.

For the fundamentalist, the truth of the Bible, its inerrancy, is understood mainly as a direct correspondence of the Bible with external reality and events. Wherever the Bible refers to an external event in space and time, the correspondence between the Bible description and the actual event is held to be exact. For example, the description of the resurrection of Jesus is judged to correspond to the fact that he became alive again in his physical body and emerged from the grave. Fundamentalist interpretation stresses more the actuality of the physical events than their significance. The principles of the inerrant correspondence between the Bible and actual physical events is a presupposition adopted from the beginning and superimposed on all passages. This means that questions such as "Might the linguistic and literary form suggest that the passage is a myth or legend?" "Might the passage be mistaken in matters of historical detail or fact?" are simply ruled out of the interpretive process from the beginning. The fact that modern biblical scholars sometimes occupy themselves with the study of such questions has led fundamentalists to conclude that modern criticism is directed to proving errors in the Bible.[137] The anxiety over the finding of errors relates to the fundamental principle of inerrancy, which, if rigorously applied, means that the finding of even a small error could put the inspiration and truth of the whole of the Bible in question.

Harmonization becomes a major part of fundamentalist exegesis so as to maintain the principles of inerrancy in situations where two or more passages seem to differ with each other in the historical events to which they refer. The harmonizing of biblical passages that appear to refer to the same realities but to differ with each other, is one of the most crucial aspects of fundamentalist interpretation. For example, if two passages in the Gospels describe the same event differently, they are harmonized usually by adding the two together as complementary appearances of the same event. If Jesus cleansed the Temple at different times in the different Gospels, this difficulty is harmonized by having him cleanse the Temple on more than one occasion.[138] Since everything in the Bible is judged to be authored by God, everything in the Bible is seen to be of equal importance—all of it is divinely inspired. In practice, however, there is some grading by virtue of the fact that certain books are given more attention, for example, the Gospels, while others receive less attention, for example, Esther or Ecclesiastes.

The fundamentalist believes in the truth of the entire Bible because every portion of it brings him or her into a living experience of God in Jesus Christ. In addition each person, not just the clergy, has a responsibility to teach and preach the Bible to all the world. There is a strong missionary drive behind the interpretation of the Bible. In the fundamentalist view those who do not share their experience of the gospel with others are not true Christians. To enable the Bible to be shared effectively with others and understood for oneself, it must be read with prayer. Even with all its infallibility, it is only when the Bible is read prayerfully and with the presence of the Holy Spirit that it acts upon the heart and is understood rightly.[139]

For the fundamentalist the Bible is more than just the source of truth; it functions as a kind of visible symbol of Christ. While Christ is the personal Lord and Savior, the Bible is the supreme religious symbol that is tangible, articulate, and accessible to people on earth. For fundamentalists it is the Bible that is the visible symbol, and as such it is infallible and inerrant. This tradition of the inerrancy of the Bible is so crucial that it dominates the whole of fundamentalist exegesis and insists that all interpretation accord with it. In this sense the Bible functions for the fundamentalist as a dogmatic symbol of Christ's presence, which must be protected from any interpretation that would introduce doubts or conclude otherwise. This can mean that people concentrate on protecting the Bible as their dogmatic symbol with its infallibility and inerrancy, but have a poor knowledge of it to the point of having hardly read it. Many fundamentalists, however, are avid readers of the Bible and have an excellent knowledge of it. Devotion to it is often based on deep personal experience of help, encouragement, and inspiration gained from certain biblical texts.

FUNCTIONS OF SCRIPTURE IN CHRISTIAN LIFE

From the beginning, the primary use of Christian scripture has been in the service of worship. This practice was present in the early Christian church and was taken over with Christianity's earliest scriptures from Judaism. In the Jewish synagogue a major portion of the Sabbath service included readings from the law and the prophets, which were then interpreted to the congregation. In the first Christian worship, the synagogue practice was followed almost exactly: the scriptures of Judaism were read and commented on—as yet no distinctively Christian scriptures were available. As the Gospels were written down and letters such as those of Paul began to be circulated, they were added to the readings from the law and the prophets and were read in the worship setting. Eventually the use of these new Christian writings in worship led to the formation of the canon of the Christian Bible, which then enabled the development of a lectionary system providing a fixed schedule for the reading of scripture passages throughout the year.[140] Over time the lectionary readings gave to the worshiping community a broad acquaintance with scripture. However, while the first lectionary readings were quite lengthy, they were gradually reduced in size so that other liturgical elements could be included. Eventually only brief sections were read, with little attention to their larger contexts. As a result the scripture was heard only in bits and pieces, which sometimes were experienced as disconnected divine words descending directly from heaven.

The oral character of the scripture was preserved, and care was taken to train readers in rhetoric so that the full power of parable, story, poem, and so forth would be made present in the hearing of the congregation. Translations such as the King James Version were made with an ear to the "oral music" of the scriptures when read. Recently, however, translators have focused on the meaning and lost their sensitivity to the oral performance of the word, and ministers and lay readers lack training in rhetoric and therefore often read poorly.

In its classical form the sermon, which accompanied the reading of scripture, involved an interpretation, exposition, and application of the texts previously read. Thus the sermon traditionally provided the occasion for the interpretation of scripture within the church. While the sermon may engage in teaching, its main aim is to make scripture relevant to the lives of the members of the congregation and the church itself. It is through the preaching of the word that the church tradition is formed and influenced, and it is that same tradition that guides the hearing and teaching of the word (as exemplified in the formation of the canon). In the life of the community, therefore, the relationship between scripture and tradition is one of mutual reciprocity under the overall guidance of the Holy Spirit.[141] At times the doctrinal pronouncements of theology have seriously hampered the creative, reciprocal interchange between scripture and tradition, for example, the doctrine of inerrancy, which demanded a notion of biblical truth fixed once and for all time. Such "hampering" has occurred in both the Roman Catholic Church and fundamentalism. The biblical word has functioned effectively when it has been freed from fixed dogmas and allowed to function in historical continuity with the biblical message of the original author. In such freedom the preaching of the Sermon on the Mount or Paul's letter to the Romans may result in a new hearing of the truth of scripture—but one that is not radically out of context with previous hearings of the same passage by the church.[142] Different Christian denominations place differing emphases on scripture and tradition, but the major denominations see a need for a dynamic balance between the two.[143] Avery Dulles notes that recent Catholic and Protestant scholars see scripture and tradition not as competing authorities but as being in dynamic interaction, each being corrected and inspired from the action of the other.[144]

The role of preaching has frequently followed the prophetic pattern of Amos (5:21–24) in criticizing church practice and dogma, and in so doing infusing new life. But preaching has equally often been helpful and inspiring in nature. Witness, for example, the report we have from Philo of a sermon in the context of an early Christian "feast of Pentecost":

> . . . when a general silence is established . . . he [the preacher] discusses some question arising in the Holy Scriptures or solves one that has been propounded by someone else. In doing this he has no thought of making a display, for he has no ambition to get a reputation for clever oratory but desires to gain a closer insight into some particular matters and having gained it not to withhold it selfishly from those who if not so clear-sighted as he have at least a similar desire to learn. His instruction proceeds in a leisurely manner; he lingers over it and spins it out with repetitions, thus permanently imprinting the thoughts in the souls of the hearers, since if the speaker goes on descanting with breathless rapidity the mind of the hearers is unable to follow his language, loses ground and fails to arrive at apprehension of what is said. His audience listen with ears pricked up and eyes fixed on him always in exactly the same posture, signifying comprehension and understanding by nods and glances, praise of the speaker by the cheerful change of expression which steals over the face, difficulty by a gentler movement of the head and by pointing with a finger-tip of the right hand. The young men standing by show no less attentiveness than the occupants of the couches. The exposition of the sacred scriptures treats the inner meaning conveyed in allegory. For to these people the whole law book seems to resemble a living creature with the literal ordinances for its body and for its soul the invisible mind laid up in its wording. It is in this mind especially that the rational soul begins to contemplate the things akin to itself and looking through the words as through a mirror beholds the marvellous beauties of the concepts, unfolds and removes the symbolic coverings and brings forth the thoughts and sets them bare to the light of day for those who need but a little reminding to enable them to discern the inward and hidden through the outward and visible.[145]

For the early Christians, the church fathers, and the medieval church, it was the preached scripture that was alive and filled with the Holy Spirit.

Luther was emphatic that God's word as written scripture is dead, only when preached can it be heard. In his preface to the *New Testament*, Luther states that the "Gospel" is not a book but a message, a news story which must be reported from one person to another. God's dealing with us takes place through his word. Its purpose is not just to transmit truth, but to establish a personal fellowship between God and his people. "For this reason the Word must be spoken to us personally and verbally in God's name, through the *viva vox*, the living human voice."[146] The Gospel is not really a book, for Luther, but the message that Christ did not write but spoke. Luther uses the term "scripture" to refer to the written text of the Old Testament, which Christ brought back to life by reciting its contents in his oral preaching. Christ did not call his teaching scripture but gospel, that is, good news or proclamation. "That is why it must not be described with the pen but with the mouth."[147] This oral word of the gospel is heard in the church both in the preaching of scripture from the pulpit and in the exchange of mutual comfort. "Where God's word is not preached," says Luther, "it were better if people did not sing, read, or assemble at all."[148] In Luther's view, when we write and read books, we have not fulfilled our responsibility as Christians—it is essential that the gospel be spoken and heard. Thus it is more important to have good speakers than good writers in the church. The church is a "mouth-house, no pen-house,"[149] and today Luther would surely add, "or computer house."

Luther constantly reminds us that in contrast to the written scriptures of the Old Testament, the gospel was a spoken and preached word. Jesus and the apostles did not intend to attach an appendix to the Old Testament, which was for them "scripture." Rather, in their preaching they wished to interpret and apply the Old Testament. For Luther, the early oral gospel was not inadequate but the correct form of the word. Putting the oral gospel into written form was a necessary evil to meet an emergency situation (the danger of the verbal word being lost as a result of heresies). But we must always remember, says Luther, that the written and published New Testament exists only as a prop for the spoken word of the gospel. "The written Word originates in the spoken Word which now must again come forth from the written Word."[150] The written text of the gospel is merely a tool through which, when preached, God speaks powerfully to us in the here and now. Luther indeed embodied the dictum of Paul, "So faith comes from what is heard, and what is heard comes from the preaching of Christ" (Romans 10:17).

The Protestants of England seem to have carefully followed Luther's lead with regard to the importance of the preached word. Indeed, as Ronald Bond has shown, well into the seventeenth century a strong tradition of oral preaching prospered.[151] The merit of preaching was not at issue but, rather, the question of the authenticity of two styles of preaching. In its preaching the Church of England prepared thirty-three official homilies, which were printed and distributed in two books, to aid the barely literate parsons and curates "who were required by royal injunctions and ecclesiastical canons to read them plainly, distinctly and regularly to their even less literate parishioners for much of the sixteenth and seventeenth centuries."[152] The Puritans opposed this practice because, in their view, "the lively word of the spirit, breathed through the preacher's utterances, was superior to the dead letter of the written word merely read."[153] The Puritans saw the printed and read homilies as obstructions coming between the scripture and the fresh oral exposition of it by the preacher under the impulse of the Holy Spirit. These printed homilies read in rotation by the Church of England preachers were, in the Puritans minds, merely muffled and muzzled expressions of the gospel's living word. Unless each preacher made the scripture text relevant to the lives and situation of his listeners, the congregation would not hear the word speaking to them through the preacher. This could not be accomplished if the pastor had to read a homily prepared for general distribution. "Lively preaching" required freedom from a text, so that the living scripture could be given careful application to the personal lives of the hearers.

At the turn of the twentieth century a renewal of preaching was again being counseled, but now arising from the new historical scholarship that was making the Bible a new book. The view of P. T. Forsyth, given in 1907 lectures at Yale University, may be taken as representative of the Protestant thinking of the day. "Preachers," says P. T. Forsyth, "are inspired by the historic freshness of it, as the public are interested by its new realism. . . . For the Bible is the book of that Christian community whose organ the preacher is."[154] The Bible is not a book of history; rather, it is history preaching. The object of the New Testament writers was not to provide biographical material of Jesus but evangelical testimony. The Bible is to be understood as "a preacher" rather than as historical evidence. In this sense, says Forsyth, the Bible is a sacrament, "the active grace of God."[155]

In modern times, scholars such as Walter Ong and Paul Ricoeur have emphasized the importance of the preaching of the scripture. Ricoeur describes preaching as "the permanent reinterpretation of the text which is regarded as grounding the community," and the function of preaching as "to bring back the proclamation from the written to the oral."[156] Ong observes that Protestant sacramental theology places a strong stress on the efficacy of the word of God in preaching. In Protestantism, God is powerful through the spoken word, which may be heard in sermons or in prayer or in the imagination of the devotee reading the Bible in print.[157] We are reminded of Paul's description of "gospel" through the use of the verb "is being revealed." Paul does not say that the gospel is *about* revelation; rather, that when the gospel is preached, revelation happens.[158]

In addition to the preaching of the word, the scripture also appears in other parts of the service of worship. Psalms are repeated responsively, and often provide the words for some of the most powerful hymns of the church. Indeed the combination of scripture and music sung by a congregation can be a most powerful oral-aural experience of the word. In Orthodox worship, the scripture is virtually always prayed. One is constantly "washed" in the text. The speaking of the text is the way the devotee addresses God. As the Orthodox liturgy puts it, "Thine of Thine own we offer to Thee."

Private devotional reading of scripture has also had a long history in the Christian tradition. This practice has been constrained by three factors: the availability of Bibles for private use, the availability of Bibles in the vernacular, and the literacy of the people. During the medieval period few people could read, and since all copies had to be made by hand they were generally available only to scholars and priests. However, with the advent of printing, the possibility arose of making large numbers of copies of the Bible available. This possibility became even more promising when translations were made available as printed books, in English from 1526 on and in German from 1461, with Luther's translation appearing between 1522 and 1546. The passion that pushed Luther to complete his German translation was "that every Christian should consider nothing but the simple scripture itself and the pure Word of God . . . accept it for our own, and hold it fast."[159] It is clear, however, that Luther's vision of the use of the Bible by individuals in devotion was still to be oral in nature: "Would that the farmer at the handle of his plow and the weaver at his loom repeated by themselves a text and that the traveler overcome the tiresomeness of his journey in this way. Might the conversations of all Christians be full thereof."[160] Following Luther's lead, the Protestant Reformation energetically promoted the translation and printing of the Bible in all languages and prescribed an intimate firsthand knowledge of scripture as a religious duty of each devotee. Consequently, for many Protestants the Bible is consulted for guidance in everyday life and studied devotionally each day. This Protestant focus on the words of the scripture in their written form had the effect, says Ong, of reinforcing the early Christian attitudes regarding the power of God's word. Attention is shifted from other aspects of the tradition and focused on the word. For Protestants the word assumed a kind of sacramental power. Sensing the fact that the written word was altering the oral experience of the word, Protestants overemphasized the power and authority of the word—to compensate for this subconsciously sensed tendency of print to weaken the word's power. Because the Roman Catholic Church retained a strong sense of power in its sacraments, says Ong, it did not feel the need of this Protestant compensation.[161]

In the Protestant conviction, the power of the word and its truth for the individual comes through the activity of the Holy Spirit within each person. Biblical criticism can help one to understand the original historical context of a biblical passage, and the traditions of the Church can enable one to perceive the range and depth of biblical truth. But the lifeless written word becomes the living word only when the Spirit illumines the mind of the person and convinces one in one's heart that God is speaking to one directly through the words of scripture.[162] For this to happen requires sincerity, openness of mind, and a fundamental reverence from the reader. As C. H. Dodd puts it, "for those who approach the Bible in this spirit (which Jesus described as that of a child), it is capable of awakening and redirecting the powers of mind, heart and will."[163]

THE NEW TESTAMENT IN RELATION TO OTHER SCRIPTURES

When other scriptures are considered in relation to the New Testament, the Torah of Judaism must be given special consideration. We have seen that for Jesus and the early Christians, the Torah was their only scripture. But Christian use and interpretation of the Torah was quite different from that of Judaism. For Christians the history of God's interaction with his people reaches its crowning climax and fulfillment in Jesus Christ. Thus the Torah is read as preparing the way and foretelling the coming of Jesus. Because Christians looked back to the Hebrew Bible through the presupposition of Jesus as the Christ, the Christian use of the Jewish scriptures was selective in both content and method of interpretation. There was a bias in favor of the prophetic books and the Psalms over the books of Moses. At the same time Christian interpreters had a definite preference for certain books—for example, Genesis, Exodus, Isaiah, Jeremiah—and neglected others. Allegorical and typological interpretations were used to elicit specifically Christian meanings from the Hebrew Bible. In this way the early Christians appropriated the Jewish scriptures for their own purposes and invested them with a very different meaning. The perspective that furnished this new meaning was the experience of Jesus as Messiah. The Hebrew scriptures were seen to prefigure him, and he was seen to fulfill them.[164]

As Christian writings were composed and circulated in the last decades of the first century C.E., they began to be employed in worship and teaching along with the Jewish scriptures. Eventually they came to be regarded as scriptures in their own right with religious authority like that given to the Hebrew Bible. The Christian Bible is divided into two parts reflecting the foregoing process. The Hebrew Bible is called the Old Testament, while the Christian writings in the canon are called the New Testament. The word "testament" refers to the covenants made between God and his people: the Old Testament, or covenant, referring to the agreement God had made with the Jewish people through Moses; the New Testament referring to the new covenant through Jesus Christ (Jeremiah 31:31–34). In the Christian view, the old covenant gives place to the more inward and personal one instituted through Jesus Christ. Although both books are judged to be revelations of God's divine activity with his people, for Christians the criterion revelation is found in the activity and teaching of Jesus Christ as recorded in the New Testament, which is judged to be a continuation and fulfillment of the Old Testament. Thus taken together, the two provide a unity of saving and revealing activity of God.

With regard to scriptures other than the Torah (e.g., Qur'an, Veda, Sayings of the Buddha), the situation is quite different. The traditional attitude of Christianity has been to distinguish between general revelation (or natural religion) and special revelation (or revealed religion). The Bible (which includes the Torah) is classified as special revelation, whereas the scriptures of Islam, Hinduism, and Buddhism are classified as general revelation. This classification is based not so much on an abstract idea of revelation (as the communication of propositions about God to be believed); rather, revelation is seen in the confrontation of God and people through actual historical events such as the escape from Egypt, the Babylonian exile, and the life of Christ. In the Christian view, what is disclosed in such revelation is "not truth about God, but the living God Himself."[165] God guides events, inspires prophets to appreciate and record the meanings of events, and opens the eyes and ears of the readers and hearers to his presence in these events and their implication for each person. Although all events in the world process are potentially pregnant with divine meaning (and are thus general revelation), certain key events in human history have the ability to bring out the meaning in all other events (and are thus called special revelation). This is true in the history of Israel as recounted in the Old Testament, but supremely and uniquely true of the events of the life of Jesus Christ recorded in the New Testament. For the Christian, God's acts and the interpretation of their meaning coincide completely in Christ so that in him we encounter "the Word made flesh" (John 1:14). As the classification above is usually interpreted, the scriptures of Islam, Hinduism, Buddhism, and other religions are usually judged to be "general revelation." Along with other parts of the world process, such scriptures are potentially pregnant with divine meaning. Alone, however, these scriptures would be unable to understand that meaning clearly and completely. Only by encountering the special revelation of Jesus Christ, as recorded in the Bible, can the potential meanings present in other scriptures be made manifest.

Some recent thinkers, however, have tried to go beyond the traditional interpretation. W. M. Horton has suggested that revelations of God in other scriptures may be given a status somewhere between general and special revelation. Even though most scriptures have no such sense of the presence of God in history (as is found in the Jewish and Christian scriptures), since God is truly present in all history he must be acting in events (recorded in other scriptures), whose meaning may be only dimly discerned. Yet still these "dim intimations could be classified as *preparatory revelations* leading up to the definitive revelation in Christ, or *secondary revelations* permitting this primary revelation to be differently applied and interpreted in different cultural environments."[166]

The Roman Catholic theologian Karl Rahner and the Roman Catholic Church at the Second Vatican Council take a similar position. Rahner affirms the unique and universal revelation of God in Christ and yet at the same time emphasizes that God has fully intended salvation for all people. In Rahner's view these two requirements for Christian belief "cannot be reconciled in any other way than by stating that every human being is really and truly exposed to the influence of divine supernatural grace."[167] Rahner's resolution leads him to state further that until a person encounters the gospel, the scriptures of another religion can contain, for that person, not only natural knowledge of God (general revelation), but also supernatural elements of grace (a free gift from God on account of Christ). This means that in such circumstances the other religion and its scripture can function as a revelation of God's grace, and can lead to salvation. This salvation, however, must be regarded as an experience of anonymous Christianity since salvation can be gained only through Christ.[168] The Second Vatican Council, in its "Declaration on the Relation of the Church to Non-Christian Religions" also emphasizes the universal nature of God's grace for all peoples, and acknowledges in the various religions and their scriptures a deep and pervading religious sense. After discussing Hinduism and Buddhism, and alluding to other religions, the document states, "The Catholic Church rejects nothing which is true and holy in these religions . . . but she proclaims . . . Christ who is 'the way, the truth and the life' (John 14:6)."[169] For Rahner and the Catholic church the approach to be taken would seem to be one of employing the revelation of the New Testament as a yardstick for identifying the presence of God's grace in the scriptures of other religions.

Moving to the Reformed Protestant tradition within Christianity, a much more exclusivistic approach to other scriptures is encountered. For the theologian Karl Barth, the revelation by which people can be saved comes only through the word of God in Jesus Christ.[170] In Barth's view all religions, including the Christian religion, are futile human attempts to know God. By their nature they are sinful and, alone, are doomed to failure. Christianity is like the other religions in this regard. But by abandoning its own claim to superiority or absolute truth, and by relying on God's grace in the revelation of Jesus Christ, Christianity may be judged by God as the right and true religion. It is not by virtue of anything Christians have done right or other religions have done wrong, but merely as a result of God's act of divine election that the light of Christ happens to shine in the scriptures of Christianity rather than in the scriptures of another religion.[171] The uniqueness of Christ and his presence only in Christian scriptures is also emphasized in the evangelical Lausanne Covenant, which states: "To proclaim Jesus as 'the Saviour of the World' is not to affirm that all religions offer salvation in Christ. Rather it is . . . to invite all men to respond to him as Saviour and Lord in the wholehearted personal commitment of repentance and faith."[172] This declaration is understood by the evangelical Christians as arising directly out of Christian scripture. It clearly rejects the finding of God's revelation in Christ in any other scripture.

Within the New Testament itself may be found passages that provide a basis for both the narrow evangelical approach and the more open outlook of Rahner and the Second Vatican Council. Evangelicals point to passages such as Peter's statement about Christ, "There is no other name under heaven given among men by which we must be saved" (Acts 4:12), and the statement of Jesus in the Gospel of John, "I am the way, and the truth, and the life; no one comes to the Father, but by me" (John 14:6). Those favoring a more open approach quote those passages where God is seen to have made all races of people and given them the whole earth to inhabit (cf. Acts 17:26) and where God's providence, his evident goodness, and his plan of salvation extend to all people (cf. Acts 14:17; Romans 2:6–7; 1 Timothy 2:4). Passages in which attention is drawn away from Jesus and toward God (e.g., "When all things are subjected to him, then the Son himself will also be subjected to him who put all things under him that God may be everything to everyone," 1 Corinthians 15:28) are also highlighted. By seeing such passages as shifting the focus from Christ to God opens the way to conceive of God acting through other religions and their scriptures.[173]

3

SCRIPTURE IN ISLAM

Although scripture occupies a central place in all major religions, in Islam its function is supreme. Out of the Qur'an arises the Islamic community, its law, literature, art, and religion. Perhaps more than any other religious community, Muslims are a "people of the Book." The beginning of the Muslim community and its continued existence come in response to the call of the Qur'an.[1] Although it recognizes that others such as Jews and Christians have received books from God, the Qur'an sees itself as superseding all previous books and creating a new "people of the Book" from a community that, until then, had had no book. Instead of sending to the Arabs a missionary from those who had already been given the book, God sent Muhammad, the prophet chosen from among those who had previously not been given the Book of God.[2] This new scripture, the Qur'an, does not conform easily to the literary styles and religious functions common to other scriptures. Its uniqueness is observed by Kenneth Cragg:

> Islam is . . . the world's most striking expression of . . . documentary faith. Response to the book's meaning creates the Ummah, or household of belief, the society of the Scripture and the scriptured. . . . Committing the words to heart in memory and recitation, the Muslim believer participates in the mystery of the divine concern with man. The Qur'an is, literally, "The Reading," and Muslims are "the readers."[3]

For Muslims the Qur'an is experienced as the eternal speech of God,[4] the ultimate source of all truth and the original basis of all authority both religious and secular.[5] In an attempt to sense the uniqueness of the Qur'an as the scripture of Islam, we shall study the following: (1) Muhammad and the revelation of the Qur'an, (2) the oral or recited text, (3) the written text, (4) exegesis, (5) the Qur'an in daily piety and practice, and (6) the Qur'an in relation to other scriptures. Special emphasis will be placed upon the primacy given to the oral or recited text in Muslim experience. Under the heading of "Exegesis," attention will be given to the topics of translation and inimitability, and Sunni, Sufi, Shi'i, Isma'ili, and modern interpretations. The fascinating concept of the "Mother of the Book" in heaven is shown to provide a powerful basis for Islam to relate the Qur'an to other scriptures in today's context of religious pluralism.

MUHAMMAD AND THE REVELATION OF THE QUR'AN

> It belongs not to any mortal that God should speak to him, except by inspiration (*waḥy*), or from behind a veil, or that He should send a messenger and He reveals whatsoever He will, by His leave; surely He is All-high, All-wise.[6]

Cragg observes that there is no satisfactory English word to translate *Rasūl*, the creedal description of the status of Muhammad in relation to the Qur'an. What is needed is a word to convey the "doer" or the "doing" within the root verb of "sentness." "Prophet" translates another inferior Arabic word and is associated with the biblical notion of "inspiration," which is also inferior. Although often used, "Messenger" is judged by Cragg to be too minimal, suggesting a negligible errand. "The Qur'ān as Scripture comes only to him [Muhammad]: it has penmen other than himself but does not come from their pens, nor is it *about* him. 'Herald,' 'emissary,' even 'commissioner,' would all possibly serve, were they not encumbered by associations that are too sentimental or too vulgar."[7] God is the speaker of the revelation, the angel Gabriel is the intermediary agent, and Muhammad is the recipient. Not a passive recipient, however, for God's word acts by its own energy and makes Muhammad the instrument, the "sent-doer," by which all people are warned by God and called to respond. The command to Muhammad is "Recite" (*iqra'*). Muhammad is not to speak in his own name but, rather, to repeat something that has been conveyed to him word for word. Here there is no notion of an inspiration from God that is then clothed and uttered in the best words a human mind can create. In the Qur'an, Muhammad receives a direct, fully composed revelation from God, which he then recites to others. Indeed "recitation" or "something to be recited" is probably the basic meaning of the Arabic word *qur'ān*, which came to signify the revelation in its totality as well as single parts of it.[8] The single parts of the Qur'an, as direct words of God, are thus very suitable for use in liturgy and private prayer. Such is the view of orthodox Muslims.

For some modern scholars, the situation may not be quite so clear-cut. Alford Welch, for example, finds that in many of the early passages (in the Meccan years) God spoke directly to Muhammad and not through some intermediary. Other passages, he suggests, have the effect of elevating God from direct revelation by having the message brought down by an intermediary, for example, an angel.[9] This heightening of God has the psychological effect of ensuring a distinct separation between persons and God, and increasing the numinous or awesome quality of the divine. Welch also suggests that the real formalizing and assembling of the revelations into a book occurs as Muhammad attracts followers and they demand a book of their own, like the books possessed by the Jews and the Christians. He notes that the establishment of an independent Muslim community in Medina, distinct from the Jews and the Christians, "was marked by the granting of a separate Islamic scripture that was to serve as a criterion (cf. *furḳān*) for confirming the truth of previous scriptures (II, 3, IV, 105, V, 48, etc.)."[10] There is also the difficulty of later revelations that caused earlier revelations to be changed or abrogated. This would seem to call into question the orthodox view that every word of the revelation is God's eternal truth. Three solutions to this problem are found in the Qur'an: (a) Muhammad sometimes forgot parts or was caused to forget parts so that God could substitute like or better ones, (b) Satan when he was yearning for a message from God inserted something into Muhammad's thoughts (which God later abrogated), and (c) sometimes God simply replaced some parts with others as good or better.[11] Some modern scholars question the historicity of the Satan explanation; however, most accept it as historical.[12] This is also a contentious interpretation for most modern Muslims with few accepting it while others reject it.

While orthodox scholars agree that the revelation was spread over many years, the explanation they offer is quite different from the suggestions above of some modern Western scholars. Ahmad von Denffer, for example, says that the Qur'an was revealed to Muhammad over a period twenty-three years for a number of reasons, the four most important being:

1. To strengthen the heart of the Prophet by addressing him continuously and whenever the need for guidance arose.
2. Out of consideration for the Prophet since revelation was a very difficult experience for him.
3. To gradually implement the laws of God.
4. To make understanding, application and memorization of the revelation easier for the believers.[13]

As an illustration of how difficult the revelation experience sometimes was, we have Bukhārī's account of the beginning of the revelation in the cave of Ḥirā on a mountain near Mecca (ca. 610 C.E.):

> He used to go in seclusion in the Cave of Hirā, where he used to worship (Allah alone) continuously for many days before his desire to see his family. He used to take with him food for the stay and then come back to (his wife) Khadija to take his food likewise again, till suddenly the truth descended upon him while he was in the Cave of Hirā. The angel came to him and asked him to read. The Prophet replied, "I do not know how to read."
>
> The Prophet added, "The angel caught me (forcibly) and pressed me

> so hard that I could not bear it any more. He then released me and again asked me to read and I replied, "I do not know how to read." Thereupon he caught me again and pressed me a second time till I could not bear it any more. He then released me and asked me to read, but again I replied, "I do not know how to read" (or what shall I read?). Thereupon he caught me for the third time and pressed me, and then released me and said: "Read, in the name of Your Lord, who created, created man from a clot. Read! And Your Lord is the most bountiful."[14]

After the first few revelations Bukhārī claims that revelation came regularly and strongly to Muhammad.[15]

A major reason for the divergence of the modern Western scholars may be attributable to the different perspectives they bring to the Qur'an. The modern scholars approach it as a written text to be unraveled through the methods of historical literary criticism. From this perspective the findings such as those reported by Welch are certainly reasonable. For Muslims, however, the Qur'an is first a recited and memorized text that is transmitted to the believers orally. From this perspective the reasoning of von Denffer as to why the Qur'an was revealed in stages is very acceptable. Even modern Western scholars admit that in the reception of the revelation within Islam, the oral experience was parallel and perhaps primary to the written text.[16] Let us then give our attention to the uniquely Muslim experience of the oral or recited Qur'an.

THE ORAL OR RECITED TEXT

Muhammad's initial experience in which he was commanded to "read" (recite) seems to have steadily grown into a conviction that through him a series of scriptural revelations were forming themselves into a book in the tongue of his own people.[17] It is upon the oral Arabic character of the revelation that much of the claim for uniqueness of the Qur'an is based. The proof that this was indeed God's word is seen in the surpassing eloquence of language and rhythm embodied in the Arabic words of these revelations when recited aloud by Muhammad. This Arabic Qur'an responded both to the Arab love of language and to the Arab yearning for its own scripture, and the unity that might bestow.[18]

The importance of the oral or recited Qur'an in Islam is hard for modern persons, with their emphasis upon written text, to appreciate. The primary significance of the Qur'an for the vast majority of Muslims through the centuries has been in its oral form—the form in which it first appeared as the recitation (*qur'ān*) chanted by Muhammad to his followers over a period of about twenty years. Welch summarizes the central place of the oral Qur'an as follows:

> The revelations were memorized by some of Muhammad's followers during his lifetime, and the oral tradition that was thus established has

> had a continuous history ever since, in some ways independent of, and superior to, the written Kur'ān. During the early centuries when the written Kur'ān was limited to the *scriptio defectiva* of the period, the oral tradition established itself as the standard by which the written text was to be judged. Even when the Egyptian "standard edition" was prepared in the early 1920s, it was the oral tradition and its supporting *kirā'āt* literature (rather than early Kur'ān mss.) that served as the authority for determining the written text.[19]

Down through the centuries the complete oral Qur'an has been maintained in unbroken chains with professional reciters (*ḳurrā*) learning the sacred text by memory from their teachers and then passing it on to their students in the same way.[20]

The first committing to memory of the revelation was by Muhammad who, tradition tells us, was commanded to do so by the angel Gabriel. Following the example of Gabriel, Muhammad then recited the revelation he had received to his followers and instructed them also to memorize it. Such passages were recited during daily prayers, which reinforced their retention in memory. As a check on the process, Muhammad often had his companions or close followers recite the Qur'an for him. Several of them apparently recited the entire Qur'an for or with Muhammad in the year before his death. This also follows upon the example of Gabriel who, according to Bukhārī, used to recite the Qur'an with Muhammad once a year (twice in the year he died).[21] These companions were then instructed to recite the Qur'an publicly to others, and in this way Islam was spread. Emphasis on the memorization and public recitation of the Qur'an has continued right up to today within Islam.

According to Islamic tradition, the reciting of the Qur'an brings blessings not only upon those doing the chanting, but also to the whole world. It is a guide through this life and into the next, and is an intercessor with God on the day of judgment. About the Qur'an, Muhammad said:

> The Qur'an is right guidance from error and a light against blindness. It is a support against stumbling . . . a source of illumination against sorrow and a protection against perdition. It is the criterion of truth against sedition and the best way of leading from this world to the next ['Ayyāshī, I].[22]

In its function of giving guidance and support, the importance of the oral nature of the Qur'an has not been fully appreciated in the modern West, especially its role in Islamic personal piety.

The traditional recitation of the Qur'an in public liturgy and witness as well as in personal prayer is grounded upon a well-developed theology of the oral word. The Qur'an is uttered to call others to it, to expiate sins, to protect against punishment, and to ensure blessings in paradise. "He who recites it [the Qur'an] shall have the reward of a thousand martyrs, and for every *surah* the reward of a prophet."[23] Like a prophet, the pious person will be called on the day of resurrection to rise up and recite. With every verse that is recited the person rises up one station until the rewards of everlasting life and the bliss of paradise are received.[24] In this way the pious reciter, to the extent that he or she knows the Qur'an by heart, shares in the status of the prophets. The difference between the pious person and the prophet is that, unlike the prophet, the reciter does not receive the Qur'an as revelation. But to the extent the reciter memorizes it, he or she is said to "live in the Qur'an."[25] Mahmoud Ayoub observes that this is a very close parallel to the New Testament idea that the pious Christian is one who lives "in Christ."[26]

As the direct word of God, the uttered words of the Qur'an are judged to possess powerful numinous qualities. For example *sūra* 59:21 states, "Were we to cause this Qur'ān to descend upon a mountain, you would see it humbled, torn asunder in awe of God."[27] In addition to its creative and destructive power, the words of the Qur'an are also a positive source for healing and tranquillity. According to tradition when the Qur'an is recited divine tranquillity (*sakīnah*) descends, mercy covers the reciters, angels draw near to them, and God remembers them.[28] Tradition also tells how one of the companions of Muhammad came to him and reported seeing something like lamps between heaven and earth as he recited while riding horseback during the night. Muhammad is reported to have said that the lights were angels descended to hear the recitation of the Qur'an.[29] For the pious Muslim, then, the chanted words of the Qur'an have the numinous power to create and destroy, to bring mercy, to provide protection, to give knowledge, and to evoke miraculous signs. Because they contain such power, the words of the Qur'an are described as a heavy burden for those who take them to heart. To bear this holy burden requires that the reciter be pure in heart, mind, and action. The reciter must be prepared to sacrifice for the holy word by fasting, by chanting through the night, and by giving thanks. The possibility of spiritual pride infecting the chanting of the Qur'an has been recognized by the tradition. Is the virtuosity of the chanter designed to draw attention to the person or to the holy words? Qur'an scholars have been of two minds on this question.

> Some have adduced *hadīths* extolling musical chanting (*taghanni*) of the Qur'an, and others have cited equally accepted traditions enjoining a simple chant (*tartil*). Two modes of Quranic recitations came to be accepted: *tajwid* (making good, that is musically beautiful) and *tartil* (a slow and deliberate, simple chant).[30]

Musical styles used in secular singing are ruled out. The Qur'an is to be recited with dignity of demeanor, softness of voice, and a sorrowful tone. Within Islam the argument is between those who would adorn the Qur'an with their voices, and those preferring the simple mode who reverse the injunction to read "adorn your voices with the Qur'an."[31] The latter see themselves as putting the emphasis upon the beauty of the sacred word rather than upon the reciter's voice, thus guarding against the sin of pride. The emotion to be evoked in chanting is one of subdued sadness rather than joyful ecstasy. Because God sent down the Qur'an in sorrow due to the sinfulness of people, Muhammad charged his followers: "Weep, therefore, when you recite it."[32]

The pious and correct chanting of the Qur'an has been understood as meritorious within the tradition. Completing a recitation (*khatm*) of the full Qur'an is a time of celebration. For the Muslim the Qur'an is not seen as a book in the usual sense, but as a living word and faithful companion in the journey through this life to the hereafter. As Ayoub puts it, "a Muslim journeys through this life in the Qur'an."[33] This recitation of the holy word not only purifies the life of the devotee but also is seen to be necessary for the well-being of the rest of humanity and the maintenance of order in nature. Such an exalted view of the power of holy word parallels the Hindu experience of revelation as *mantra*, which maintains both personal and cosmic order (*ṛta*).[34]

A contemporary Muslim, Labib as-Said, in his book *The Recited Koran,* has underlined the importance of the oral Qur'an for Islamic life. Worried about the decreasing memorization of the oral text by young children, and the falling off of good teachers and reciters, Said proposed recording the chanted Qur'an and its reproduction on audio records as a way of preserving the oral text.[35] With support from the government of Egypt and the rector of the Azhar, the recording project was begun in May 1960, using the *tartīl* (less musically dramatic) style of chanting. The *al-Muṣḥaf al-Murattal* reading of the Qur'an was made available in some twenty-eight records. Said feels that by safeguarding the oral text in this fashion the legacy of the Arabic Qur'an, which binds together Muslims from all over the world, will be maintained.[36] Said's thinking in this regard is grounded in the viewpoint that while the canonical written text has been a significant factor in the preservation of the Qur'an, equally if not more important has been its transmission from generation to generation by word of mouth. This high regard for the oral tradition also involves meticulous methods for preserving it. Transmission from the mouth of a teacher to a student through the oral mode is judged to avoid errors such as the misreading of words (*taṣḥīf*), which easily occurred in the early script when diacritical points and vocalization signs had not yet been developed (the so-called *scriptio defectiva*).[37] As a safeguard against the oral text becoming corrupted in its transmission, each trustworthy teacher had to be identifiable as being in an unbroken chain (*isnād*) of teachers reaching back to Muhammad. Said identifies ten such schools, commonly called "Readings" (*qirā'āt*).[38] Traditional scholars attribute the variations among the Ten Readings to the dialectical variation in the way they were originally spoken by Muhammad.[39] Safeguard against corruption of the original revelation or new material creeping into the oral text is achieved by application of the principle of *tawātur,* namely, that a large number of readers scattered over a wide area could not possibly concur on an erroneous or fabricated reading.[40] Said's aim in his modern project was to record all Ten Readings of the Qur'an.

It might be supposed that once the ambiguities of the early script were overcome through the use of diacritical points and vocalization signs, the oral readings would no longer be judged essential. This has not happened and the reasons offered for the continuing need for the oral text are instructive. First, since the added points and signs are not judged to be part of the orthodox written canon as such, there is a continuing need for the oral as the criterion against which the written text is to be verified. In the view of Muslims like Said, experience of the oral word is more basic and trustworthy than the written.

> Oral tradition, provided it satisfies those requirements which are subsumed under the concept of *tawātur*, is considered to be a virtual foolproof vehicle of transmission. Written marks and signs are simply a convenience to scholars who wish to study and compare the various authentic Readings. They should never be taken as a source from which to learn these Readings.[41]

"Secondly," maintains Said, "only through the oral tradition can the Koran's essential character as something recited, something orally delivered be preserved."[42] Just as the Qur'an was orally delivered to Muhammad by the angel Gabriel, so its ongoing reception and transmission must retain the oral form. In disseminating the Qur'an, Muhammad sent out reciters not books. Even later, when 'Uthmān distributed copies of the canonical written text, reciters went along as well to teach the correct recitation.

"Thirdly," argues Said, "the art of chanting the Koran, known in Arabic as *tajwīd*, cannot be conveyed except by means of oral tradition."[43] Muhammad chanted the scripture and directed the people to follow his example of melodiously reciting the Qur'an. Such speaking is not ordinary speaking but a special style of chant suitable for the sacred words.

From our modern context it is important to note the key role that memorization plays in the oral tradition. To avoid errors creeping in from the misreading of words (*taṣḥīf*), the Qur'an is not to be memorized from a written text but, rather, by the repetition of the recitation of an authoritative teacher. In traditional Islam, to learn the Qur'an is to learn it by heart. In this learning there is a personal linkage through one's teacher's chain of teachers back to Muhammad, Gabriel, and God. Thus there is an experience of spiritual psychological immediacy that memorization from a printed page cannot duplicate. Like other religions with oral text traditions (e.g. Hinduism), Islam stresses the importance of memorizing the Qur'an early in life. Psychologically this is sensible for two reasons. First, children possess the ability to memorize large amounts of text easily and, once learned, it stays with one for life. Second, having learned the text by heart at a young age, it is intimately with one for the rest of one's life. Being present within the unconscious, assuming that we sleep and occupy our conscious minds with other activities, the text in the unconscious is—as Freud has shown us—all the while influencing our thought and action. Learned by rote in childhood, the meanings of the words are then gradually appropriated by a pious or reflective person throughout the adult life. Memorization of the Qur'an by children has been taught privately by parents and publicly in the *makātīb katātīb*, or schools devoted to memorization of the text. First established by 'Umar in 634, these schools have flourished wherever Muslim civilization was dominant.[44] This practice, however, is being challenged in some modern Islamic cultures (e.g., present-day Egypt), thus leading to the worries that Said, through his recording project, is attempting to address.

The special eloquence and power of the oral recitation of the Arabic Qur'an has fostered the doctrine of its incomparability (*i'jāz*). Together with the tradition that Muhammad was an unlettered man, the idea that the verses he recited were so uniquely beautiful and powerful has led to the Qur'an being seen as a miracle that only God could have authored.[45] Indeed the Qur'an itself challenges others to bring forward revelations that could equal the Qur'an (e.g., *sūra* 2:23–24). According to the Islamic tradition, this challenge has never been met and in fact cannot be met.[46] The Muslim scholar al-Qurṭubī in his commentary lists characteristics of the Qur'an's *i'jāz*, or incomparability, such as: its language excels all other Arabic language; its style excels all other Arabic style; its comprehensiveness cannot be matched; it has no contradiction with natural science; it has a profound effect upon the hearts of people.[47]

Given that it is the eloquence of the chanted Arabic Qur'an that is unique and incomparable, it stands to reason that it should be judged also to be untranslatable. This is certainly the view of traditional scholars, and it is a position shared by many Western scholars. One of the most successful Western scholars in this regard, Arthur Arberry, carefully distinguishes his English rendition from a translation by titling it *The Koran Interpreted*.[48] Commenting on the special qualities of the Arabic Qur'an, Arberry uses a music analogy.

> There is a repertory of familiar themes running through the whole Koran. . . . Using the language of music, each Sura is a rhapsody composed of whole or fragmentary *leitmotivs*; the analogy is reinforced by the subtly varied rhythmical flow of the discourse.[49]

When to this literary insight the intangible qualities imparted by a well-trained chanter are added, the claim that the total Arabic experience of the Qur'an is untranslatable appears quite reasonable. This should caution those who, upon reading an attempted translation and finding it dull or repetitious, are then tempted to dismiss it as incongruous or lacking in aesthetic qualities, to think again. The strength of Arberry's rendering is that he has tried to transpose the rhapsodic patterns of the Arabic Qur'an into English parallels, thereby conveying much more of the lyrical style of the original. The message of the Qur'an, it seems, is contained both in its lyrical style and in its word meanings. Cragg captures this understanding effectively:

> The scripture is a miracle of eloquence and diction, as well as the repository of final truth. Meaning cannot be assured in such sacred and crucial fields of truth unless language is also verbally inspired and given. Once given, in the revelatory particular, which is Arabic, it cannot be undone or transposed.[50]

And, as we shall now see, the need for the Qur'an to be in the original recited or oral Arabic quickly gets extended to include the necessity for a written Arabic text as well.

THE WRITTEN TEXT

In addition to having his followers memorize his recitations, Muhammad seems also to have dictated sections of the revelations to be written down by scribes. What the scribes wrote down, however, appears to have remained fragmentary, awaiting collection and organization by later scholars. Muslims believe that virtually all of the Qur'an was committed to writing during Muhammad's lifetime. Islamic tradition argues that although Muhammad started to compile the dictated *sūras* and indicate their correct order, this task remained unfinished at his death.[51] It has been suggested that the reason Muhammad never completed the organization of the written text was that the revelations were received by him piecemeal over a twenty-year period, so that as long as he lived the possibility of fresh revelations existed and therefore the collection of *sūras* could not be closed for final compilation. Also, as long as Muhammad was alive the community had in him an authoritative guide as to the correct recitation of the Qur'an, and with the oral text so secure, no need was felt for an authoritative written text. However, the death of Muhammad, along with the deaths in battle a few months later of a large number of persons who knew the Qur'an by heart, led to the worry that portions of the oral text might ultimately be lost.[52]

In response to this concern the Caliph Abū Bakr undertook to gather together all the written fragments of the Qur'an and compile a complete written text. In accepting a verse the compilers apparently insisted on certain principles as a safeguard against error: (1) it must have been originally written down in the presence of Muhammad, (2) it must be confirmed by two witnesses who would testify that they themselves heard Muhammad recite the passage in question, and (3) it must not represent portions of the Qur'an that had been abrogated by a subsequent revelation to Muhammad.[53] It is also maintained that, since those involved in the compilation (the chief person being Muhammad's scribe Zayd ibn Thābit) knew the complete Qur'an by heart and had chanted it through with the Prophet during his final year, there was little opportunity for error to occur unnoticed.[54] The completed text was kept first by Abū Bakr and, after his death, in the possession of the second Caliph 'Umar. When 'Umar died and 'Uthmān became Caliph it was entrusted to Ḥafṣa, the daughter of 'Umar who was also Muhammad's wife. At this time there was apparently no attempt to establish this first recension of the text as a sole authorized canon or to prevent others from developing and keeping their own compilations of the written text. And since the oral text was present in several different readings (as indicated above), different written recensions based on the various oral readings would not be seen as incorrect. Abū Bakr's motivation was apparently not standardization of the written text but, rather, "to produce, in response to the crisis posed by the death of many Koranic readers, a text which was indisputably authentic and publicly endorsed as such, as a safeguard against the possible loss of other Koran readers."[55]

It was the advent of a new kind of crisis that led to efforts to standardize the written text. The expansion of Islam beyond the Arabian community led to a situation where factions representing different ethnic communities began to dispute over the Qur'an and thus to threaten the unity of the Muslim community. For example, the Syrians following the text of Ubayy ibn Ka'b quarreled with the Iraqis who followed the text of 'Abd Allāh ibn Mas'ūd, with each party accusing the other of unbelief (*kufr*). In other situations certain groups boasted that their oral reading or written text was a superior Qur'an to the oral or written versions of others. It is reported that such internal dissension finally drove the governor of al-Madā'in to go in disgust to the third Caliph 'Uthmān beseeching him, "O Commander of the Faithful! Save this people before it is torn asunder in strife over the Holy Book."[56] In response to this threat to Muslim unity, 'Uthmān decided "to undertake that which had seemed unnecessary to his predecessors, namely, the standardization of the written text of the Koran through the institution of a sole authorized canon."[57] A council of prominent scholars, including Zayd ibn Thabit, was appointed around 650 in Medina to carry out the task. The new version was based heavily on the earlier recension by Zayd, which had been kept by Ḥafṣa. To a large extent the task of the council was to copy and distribute the previous text. To eliminate some of the variant readings contained in the earlier text, 'Uthmān decided that in such cases the reading following the Quraysh dialect should be employed, since that was the dialect spoken by Muhammad. The principles followed by the council were:

1. The earlier recension was to serve as the principal basis of the new one, since it had been compiled from original materials written down during Muhammad's lifetime.
2. Additional written material not previously submitted was solicited, so that a wider range of material could be considered.
3. Variants conforming to the dialect of Quraysh were to be chosen over all others, because Quraysh was the dialect spoken by Muhammad.
4. The entire community was to be apprised of what was submitted, so that the work of final recension would be in effect a collective enterprise, and no one who possessed a portion of the Qur'an passed over.
5. Any doubt that might be raised as to the phrasing of a particular passage in the written text was to be dispelled by summoning persons

known to have learned the passage from Muhammad. Thus, as before, the written text was to be confirmed by oral tradition.

6. The Caliph was to supervise the work of the council.[58]

When the task of the council was finished, it is reported that 'Uthmān kept one copy of the new recension in Medina and sent others to Kūfa, Baṣra, Damascus and Mecca (the number of cities listed varies), along with an order that all other copies of the Qur'an were to be destroyed. According to one tradition this was done everywhere except in Kūfa, where Ibn Mas'ūd and his followers refused to comply.[59]

Within Qur'anic scholarship there is considerable debate over the reliability of the explanation above of the formation of the 'Uthman written text. Traditional Muslim scholars generally accept it, whereas it is seriously questioned by modern Western scholars. The various views of Western scholars are summarized by Welch. What, he asks, are modern scholars to make of the vast literature relating to both oral and written texts of the Qur'an reporting several readings of individual words or phrases that differ from what is our present text of the Qur'an, as well as different arrangements of the *sūras* and even disagreement as to which *sūras* are part of the Qur'an, and which are not.

> First, the problem needs to be stated clearly. Simply put, it is this: the extant manuscripts available to Western scholars represent a single text tradition, commonly known as the 'Uthmanic text, while the classical literature on the Qur'an presents the opposite picture, with countless reports of readings that differ significantly from the text we now have. How are we to explain this contradiction? One possible answer is that the manuscript evidence points to the truth, that only one text of the Qur'an ever existed, either the text that was completed and left by the Prophet (the view of Burton[60]) or a text that was not even compiled and arranged in its present order until long after Muhammad's death (the view of Wansbrough[61]). According to this view, virtually all of the early Muslim reports on the Qur'an and its history must be rejected and regarded as having been fabricated for one reason or another. Another possible answer is that the diverse reports in the literature point to the truth, that a number of different texts of the Qur'an once existed, but no longer survive, or at least are no longer available to Western scholars. This latter view is the one that I find most feasible.[62]

In contrast to the divided opinion among Western scholars, contemporary Muslim scholars such as Ahmad von Denffer and Labib as-Said accept the traditional account of the compilation of the 'Uthmanic text and its authoritativeness for Islam. In his book *The Recited Koran* Labib as-Said devotes a chapter to rebutting the questions raised by Western scholars—questions Said feels to be inadequately based in fact and to call into question centuries-old

Islamic practice. Whatever status scholars may attribute to other texts, says Said, none of them gained the status and confidence that Muhammad's close followers accorded the 'Uthmanic text. Over the centuries, Muslims have seen other texts as belonging to single individuals and kept solely for their personal use.

> Any additional or divergent material which these texts might have contained has been explained as material recited only by a few individuals (and transmitted to later generations via a single chain of authorities), and therefore not fully authenticated but worth preserving for its possible exegetical value; or as abrogated material which was not included in the final corpus recited by the Prophet; or as explanatory notes inserted by the Companions but not intended to be taken as Koranic; or, finally, as variants from non-Qurayshite versions which, though part of the original Revelation, were excluded from the 'Uthmānic canon.[63]

The 'Uthmanic text is divided into 114 *sūras* of various lengths.[64] Within the *sūras* the verses (*āyāt*) are formed on the basis of the prose rhymes. The material is not arranged chronologically but on the basis of length, with the longer *sūras* coming first. The phrase "in the name of God, the Merciful, the Compassionate" (the *basmala*) serves as an introductory formula and divider for the individual *sūras*—except in the case of *sūra* 9. It appears that Muhammad used this formula and himself placed it at the beginning of the separate *sūras* when they were written down. Also, in the case of some twenty-nine *sūras* one finds certain letters or groups of letters—the so-called mysterious letters. Although their meaning is not clear, these letters are considered part of the revelation and may relate to the actual notion of scripture in the Qur'an. In line with the Islamic emphasis upon the oral tradition, the *sūras* are not usually referred to by number but, rather, by names that were added as a later supplement to the 'Uthmanic text. These names were not titles but striking words taken from somewhere in the *sūra* for the purpose of making reference to it.

Even the standardization of the 'Uthmanic edition did not completely prevent the appearance of variants within the written text after it was distributed to the various regional centers. This was due less to scribal errors than to the inadequacy of the Arabic script of the day. Vowels were expressed either inadequately or not at all—the reader had to insert them as the text was read. Also some consonantal symbols were almost indistinguishable from one another. Additional symbols for vowels and other sounds, although developed in the first century after the Hijra (623–723 C.E.), came to be used only gradually in the written Qur'an. An additional factor was that during the first four centuries of Islam, copies of the Qur'an were written in a script called Kufic, a style that differed from the cursive Arabic. Given these difficulties it is not surprising that the oral text continued to be the authority. A person who had learned to recite the Qur'an orally had hardly any textual problems. The written text was simply an aid to scholarship and helped to arbitrate in disputes—it had a functional value. When a reliable written text was finally achieved, its authority was seen to exist in tandem with the authority of the oral text within Islamic tradition.

In the early Islamic centuries, schools for Quranic study developed in Medina, Mecca, Kūfa, Baṣra, and Damascus. At these schools the variant readings of the written text preferred by the leading teachers assumed priority. Criteria for the reliability of a variant reading included correct language, assurance based on a tradition of teachers reaching back to Muhammad, and a consensus of the majority. Gätje describes the outcome:

> The result was similar to that of law: one did not propagate the exclusivity of a single form of the text, but rather permitted different canonical groups of variants to be valid alongside each other, the knowledge of which belonged to the armour of the Qur'ānic teacher.[65]

Just as God's word was understood to have been revealed to Muhammad in several ways, so the same written text could be presented through several variant versions without serious internal conflict or inconsistency. Such was the evolved orthodox view.

Due to the intense sensitivity against anything that might be interpreted as idolatry, Islam totally rejected the use of art in image, music, and iconography. All artistic expression was reserved for religious objects in the mosque, for the margins of the written text, and the calligraphy of the text itself. The written text thus became a major expression of art in the praise of God.[66]

EXEGESIS

Although complete within itself, the Qur'an in its oral and written forms relates to a setting that was limited to the time of Muhammad and could not anticipate the many issues encountered by Islam in its expansion into new areas and its existence in future times. As a second source to be used in interpreting the primary revelation in these new circumstances *Ḥadīth* (tradition) was developed. *Ḥadīth* is based on the sayings and actions of Muhammad, which are judged to be inspired but not revealed—the latter category being reserved for the direct revelation of the Qur'an itself.[67] Technically, *Ḥadīth* includes reports, both oral and written, about what Muhammad and his Companions (i.e., close followers) said, what he did, and what he approved of in the actions of others. There are also reports about what he was like. A clear distinction between Qur'an and *Ḥadīth* is made by the Muslim scholar von Denffer as follows: "The contents of the *sunna* (*Ḥadīth*) are . . . expressed through the prophet's own words or actions, while in the case of the Qur'an the Angel Gabriel brought the exact wording and contents to the Prophet, who received this as revelation and announced this in the very same manner that he received it."[68] Whereas the Qur'an is revealed, *Ḥadīth* is inspired. *Ḥadīth* is the words or actions of a human being (not God) and as such it is not necessarily reported in its precise wording—as the Qur'an is—and is not protected against corruption by God—as the Qur'an is. Whereas the words of the Qur'an are trustworthy by virtue of having been memorized from Muhammad and passed on by a large number of persons, *Ḥadīth* sayings or events arise often from the experience of only one person or a small group with Muhammad.[69]

In the early decades of Islam the *Ḥadīths* were primarily oral rather than written, and "The distinctions between revelation and prophetic inspiration were, though present in some degree, less absolute, and certainly less important than the overwhelming awareness of one's being close to what has been termed 'the prophetic-revelatory event.' "[70] Both Qur'an and *Ḥadīth* were perceived as complementary but integrated aspects of a single phenomenon. But also from the very beginning there was a clear awareness of the danger of confusing any of Muhammad's words or actions with the word of God. Muhammad repeatedly stresses that as a man he has no special power or knowledge. Both the words of Muhammad and the words of the Qur'an stress the unimportance of the messenger in relation to the divine message.[71] In Islam, idolatry was safeguarded against by keeping even as important a person as Muhammad totally separated from God. For Islam, the Christian notion of Christ as God's word incarnate (John 1:14) is anathema, as is the Hindu notion of *avatar* as the incarnation of the Veda.[72]

The formalizing of this clear separation between the person of Muhammad and the *qur'āns*, or revelations, that he had spoken was probably aided by their collection into a written book by the 'Uthmanic redactors some two decades after the Prophet's death. The formalization of the *Ḥadīth,* however, developed much more slowly over the course of the first one hundred or one hundred and fifty years of Islam. In its evolved technical sense within Islam, *Ḥadīth* refers to any report or narrative that is ascribed to Muhammad or one of his close followers (Companions), and which is attested to by a chain of supporting authorities (*isnād*) reaching from the present day right back to Muhammad or a Companion.[73] In reality, however, the *Ḥadīth* literature is voluminous and much of it does not seem to go back to Muhammad or his Companions but, rather, conveys the opinions of the transmitters. That Muslim scholars themselves recognized this fact is evidenced by the development of *Ḥadīth* criticism within Muslim scholarship as early as the ninth century.[74]

As long as Muhammad was living, one could turn to him for an interpretation of a verse from the Qur'an. In the traditional view, it is his statements of this kind and those of his Companions as preserved via *Ḥadīth* that provided the beginning point for Muslim exegesis. This *Ḥadīth* was of several kinds.[75] A common type involved Muhammad's predictions about future events that would befall his community after his death, or about the day of resurrection. Through the *Ḥadīths,* Muhammad is able to assure his people that although they may be the last to receive a prophet they shall be first on the day of resurrection. Another type of *Ḥadīth* is Muhammad's interpretations of specific verses of the Qur'an for his followers. These explanations formed the basis of the earliest exegesis, or *tafsīr.* One *Ḥadīth*, quoted by Ibn Abdalbarr, goes so far as to suggest that whenever a revelation was sent down to Muhammad, Gabriel also provided the appropriate words to explain it.[76] A most interesting kind of *Ḥadīth* material is that designated *ḥadīth qudsī* or Divine Saying in which direct words of God not found in the Qur'an are quoted on the authority of Muhammad. Included in Divine Sayings may be divine words to a previous prophet, for example, Moses or Jesus. William Graham has completed a fine study of these interesting Divine Sayings.[77] Of course, this special revealed *Ḥadīth* seems to be in a quite different category from ordinary, merely inspired *Ḥadīth* described above.

After the death of Muhammed and his Companions these materials were turned to for the solving of doubts about the meaning of particular passages in the Qur'an and their application to new situations faced by Muslims. The theological motifs of Islam and the community's practical needs resulted in an early emphasis on law (*shari'a*). When neither the Qur'an itself nor *Ḥadīth* provided the requisite regulations, it became necessary to develop additional sources for reaching legal decisions. Muslim jurists, like Muslim thinkers in general, used the principle of private interpretation (*ijtihad*) to think through questions of faith and life. The application of reason resulted in a third source of legal development, namely, analogy (*qiyas*). This, in turn, called for a methodology for resolving the variety of personal opinions that ran through early Islamic thought. Thus the idea of *ijma'* developed, the consensus of the Muslim community. Through consensus—meaning primarily the agreement of the learned doctors of the law—the Muslim community would finally decide the meaning of God's word. Although, ironically, this complex process resulted in Muslims becoming ever more distant from the actual words of the Qur'an, the intention was clear: God's word had to be heard, its practical implication had to be made clear, and it had to be translated into a comprehensive code for life.

Theology followed a path similar to that of law. The same supplementary sources of faith that were applied to the Sunni development of the *sharī'a*—tradition, analogy, consensus—also came to be applied to the development of scholastic theology (*kalam*). Not only did daily and community life need to be regulated according to the Qur'an, but beliefs and doctrines had to be clarified. The Qur'an needed to be interpreted to meet this need, and this whole process of interpretation was designated by the term *tafsīr* (explanation).[78] To obtain a brief overview as to how *tafsīr* developed within Islam, we shall look at the different kinds of exegesis that have developed in Sunni, Shi'i, Sufi, Isma'ili, and modern interpretation.

The traditional Sunni approach to exegesis or *tafsīr* is exemplified in the commentary on the Qur'an written by a Persian scholar named Abū Ja'far Muhammad aṭ-Ṭabarī (died 923).[79] Ṭabarī's method is to exegete each verse of the Qur'an by citing in encyclopedic fashion all the *Ḥadīth* material available including the exact chain of authority (*isnād*) for each comment. To illustrate the verse, Ṭabarī provides simplifying paraphrases and lexical references including many poems. Technical issues of grammar are discussed with references back to Baṣran and Kūfan linguistics. In judging between various interpretations, Ṭabarī follows the principle that the clear and easily seen meaning should take precedence. Deviation from the evident interpretation may occur only when convincing reasons for doing so can be given. Ṭabarī places himself consciously on the foundation of inherited interpretations and, when faced with divergent positions, adopts a moderate middle view.

Sunni exegesis is considered to have reached its height with the commentary of Fakhr ad-Dīn ar-Rāzī (died 1209). Rāzī not only follows Ṭabarī's lead in including the *Ḥadīth* material, Rāzī reaches out widely and brings into consideration philosophical thought particularly in reaction to the rationalistic emphasis of Mu'tazīli commentators contemporary with him. Rāzī's exegesis is distinguished by its attempt to interpret difficult or ambiguous verses with novel suggestions couched in painstaking arguments. Some Muslim scholars feel that Rāzī goes too far in this philosophic direction and sometimes loses touch with the actual verse.[80]

The Qur'an is understood within Islam as having been revealed for guidance for all times and situations to come. One scholarly tool used in interpretation is *sabab*.[81] *Sabab* (perhaps best understood as "the occasion of revelation") has the function of helping one to understand the circumstances in which a particular revelation occurred; this sheds light upon its implications then, as well as upon the application of the particular passage for other times and situations. *Sabab*, in this context, seems to have a limited and specific meaning, namely, knowledge about the particular events and circumstances in history that are related to the revelation of particular passages in the Qur'an. It is not the free use of speculative reason that is employed; rather, it is the use of reason in (a) understanding the meaning of a verse in its original context, (b) showing whether the meaning of a verse is specific or general in its application and under which circumstances it is to be applied, and (c) in determining the historical situation at the time of the Prophet and the development of the early Muslim community. An example will make this very limited use of reason clear. *Sūra* 2:115 states, "To God belong the East and the West: whithersoever ye turn, there is the presence of God, for God is all-pervading, all-knowing." Without knowing the reasons or circumstances involved in this revelation, one might interpret it as allowing a Muslim to face in any direction when performing prayer. However, the circumstances in which this revelation occurred explain its proper interpretation. According to Wāqīdi, a group of Muslims traveling on a dark night did not know the direction of Mecca and later came to realize that they had prayed in a wrong direction. They asked Muhammad about it and he apparently kept silent until the verse above was revealed. Taking into account the circumstances of the revelation, *sabab* provides the interpretation that this verse excuses the mistake of those who unwillingly and under adverse circumstances fail to pray facing Mecca, the correct direction.

Sabab (the reasons or causes that occasioned a particular revelation) is said to be known to us via the reports of Muhammad's Companions. Such a report must be reliable, however, which requires that the person making the report should have been present with Muhammad at the time of the revelation. The examination of the reasons surrounding a revelation can lead to the conclusion that it was meant to give guidance to more than one situation or question—one revelation can be applied to interpret several different situations.[82] There are also situations in which several revelations may be connected with one particular circumstance, for example, as when Umm Salama asks why only men had been referred to in the Qur'an as being rewarded—several verses (3:195, 4:32 and 33:35) were judged by the exercise of *sabab* to have been revealed in response to this question. *Sabab* is also used to decide whether a specific revelation has implications only for the historic situation to which it was connected or whether it is of general application to the needs of Muslims in future situations. The role of *sabab*, then, in Islamic interpretation is to help distinguish between the part of the revelation that is attached only to the historical event, and the part that, although attached to the historical event, also has wider implications.

Modern Western historical scholars are critical of traditional Sunni commentaries for their assumption that all of the Qur'an is divine speech, which leads to the glossing over of difficult or ambiguous passages by relating them to *Ḥadīth* contents that are clear and unambiguous.[83]

A fundamental difference in basic assumptions lies at the heart of the difference of Shi'i exegesis from that of the Sunnis. The difference centers on the Shi'i understanding—rejected by the Sunnis—that revelation or special inspiration outside of the Qur'an has been granted to some of those around the Prophet and to the Shi'i imāms.[84] Thus the Shi'i idea is of a continuing inspired or infallible guidance through the imāms after the death of Muhammad. This is rationalized with traditional Sunni principles (which are also accepted by the Shi'i) in the following way.[85] The Shi'i have agreed that Muhammad was the only true interpreter of the Qur'an and that therefore any trustworthy interpretation has to go back to him. But the Shi'i have further maintained that the Qur'an has two distinct levels of meaning: one that could be known by everyone who knows the Arabic language (*tanzil*) and the other safeguarded by God (*ta'wil*). The latter is known only to those whom God has specially chosen, namely the imāms—Ali (cousin and son-in-law of Muhammad) and the eleven imāms (who through Ali stand in a family descending from Muhammad). According to Shi'i thought, Ali and his eleven descendants have inherited the inner (*ta'wil*) knowledge of Muhammad. This knowledge is not closed and static but continually changing so as to make the eternal truth of the Qur'an relevant to current situations. Because only the imāms have this special and relevant knowledge, the Qur'an is understood as revealed by God first to them and then by extension through them to the rest of humanity. The function of the imām in making the revelation of the Qur'an relevant to changing situations is paralleled within the Sunni tradition by the role of law, or *sharīa*, which makes judgments to interpret and relate the original Qur'an to succeeding generations. By its very nature Shi'i exegesis leads to the view that the Shi'i are a special community within Islam and the world—specially chosen and favored by God. Since in this view the Qur'an is primarily addressed to the imāms, it is only through them and their followers that the inner meaning of the revelation for the present situation is given to the rest of Islam and to the world. In response to charges of "addition" or "omission" in their interpretation, Shi'i scholars have mainly asserted that only the *ta'wil*, or inner meaning, has been altered, while the *tanzil*, or outer text, which is in our hands has not been changed. Within the Shi'ite tradition *tafsīr*, or exegesis, consists mainly of imāms' *Ḥadīths*, which are given equal weight with those of Muhammad because it is assumed that they inherited their knowledge from him. The Shi'i also depend on a somewhat different corpus of *Ḥadīth*.

In the opinion of Helmut Gätje, Shi'i interpretation tends to choose from among the Qur'anic variants those which are favorable for their theology. He suggests that they sometimes go so far as to undertake changes and expansions to the 'Uthmanic text, which they claim to have obtained from the "genuine" Qur'an of the imāms.[86] Shi'i exegesis also makes more use of allegory and levels of meaning than does Sunni interpretation. Kenneth Cragg summarizes the difference between the two approaches effectively:

> The Sunnī scheme took the lengthening ages of Islam back, as it were, horizontally in the plane of history to the fountainhead in the Prophet, and bound them into one by the criterion of the *Sharī'ah*. Shi'ah Islam saw that final source linked afresh to each generation, vertically, through the Imām, without whom the faith and the faithful could not coinhere. In doing so, they did not impugn the finality of the Qur'ān: they believed they possessed it through renewed emanation of the original "light of Muhammad."[87]

While the Sunnis basically rely on law, or *sharī'a*, to interpret the fixed revelation to changing circumstances, Shi'i believe that through the mediation of the imāms Muhammad's revelation remains dynamic and relevant to every new situation. For the Shi'i, it is through the imām that the faithful in each generation stand within the authentic truth of the Qur'an.[88]

By way of passing comment it could be noted that in matters of exegesis the Ismailis Shi'i follow the same general principles as those outlined above. The main difference is that the Ismailis recognized Ja'faral Sadig's son, Ismā'īl, who had predeceased his father, as the next imām in succession (seven imāms after Ali) while the other Shi'ites, the Twelvers (twelve imāms after Ali), took Mūsā al-Kāẓim, a surviving son of Ja'far, as the next true imām in succession. Both groups ended up believing in the concealment of the true imām, to await manifestation in God's time and to guide the faithful in the meantime from his mysterious place of hiddenness. For the Seveners, the hidden imām is the lost son of Ismā'īl who was predeceased by Mūsā. For the Twelvers, it is the son of the eleventh imām, Ḥasan al-'Askarī, who mysteriously disappeared at the age of seven.[89]

In concluding this discussion of Sunni and Shi'i exegesis, it should be noted that modern interpretation in both schools is quite similar. Both are now characterized by their reaction to the challenges of Western technology, science, and education. Ayoub describes modern exegesis as rational and apologetic; its primary aim is "to present Islam to Muslims and defend it against the Western secular and missionary onslaughts."[90] Shaykh Muhammad 'Abduh (died 1905) and his disciple Sayyid Muhammad Rashid Rida (died 1935) are well known examples of this kind of reaction to modernity. Sayyid Qutb and Abul Mandrīdī may be taken as representing a more confident return to the Qur'an without the need to apologize for it. Their commentaries have a wide appeal to the youth of both Shi'i and Sunni communities.[91]

Shi'i exegesis, with its use of the idea of levels of inner meaning, leads conveniently to the Sufi approach to interpretation of the Qur'an. Within Islam Sufi exegesis is characterized as mystical and frequently integrates elements of Greek philosophy into its interpretations. The distinctive Sufi method of exegesis is well represented by the Sufi Sahl at-Tustarī, a Persian who lived in the ninth century.[92] Tustarī's Qur'anic interpretations take the form of phrases, sentences, or brief passages written down by his disciples as a result of listening intently to Qur'an recitals. "The reception of Qur'an recitals and the reaction to their impact upon the Sufi's mind involve primarily the auditive energies of the Sufi and result in Sufi speech, sometimes manifested in ecstatic utterance."[93] This listening and speaking process is transposed into a written record by a disciple noting down the Sufi master's succinct statement next to a Qur'anic phrase or word. Thus the reading of a Sufi commentary requires that the eye take in both the Qur'anic word or phrase that the Sufi heard, and the response uttered in his mystic speech.

Rather than a meditative or scholarly approach to the written text, the Sufi exegete allows himself to be inspired by a word or phrase from the oral text. The nature of the inspired response is indicated in the texture of Tustarī's commentary where the theme of a particular item in the commentary "is usually introduced by a Qur'anic keynote (a word or a phrase of a particular verse that strikes the mind of the commentator) and is taken up as the focal point of the interpretation."[94] Qur'anic keynotes can be anything from historical references to theological terms or philosophical puzzles that in one way or another have managed to awaken associations in the mind of the listening Sufi. Böwering describes the mental process as follows:

> These associations establish the essential link between the Qur'ānic keynote and the commentary. Called forth by Qur'ānic keynotes (among them certain privileged keynotes in particular), they grow out of the matrix of Tustarī's world of mystical ideas (his experience about himself, God, and the world) and find their expression in a way that can be as allusive as it is concrete, and as general as it is particular. In this process a level of synthesis is achieved which makes it impossible to discern where "exegesis" ends and "eisegesis" begins.[95]

Tustarī's Sufi method of interpreting the Qur'an is thus basically an encounter between the spoken keynote words of the scripture and the matrix of his mystical ideas. This encounter, under the influence of divine inspiration, produces associations and verbal expressions that are then recorded as the written commentary. For the Sufi these keynotes are not studied as a text, but are heard by men experienced in listening attentively to Qur'anic recital and intent on hearing God, the actual speaker of the Qur'anic word. The keynote psychologically functions to help the Sufi break through to God. This special Qur'anic word takes the Sufi beyond its outer form and sound to a direct revelation of God.

It is through this method of evoking mystical insight from the Qur'anic word that the Sufi arrives at its inner meaning. Tustarī employs a fourfold category, which resolves to two levels of meaning—the literal and moral meaning as opposed to the combined allegorical and analogical meaning. The latter, the inner meaning, is the domain of the Sufi or mystic, while the former, the literal and moral or outer meaning, is open to the ordinary person.[96]

THE QUR'AN IN DAILY PIETY AND PRACTICE

While the various approaches to exegesis within Islam have attempted to show the Qur'an's relevance to the changes of history, it is the use of the Qur'an in daily life by pious Muslims that demonstrates its continuing presence in their lives. As Wilfred Cantwell Smith has emphasized, the Qur'an is not just a seventh-century Arabian document, as modern historians of religion often seem to maintain. For the Muslim, the Qur'an is equally a ninth-, a fourteenth-, an eighteenth-, and a twentieth-century document, which has been and still is intimately involved in the life not only of Arabia but also of Africa, India, China, and elsewhere.[97] The continuing vitality of the Qur'an is well portrayed by Smith:

> The Qur'ān has played a role—formative, dominating, liberating, spectacular—in the lives of millions of people, philosophers and peasants, politicians and merchants and housewives, saints and sinners, in Baghdad and Cordoba and Agra, in the Soviet Union since the Communist Revolution, and so on. That role is worth discerning and pondering. The attempt to understand the Qur'ān is to understand how it has fired the imagination, and inspired the poetry, and formulated the inhibitions, and guided the ecstasies, and teased the intellects, and ordered the family relations and the legal chicaneries, and nurtured piety, of hundreds of millions of people in widely diverse climes and over a series of radically divergent centuries.[98]

"The meaning of the Qur'ān as scripture," concludes Smith, "lies not in the text, but in the minds and hearts of Muslims."[99]

This central role of the Qur'an is anchored and sustained in Muslim life by the practice of recitation *(qirā'a).* Recitation of the Qur'an has been the one essential element of Muslim daily worship (*ṣalāt*). In addition to the opening sentences, it is expected the one or more shorter *sūras*, or chapters, of the Qur'an will be recited. Recitation of the Qur'an is the preferred form of devotion in Islam at any time. The fact that the Qur'an is the sacred word of God has led Muslims to maintain that it should be recited in the original Arabic, even if that language is not understood. Thus Muslim children of whatever linguistic or cultural background are taught to memorize by saying aloud the words of the Qur'an. Memorized knowledge of the key passages will allow them to participate in *ṣalāt*, or daily worship, throughout their lives. As one old teacher, who was teaching children the Qur'an in Singapore, put it: "The sons of the Prophet ought to have this Word in their memory so that they can repeat it often. These words are endowed with a special virtue. . . . In translating them we might alter the meaning and that would be a sacrilege."[100] Like the Vedic *mantra*, the recited Qur'an itself has power. But even more important is its memorization, which has been basic to education throughout the Muslim world. One of the greatest accomplishments open to a Muslim is to be designated *ḥāfiz,* or one who has learned by heart the entire Qur'an. This is also a prerequisite for any accomplished religious scholar (*'alim*). In a Muslim society the lilting refrain of Qur'anic recitation occupies a prominent place, so that from birth to death people are continually reimmersed in the Qur'an.[101] This has a powerful unifying and transforming effect on both the individual and communal psyche.

William Graham reports two examples of different styles of public recitation. One is the *dhikr* (the "remembrance" of God through litanies of group recitation) practiced by Sufi brotherhoods and certain mosques, especially tomb-mosques. *Dhikr* involves the chanting of texts steeped in the language of the Qur'an and usually begins with the recitation of verses of the Qur'an itself. In contrast to such group chanting are the sessions in which listeners gather to hear the Qur'an recited by a series of individual practitioners of *tajwīd* (musical recitation of the Qur'an). Cairo is especially well known for its varied forms of this kind of session, which can take place in mosques or in private homes of devotees of the art.

In addition to sessions of public recitation, the individual activities of a pious Muslim's daily life are potentially accompanied by spoken words of the Qur'an, for example, the *basmala*, "In the name of God, the Merciful, the Compassionate" that precedes routine daily acts such as eating or drinking, just as it precedes all but one *sūra* of the Qur'an. There are also longer passages heard in daily life, for example, the Fātiḥa, *sūra* 1, which every Muslim knows by heart and recites not only in every *ṣalāt*, or daily worship, but also on virtually every formal occasion. Other *sūras,* such as "The Cow" (*al-Baqara*), contain prayers for forgiveness and are often recited before going to sleep.[102]

The result of all of this activity—the memorization of the Qur'an in early youth and the constant participation in public and private recitation of such memorized passages throughout adulthood—it is no exaggeration to say, is that Muslim life is lived in resonance to the Qur'an. What the Muslim scholar al-Ghazālī said of the Qur'an long ago still holds today: "Much repetition cannot make it seem old and worn to those who recite it."[103] In much of modern society "the book lives on among its people, stuff of their daily lives, taking for them the place of a sacrament. For them these are not mere letters or mere words. They are the twigs of the burning bush, aflame with God."[104] In addition to this oral experience of God's sacred word, its written form also forms a valued part of daily experience. The written Qur'an provides the content of Islamic art, and is visible in magnificent fashion. As Graham puts it:

> The tradition of manuscript illumination and calligraphic artistry is one of the wonders of the Islamic cultural heritage. The written qur'ānic word embellishes virtually every Muslim religious building as the prime form of decorative art. Nor is the reverence and honor shown the written Qur'ān text in Muslim piety any less striking and impressive. All such facts simply underscore what has been argued here: that the scriptural word, even where its written form is most prominent, is always demonstrably a spoken word, a recited word, a word that makes itself felt in personal and communal life in large part through its living quality as sacred sound.[105]

THE QUR'AN IN RELATION TO OTHER SCRIPTURES

Islam has within it a strong sense of the unity of all religions under one God. In his revelation activity, God created the "Mother of the Book" (*sūra* 43:14 and 13:39) or the "Hidden Book" (*sūra* 56:78) in heaven, of which all earthly scriptures are copies. So Moses received a copy as did Jesus, but the followers of Moses and Jesus are judged to have corrupted the scripture they had received. This is why the Jewish and Christian scriptures differ with the Qur'an even though all three are copies of the same "Mother Book." Only the Qur'an, through its faithful preservation by Muhammad and his Companions, presents a clear and uncorrupted copy of God's revelation. Thus the relationship of the Qur'an with other scriptures is on the analogy of siblings—all scriptures are offspring of the same "Mother Book," but only the Qur'an has remained true to its source. While this interpretation works reasonably well with the Hebrew and Christian scriptures, Islamic scholars have had to resort to considerable inventiveness in attempting to demonstrate the same kind of relationship between the Qur'an and the scriptures of Eastern religions—the Hindu Veda and the Sayings of the Buddha. In fact, since God is not accepted within the Buddhist religion, and the Vedas are seen as eternal, authorless, and at times as above God (e.g., the Mīmāṁsā school) within Hinduism, the "Mother Book" in heaven analogy breaks down when it is applied to Eastern religions.[106]

Because all prophetic messages come from a single source, Muhammad felt it was incumbent on all people to believe in all divine messages. Thus Muhammad is made to declare in the Qur'an that not only does he believe in the Torah and the gospel, but "I believe in whatever Book God may have revealed" (42:15). In the Qur'an's view, God's truth and guidance is not restricted but is universally available to all people—"There is no nation wherein a warner has not come" (35:24) and "For every people a guide has been provided" (13:7). Fazlur Rahman observes that the word "book" is often used in the Qur'an not to refer to any specific revealed book, "but as a generic term denoting the totality of divine revelations" (e.g., 2:213).[107] This idea of one a priori revelation is linked in the Qur'an with the notion of an originally unified humanity.

> Mankind were one single community. Then God raised up prophets who gave good tidings and warning and God also sent down with them The Book in truth, that it may decide among people in regard to what they differed. But people did not differ in it [i.e., with regard to the Truth] except those to whom it had been given [and that only] after clear signs had come to them; [and this they did] out of [sheer] rebelliousness among themselves (2:213).[108]

Consequently, according to the Qur'an, there was originally a unified humanity that became divided due to its own rebelliousness. Fazlur Rahman sees this divisive state as fostered by the various versions of the "one Book" brought by the different prophets. Why prophetic revelation should act as a force for disunity does not seem to be answered, except to say that it is a mystery that God could overcome if he so willed. The fact that God does not so will is explained as providing an opportunity for the various religions to compete with each other in goodness.

> If God had so willed, He would have made all of you one community, but [He has not done so] that He may test you in what He has given you; *so compete in goodness.* To God shall you all return and He will tell you [the Truth] about what you have been disputing (5:48).[109]

To all other religions then, the Qur'an invites "competition in goodness" and the invitation "O People of the Book! Let us come together upon a formula which is common between us—that we shall not serve anyone but God, that we shall associate none with Him" (3:64).[110] This challenge and invitation applies to Jews and Christians, who are obviously "people of the book," and, as noted above, there have been both earlier and recent attempts within Islam to understand Hindus and Buddhists as also "people of the Book." The logic of the Qur'an seems strongly reminiscent of the *logos* idea—one divine Book of which the prophetic utterances of the various religions are simply different deviations. The Qur'an is, of course, the complete and full revelation of the one divine Book, all other books being only partial and incomplete presentations.

4

SCRIPTURE IN HINDUISM

Like the three Western religions—Judaism, Christianity, and Islam—Hinduism has been called a "religion of the Book" in that it is founded upon a scripture that is judged to be essential to the realization of release (the Eastern parallel to salvation). Yet the Hindu understanding of scripture is in many ways quite different. Whereas the Torah of Judaism has definite beginnings reported in Genesis and Exodus, the Hindu scriptures are held to be beginningless—just as in the Hindu view the whole of the universe has existed beginninglessly as a series of cycles of creation going backward into time infinitely. Although the Hindu scripture is spoken anew at the beginning of each cycle of creation, what is spoken is identical with the scripture that had been spoken in all previous cycles, beginninglessly. The very idea of an absolute point of beginning for either creation or the scripture is simply not present in Hindu thought. A close parallel to this Hindu notion of the eternal presence of scripture[1] is perhaps found in the Western idea of *logos*, especially as expressed in the Gospel of John 1:1, "In the beginning was the Word, and the Word was with God, and the Word was God."

Another difference in the Hindu view is that its basic scripture, the Veda, is held by some schools to be authorless. The idea of an authorless scripture is of course logically consistent with the claim of its eternality, in that the identification of an author would indicate a historical point of beginning. Another consideration is that authors are human and thus capable of error. Being authorless, it is argued, therefore safeguards Hindu scripture from the possibility of human error. Some Hindu schools explicitly rule out the suggestion of God as the author of scripture, since God is seen by some philosophers as being a human personification and thus also open to error. While the majority of Hindus are satisfied to think of their scripture as in some sense identified with or authored by God, one school, the Pūrva Mīmāṁsā, goes to the extreme of denying the existence of God as author to ensure that the errorless nature of the scripture cannot be called into question.[2] If even God is open to question as author, certainly humans cannot be seen as composers of scripture. The *ṛṣis*, or seers, identified as speakers of particular Vedas are understood to be mere channels through which the transcendent word passes to make itself available to humans at the start of each creation cycle. Thus, the same *ṛṣis* are said to speak the Vedas in each cycle of creation, and the very language in which the Vedas are spoken, Sanskrit, is itself held to be divine.

For the Hindu, the spoken scripture of the tradition is the Divine Word (*Daivī Vāk*) descending and disclosing itself to the sensitive soul.[3] The "sensitive soul" was the seer, or *ṛṣi*, who had purged himself of ignorance, rendering his consciousness transparent to the Divine Word. The *ṛṣi* was not the author of the Vedic hymn but, rather, the seer (*draṣṭā*) of an eternal, authorless truth. As the modern Hindu scholar Aurobindo Ghose explains, the language of the Veda is "a rhythm not composed by the intellect but heard, a Divine Word that came vibrating out of the Infinite to the inner audience of the man who had previously made himself fit for the impersonal knowledge."[4] The *ṛṣi*'s initial vision is of the Veda as one, which is then broken down and spoken as the words and sentences of scripture. In this Vedic idea of revelation there is no suggestion of the miraculous or supernatural. The *ṛṣi*, by the progressive purifying of consciousness through the disciplines of yoga, had simply removed the mental obstructions to the revelation of the Divine Word. While the Divine Word is inherently present within the consciousness of all, it is the *ṛṣis* who first reveal it and in so doing make it available to help all others achieve the same experience. The spoken Vedic words of the *ṛṣis* act powerfully upon us to purify our consciousness and give to us that same full spiritual vision of the unitary Divine Word that the *ṛṣi* first saw. This is the enlightenment experience, the purpose for which Hindu scripture exists.

In this enlightenment experience yet another difference may be seen: for most Hindus, once the direct experience of the Divine Word is realized, the manifested forms (i.e., the words and sentences of the Veda) are no longer needed.[5] The Vedic words and sentences function only as the "ladder" to raise one to the direct, intuitive experience of the complete Divine Word. Once the full enlightenment experience is achieved, the "ladder of scripture" is no longer needed. The very idea that scripture can be transcended is heresy to Jews, Christians, and Muslims. For them the obstructions of human limitations are such that even the most saintly person would get only part-way up the ladder; scripture (Torah, Bible, or Qur'an) could never be transcended in the sense that most Hindus accept.

With this basic introduction to the different ways in which most Hindus approach their scriptures, let us now examine (1) Hindu sacred books, (2) the Hindu view of language, (3) oral texts, (4) written texts, (5) techniques of exegesis, and (6) the Veda in relation to other scriptures.

HINDU SACRED BOOKS

Orthodox Hindu scholars divide their sacred books into two classes, *śruti* and *smṛti*. *Śruti*, literally, is that which is "seen" or "heard" by the *ṛṣis* at the start of each cycle of creation and then spoken for the benefit of the people as the Veda—the scriptural ladder to release (*mokṣa*). The Veda is divided into four layers, which modern scholars see as largely successive although there is an overlap in time between the last phase of one and the early phase of the next.[6] The most ancient layer, the Vedic hymns or *Samhitās*, is dated between 1400 and 1000 B.C. While some modern scholars see these hymns as essentially polytheistic—in praise of many different gods—traditional Hindu scholars see the hymns to different deities as manifestations of the many different aspects, or faces, of the one Divine Reality, *Brahman* (monism rather than polytheism). For example, Aurobindo sees the fire [*agni*] of the Vedic hymn to Agni as symbolizing the divine creative force of the cosmos as well as the supervisor of the ritual sacrifice. Aurobindo translates verse 3 of the Twenty-First Hymn to Agni in the Ṛg Veda as follows:

> Thee [Agni] all the gods with one heart
> of love made their envoy;
> O seer, men serve and adore thee in
> their sacrifices as the Godhead.[7]

Agni appears as the one representative of all the gods to humans, and the messenger from the human worshipers to the one Godhead. The poetic form of the Vedic hymns supports the traditional viewpoint that the different gods of the various hymns simply symbolize different aspects of the one Divine. The Vedic hymns, like all poetry, can be interpreted on a surface level or at the level of deeper inner meaning.

The second layer of the Veda, the *Brāhmaṇa*, is dated from 1000 to 700 B.C.E. and takes the form of a prose discussion that enlarges on the ritual use of the original poetic hymn, setting forth its procedures and speculations as to the cosmic forces that the ritual will regulate.

The next layer of texts, the *Āraṇyakas*, continues the concern of the *Brāhmaṇas* over matters of external ritual, but also begins to shift attention from the external form of the hymn to its inner meaning in terms of human relationship with the cosmos. The *Āraṇyakas* are usually dated between 800 and 600 B.C.E. The final layer, the *Upaniṣads*, further focuses on the inner meaning of the original hymn, often brought out in the form of a dialogue between a teacher (*guru*) and a student. External aspects of the ritual are often reinterpreted to become mental exercises for meditation. Throughout the *Upaniṣads* the focus is on human beings and their relationship to the cosmos, its source, and to the ultimate and irreducible principle within each person, the *ātman*. The *Upaniṣads* are dated between 800 and 500 B.C.E.[8]

These four layers of the Veda are also "vertically" divided into four collections each of which is transmitted by a separate school. The four schools are *Ṛgveda, Yajurveda, Sāmaveda,* and *Atharvaveda*. These schools derive their distinctions from their respective places in the liturgy of the sacrifice. In the rituals employing professional priests, the division of labor took place as follows: one did the main recitation, another the main manipulations, another chanted hymns, and a fourth supervised and did acts of expiation. Later this became more complex. From these separate functions came the four schools. Those expert in the *Ṛgveda-Saṁhitā* recited the hymns contained in that collection. The experts in the actual ritual operations accompanied by sacrificial formulas (*yajus*) formed the *Yajurveda-Saṁhitā*. The priests who chanted compiled their own collection of psalms for singing (*sāman*, or melody), thus the *Sāmaveda-Saṁhitā*. While the three schools above belong intimately together as performing complementary parts of the Vedic ritual, the fourth school, the *Atharvaveda*, is quite different. These priests (*atharvan* is the name of a special priest) formed their own collection of Vedic hymns or *Saṁhitā* focusing on the day-to-day needs of people. It contains medical cures, spells, and magic, and also some hymns in which the source of being, creation, and the relation of humans to the supernatural world are speculated upon. Of the collections or schools, most modern scholars consider the *Ṛgveda* to be the oldest, dating from about 1300 B.C.E., the *Yajurveda* and the *Sāmaveda* developing before 1000 B.C.E. and the *Atharvaveda* being formed by 1200 B.C.E. Each of these collections will contain older materials (e.g., original hymns and *Brāhmaṇas*) as well as more recent materials such as *Upaniṣads*. It is in this fashion that the *ṛṣis* were founders of lineages of *Brahmins* (Hindu priests) through whom the texts have been and continue to be passed down. It is from this heritage that the *Brahmins* derive their function as ritual specialists and teachers.

The language of the Veda is Sanskrit, and it is in this language that each particular collection or school passes on its texts in oral form—the student memorizing from the teacher and then passing the same oral Veda on to his students in turn. All of this is, literally, *śruti*, "that which is heard." It is the primary and authoritative scripture for orthodox Hindus.

But there is a second category of Hindu scripture, *smṛti*, literally, "that which is remembered." *Smṛti* is used to designate all other sacred literature, principally in Sanskrit, which is considered to be secondary to *śruti* (the Veda). *Smṛti*'s role is to bring out the hidden meanings of the Vedic revelation, or to represent the original teaching in an easier-to-understand form suited to the changed conditions of the age. *Smrti* thus often takes story form as in the epic poems the *Mahābhārata* (which includes the *Bhagavad Gītā*) and the *Rāmāyaṇa*. *Smṛti* texts are said never to add any new revelation but simply to represent the teaching of *śruti* in a form more suited to a wider audience in its own particular age. *Smṛti* thus provides for an updating of the scriptural revelation and, in practice, the Hindu acquires his or her knowledge of religion almost exclusively through *smṛti*, which some take to be revealed (e.g., Saiva).

Smṛti post-Vedic scripture is extremely voluminous and may be summarized under the following headings: epics, *purāṇa*, *tantra*, and others. The two main epic texts, the *Mahābhārata* and the *Rāmāyaṇa*, were likely compiled around 400 B.C. to A.D. 200. The term "compiled" is especially appropriate to the

Mahābhārata, which is a vast library into which new material was constantly added over many years. The *Mahābhārata* is gigantic, being about seven times the length of the *Iliad* and the *Odyssey* combined. Its main story is of two rival groups, both laying claim to the throne in a region somewhere near modern Delhi. Its religious importance comes from the large number of tales that have been added into the core story of the epic. Although the characters of the main story go back to ca. 1000 B.C.E., the text we have is probably not older than ca. 400 B.C.E. Perhaps the most significant addition to the *Mahābhārata* is the *Bhagavad-Gītā*. The *Bhagavad-Gītā* is significant as a scriptural form in that it contains the idea of revelation occurring through incarnation. God (Viṣṇu) incarnates himself in the human form of Krishna, a prince and chariot driver, to teach people (symbolized by Arjuna, the warrior whose chariot Krishna drives) divine truth. Although orthodox tradition maintains that no new content is being revealed, it is certainly true that the form in which the teaching is presented, and the response required, is new. In particular there is a stress on devotion (*bhakti*) as a relationship between the devotee and a personalized God, which is open to all regardless of caste or sex. None of this was evident in the Veda. This same kind of *bhakti* emphasis is found in the *Rāmāyaṇa*, which to this day continues to be one of the most powerful pieces of Hindu scripture in its impact upon people. Unlike the *Mahābhārata*, the *Rāmāyaṇa* has a unitary style suggesting a single author, traditionally called Vālmīki. The idea of God becoming incarnated in Rāma is also present in the *Rāmāyaṇa*. Especially appropriate for today is the extension of the divine incarnation to include Rāma's wife, Sītā, thus providing a female form through which God may be approached.

Purāṇa, which literally means "ancient story," is a general name given to a long series (traditionally eighteen) of voluminous texts that contain myths and legends as well as genealogies of gods, heroes, and saints. As in the epics, the stress is on devotion (*bhakti*). *Purāṇas* can loosely be divided into three groups: those exalting the god Brahmā, those devoted to the god Viṣṇu, and those devoted to Siva. However, many deal with similar materials. The most important *Purāṇas* in their present form are *Viṣṇu, Linga, Bhāgavata*, and the *Skanda*. The *Purāṇas* are dated from 300 to 1600 C.E. "This purāṇic literature continues with Upapurāṇas ('sub-*Purāṇas*') and *Māhātmyas* (glorifications) of temples and sacred places."[9]

Tantras (literally, "looms") are texts presenting Hindu religion on a popular level, and dealing mainly with *mantras* (chants), temple ritual, and *maṇḍalas*, (drawn symbols for use in meditation). There are *Tantras* for the worship of Viṣṇu, Siva, and the goddess Śakti. They focus on practical techniques for spiritual practice rather than metaphysical ideas. In some of the Sākta *Tantras*, evidence of the "left-handed" practices (esoteric, magical, and sometimes sexual) is found, but the incidence of such material is relatively infrequent.[10] The *Tantras* are dated from 500 to 1800 C.E. They seem to have arisen outside the literate *Brahmin* tradition. Although they often criticize established religious practices and the *Brahmins* who preside over them, the *Tantras* largely support the central Hindu ideas and practices. Basic to the *Tantras* is the assumption that the individual is a microcosm of the cosmos and that by learning to unite the pairs of opposites within one's being, the goal of spiritual fulfillment may be achieved. Tantric techniques include the chanting of *mantras*, meditation on *maṇḍalas*, and yogic practices, sometimes to the exclusion of traditional Vedic rituals. It is argued that Tantric methods are more suited to the present decadent era in which people are less likely to follow the elaborate Vedic rituals of an earlier age.[11]

Other sacred texts came to be written in the many regional languages found throughout India. Of these non-Sanskrit sacred texts, mention may be made of the devotional hymns written by the south Indian Tamil poet-saints from the seventh century C.E. on in worship of Siva and Viṣṇu. The hymns of these poet-saints were collected and have provided the basis for a rich and fervent devotional Hindu practice in south India over the past one thousand years. In the north, Hindi language became dominant and there the devotional poems of Kabir (ca. 1500), the princess poetess Mīrabaī (ca. 1550), and Tulsīdās (ca. 1600), who composed a Hindi version of the *Rāmāyaṇa*, have been influential. A Tamil version of the *Rāmāyaṇa* was composed earlier in the south by Kamban (ca. twelfth century). Translations of both the *Rāmāyaṇa* and the *Bhagavad-Gītā* have been made into most of the regional languages of India. One of the best examples of a poem in which divine love is symbolized by human love is Jayadeva's *Gita Govinda*. Tagore's Bengali poem *Gitanjali*, which won a Nobel prize, must be considered a great Hindu devotional work from Bengal—although it would not be classed as *smṛti*.

Hindu sacred books embrace an enormous collection of texts of startling antiquity and variety. While the canon of the *śruti* texts is well set, the *smṛti* collection, which seeks to represent the original revelation in ways better able to communicate to local conditions, is massive and continues to expand. These sacred texts are put to a wide range of uses. Vedic texts continue to function in the formal rituals presided over by the *Brahmins* in temples, and at key points in family life. The later parts of the Vedas, the *Upaniṣads*, became the basis for various philosophical schools, each with its own method of exegesis. The epics, *pūraṇas*, and *tantras*, on the other hand, became the basis for widespread popular devotion in the many regional languages of India and the changing eras right up to the present day. Hindu texts are used in private devotions in the home (e.g., chanting of *mantras* morning and evening), and on public occasions (e.g., during temple festivals). In some temples, professional reciters have their own booths in which they patiently set forth day after day texts such as the *Bhagavad-Gītā*. Perhaps the most dramatic use of a sacred text is that of the Hindi *Rāmāyan*a by Tulsīdās. At the Rām Līlā festivals in northern India, that epic is acted out with the whole city becoming involved—much like the Oberammergau reenactment of Christ's passion in the West. Similar dramatic use of various Hindu texts takes place all over India. Today the texts are also traveling with the "Hindu diaspora" to all corners of the globe. *Mantra* chanting of sacred texts occurs in North American homes, Vedic rituals to Agni in Arya Samaj ceremonies take place throughout the Western world, and enactments of the *Rāmayaṇa* have long been a high point in Pacific islands like Bali. Many educated English homes have a copy of Tagore's *Gitanjali*, and the *Bhagavad Gītā* in translation is read around the world.

Hindu scripture thus embraces an enormous variety of texts touching upon individual, family, and public life in India and, increasingly, throughout the world. Since the Hindu religion has no institutional or church basis, these texts are the heart of Hindu life. They provide Hindu "religion with its substance, with its principal assumptions, art with its themes, literature with its topics, and music and dance with their souls."[12]

THE HINDU VIEW OF LANGUAGE

In order to understand how scriptures function for Hindus, the quite different (from the modern West) view of language assumed by traditionally minded Hindus must be set forth. Linguistic speculations were begun by the Hindus before the advent of recorded history.[13] Beginning with the Vedic hymns, which are at least three thousand years old, the Indian study of language has continued in an unbroken tradition right to the present day. Nor was the Indian approach to language ever narrow or restrictive: language was examined in relation to consciousness—consciousness not constricted even to human consciousness—and all aspects of the world and human experience were thought of as illuminated by language.

In the ancient hymns of the *Ṛgveda*, furthermore, there was also a semitechnical vocabulary designed to deal with such linguistic matters as language composition, poetic creation, inspiration, illumination, vision, and so on.[14] But even though there was this careful concern for the phenomenal, or outer, aspects of language, equal attention was always paid to its inner, or metaphysical aspects. The Indians seem to have avoided successfully the two reductionist mistakes of modern Western language speculation: they did not reduce language to the status of a merely human convention having only scientific or factual referents; nor did they fall into the error of metaphysical reductionism, which so devalues the meanings of human words that language ends up as obscure mysticism.[15] Grammarians like Pāṇini and Patanjali, and etymologists like Yāska, were clearly concerned with human speech in the everyday empirical world; but they also made room for metaphysical study. Similarly, the great Indian philosopher of language, Bhartṛhari, begins his *Vākyapadīya* with a metaphysical inquiry into the nature and origin of language in relation to *Brahman*, but then goes on to explore technical grammatical points involved in the everyday use of language.[16] In classical Indian thought on language, the study of a given phenomenon and the contemplation of it as a metaphysical mystery do not preclude each other.

The ability of language to deal with ordinary human things and yet at the same time to be metaphysically grounded is further evidenced in the distinctive Indian notion of creativity. Here again the Indian approach shows itself to be more encompassing than many views of the contemporary West. Whereas the modern person often thinks of creativity in terms of a writer articulating something "original" or "new," the classical Indian conception is quite different. As Klaus Klostermaier observes: "The great creative geniuses of India, men like Gautama the Buddha or Śaṅkara, take care to explain their thought not as *creation* but as a retracing of forgotten eternal truth. They compare their activity to the clearing of an overgrown ancient path in the jungle, not to the making of a new path."[17] The creative effort of the *ṛṣi*—the composer or "seer" of the word—is not to manufacture something new out of his own imagination but, rather, to relate ordinary things to their forgotten eternal truth. In turn, both the technical study of grammar and the philosophical analysis of language are seen by the Indian as intellectual "brush-clearing" activities, which together open the way for a rediscovery of the eternal truth in relation to everyday objects and events.

Language (*vāk*) has a prominent place in the Vedas. *Vāk* is described as the support of gods such as Mitra-Varuṇa, Indra, Agni, and the Aśvins. *Vāk* bends Rudra's bows against the skeptic and gathers up all prayers. In the *Satapatha Brāhmaṇa*, *vāk* is identified with Sarasvatī, who later becomes known as the goddess of learning, wisdom, and inspiration. The action of the sages, or *ṛṣis*, in relation to language is highlighted in Frits Staal's translation of *Ṛgveda* 10.71:

> Brhaspati! When they came forth to establish the first beginning of language, setting up names, what had been hidden in them as their best and purest good became manifest through love.
>
> Where the sages fashioned language with their thought, filtering it like parched grain through a sieve, friends recognized their friendship. Their beauty is marked on the language.
>
> They traced the course of language through ritual; they found it embodied in the seers. They gained access to it and distributed it widely; the seven chanters cheered them.
>
> Many who look do not see language, many who listen do not hear it. It reveals itself like a loving and well adorned wife to her husband. . . .
>
> Though all the friends have eyes and ears, their mental intuitions are uneven. Some are like shallow ponds, which reach up to the mouth or armpit, others are like ponds which are fit for bathing.[18]

Here the power of language is clearly contrasted in its two forms. To those who "see," as Staal explains, language (and meaning) is a manifestation, is widely distributed by the *ṛṣis*, is seen and heard with understanding, is self-revealing and provides for deep intuitions; in contrast, to those who do not "see," who are obstructed by their own ignorance, language (and meaning) is hidden, is mysteriously possessed by the ṛṣis, is looked at and listened to (without understanding), is wrongly used and is hidden in shallow intuitions. According to this hymn, the nature and function of language is to manifest or reveal the meaning of things.

In the Vedas, language is also directly identified with the divine (*Brahman*). The *Ṛgveda* states that there are as many words as there are manifestations of *Brahman*.[19] Even in the *Āraṇyakas* and *Upaniṣads*, there is a continued equating of speech and *Brahman*. "The whole of Speech is *Brahman*."[20] In this respect, there seem to be close parallels between the Brahmanical view that the Veda and *Brahman* are one, and the viewpoint expressed in Christian scripture: "In the beginning was the Word, and the Word was with God, and the Word was God" (John 1:1). Both the Christian and the Brahmanical viewpoints seem to agree that speech and the Divine are synonymous. Because the words of scripture are directly linked with the Divine, it is not surprising that they are experienced by the Hindu as having the power to transform one's consciousness. For example, the words (*mantras*) the *ṛṣi* spoke were not his own, but divine words. This suprahuman origin lent his words a healing power and made them into a deed of salvation. It is this understanding of scriptural words (*mantras*) as being at once inherently powerful and teleological that is so difficult for modern minds to comprehend. Yet these are the very characteristics that underlie Hindu ritual and chant.

In his classic article "The Indian Mantra," Gonda points out that *mantras* are not thought of as products of discursive thought, human wisdom, or poetic fantasy, "but flash-lights of the eternal truth, seen by those eminent men who have come into supersensuous contact with the Unseen."[21] By concentrating one's mind on such a *mantra* the devotee invokes the power inherent in the divine intuition and so purifies the consciousness.

Because the *mantra* is understood as putting one in direct touch with divine power,[22] it is not surprising that *mantra* chanting is controlled with strict rules. A. S. C. McDermott[23] has emphasized that attention must be given not only to the content of the *mantra* but also to its context. The reciter of the *mantra* must have met certain prerequisite requirements: (a) purgation, (b) a proper moral basis, (c) requisite practical skills, (d) adequate intellectual grounding, and (e) the status of an initiate in an esoteric tradition. Conventional procedure requires "that the *mantra* be imparted to the disciple by one who is duly certified to do so and who pays meticulous attention to the minutiae of its proper transmission."[24] The correct procedures for the actual reciting of the *mantra* (e.g., sincerity of the utterer, loudness of voice, proper breathing, etc.) are also carefully controlled.[25]

Frits Staal has argued that there is a direct relationship between ritual actions and *mantras*. He suggests that *mantras* began as sentences attached to ritual actions, and that these *mantra*/ritual-action units were the raw data from which language arose. In India, according to Staal, language is not something with which you *name* something; it is something with which you *do* something.[26] The orally transmitted Vedic *mantra* is at least as long as a sentence or line of verse that corresponds to one ritual act. Even if the rites are modified or abandoned, the action of *mantra* recitation is retained.[27] Gonda points out that in post-Vedic India activities such as bringing the goddess Kālī into a stone image, bathing to wash away sins, sowing seeds in the fields, guarding the sown seeds, driving away evil spirits, and meditating to achieve release—all had to be accompanied by the action of chanting *mantras* in order to achieve success.[28]

The question as to whether *mantras* are meaningful or meaningless has produced much debate. On the one extreme, Vasubandu maintains that the true meaning of *mantras* is to be found in their absence of meaning.[29] Staal draws our attention to the teaching of Kautsa who viewed Vedic *mantras* as effective but meaningless.[30] It is this understanding of *mantras* as meaningless that appears to dominate much Tantric thinking.[31] The opposite position is taken by the Mīmāṁsakas who argue that *mantras* are not meaningless but expressive of meaning. Sabara, following Jaimini, asserts that *mantras* express the meaning of *Dharma*: "In cases where the meaning is not intelligible, it is not that there is no meaning; it is there always, only people are ignorant of it."[32] Much of the modern confusion over *mantras* results from this controversy as to their inherent meaningfulness or meaninglessness. The root of the problem is the modern view of language commonly adopted. Whereas in the Indian tradition language is thought to be truly and most fully experienced in its oral form, the modern view tends to restrict language to the printed word and then analyze it for a one-to-one correspondence with objective reality.[33] As Klostermaier has observed, contemporary linguistic philosophy sees the word only as a carrier of information and basically studies those aspects of language that a computer can store and retrieve.[34] Emphasizing the computerlike function of language, modern man tends to consign all other dimensions of the word to the unreality of a mystic's silence; either the word is factual and scientific in its referent, or it is mystical and has no real function in life. Indian speculations on the nature of language have made room for both the discursive and the intuitive experience of the word. Bhartṛhari, the fifth-century systematizer of the Hindu Grammarian School, presents a philosophy of language that proves helpful in understanding both the factual and the intuitive levels of language. Bhartṛhari's *Vākyapadīya* offers a metaphysical, philosophical, and psychological analysis of language that spans the Vedic through to the Tantric experience of *mantra*. All the views of *mantra* summarized above (including *mantra* as "meaningful"and *mantra* as "meaningless") are encompassed by Bhartṛhari within one understanding in which language is seen to function at various levels.[35] In an article on "Scripture in India," Thomas Coburn adds a helpful suggestion, which supports the view of Bhartṛhari that all *mantras* of scripture are meaningful. Coburn says:

> . . . the major thing Hindus are saying when they call certain verbal events "*śruti*" is that they are eternally, intrinsically powerful and supremely authoritative. They are never outmoded. They are worthy of recitation regardless of whether they are "understood." Indeed, *mantras* do not mean anything in the conventional semantic or etymological senses. Rather, they mean *everything*.[36]

While Coburn may be overstating the case for Vedic *mantras*, which use perfectly ordinary and understandable words, what he says applies perfectly to the so-called seed *mantras* such as AUM—understood as the fundamental *mantra* or word sound that contains within itself in "seed state" all other scriptural *mantras*.[37] By chanting "AUM" one is simultaneously evoking all the words of scripture in "seed" or "short-hand" form. Thus, as Coburn suggests, "AUM" does not mean any one thing; rather it symbolizes "everything." To come to experience "AUM" as "everything," however, requires more than merely just reading or saying the word—although even that will help. Rather, what is required, in the Hindu view, is that each of us find a *guru*, or teacher, who already has the realization of "AUM" as everything. The *guru*, through careful guidance in prescribing *mantras* for us to chant will gradually lead us up the "ladder of scripture," which removes the veiling ignorance from our consciousness until we too see clearly revealed all of the Veda, all of the Divine Word, in the one syllable "AUM." This sacred syllable is held to have flashed forth in the heart of *Brahman*, while absorbed in deep meditation, and to have given birth to the Vedas, which contain all knowledge.

The meaningfulness of *mantras* is not of the merely intellectual kind, it is meaning which has power (*śakti*). *Mantras* have the power to remove ignorance (*avidyā*), reveal truth (*dharma*), and realize release (*mokṣa*). *Vākyapadīya* 1:5, *Vṛtti*, states it clearly: "Just as making gifts, performing austerities and practicing continence are means of attaining heaven. It has been said: When, by practicing the Vedas, the vast darkness is removed, that supreme, bright, imperishable light comes into being in this very birth."[38] It is not only this lofty goal of final release that is claimed for the power of scriptural words, but also the very availability of human reasoning. Without the fixed power of words to convey meaning, inference based on words could not take place.[39] Because of the power inherent in *mantras* for both human inference and divine truth, great care must be given to the correct use of words. In Vedic practice, the importance of this *mantra śakti* is recognized in the careful attention given to the correct speaking of the Vedic verses so as to avoid distortions and corruptions. And, as McDermott observes, in view of the Tantric perception of *mantra* as "the sonic reverberation of divine power, it is hardly surprising that quality control of its components cannot be left to the caprices of the individual reciter."[40]

From Bhartṛhari's perspective, the special role of grammar (*Vyākaraṇa*) is to control and purify the use of *mantra* so that its powers will not be wasted or misused.[41] Proper grammatical usage, correct pronunciation, and so forth are crucial not only for the success of the Vedic rituals, but also for all other branches of knowledge. Whether it be the communication of meaning within the human sciences or the identification of ritual action with the Divine, it is *mantra śakti* that enables it all to happen. As Wheelock notes, in both Vedic and Tantric ritual *mantra* is the catalyst that allows the sacred potential of the ritual setting to become a reality.[42] Especially important in this regard is the contention of *Vākapadīya* 1:62: "It is with the meanings conveyed by words that actions are connected." Were it not for the power of word meanings, no connection would be made between the ritual action and the Divine, and then both Veda and Tantra would be powerless.

In the Indian experience, the repeated chanting of *mantras* is an instrument of power. The more difficulties there are to be overcome, the more repetitions are needed. *Vākyapadīya* 1–14 makes clear that repeated use of correct *mantras* removes all impurities, purifies all knowledge, and leads to release. The psychological mechanism involved is described by Bhartṛhari as a holding of the scriptural revelation (*sphoṭa*) in place by continued chanting. Just as from a distance, or in semidarkness, it takes repeated observations of an object before one sees it correctly, so also concentrated attention on the *sphoṭa* by repeated chanting of the *mantra* results in the revelation finally being perceived in all its fullness.[43] Mandana Miśra describes it as a series of progressively clearer impressions until a clear and a correct apprehension takes place in the end.[44]

In summary, then, it is the Hindu view of language, which sees all words as manifestations of the Divine, that gives ordinary words and the special words of scripture their meaning and power. Until this quite different view of language is understood, the Hindu experience of the nature and function of scripture will remain an enigma to the modern Western mind. Once understood, however, much of the mystery associated with such Hindu practices as the chanting of *mantras* is removed, and a basis is given for scripture to function as a powerful transformer of human consciousness.

ORAL TEXTS

The Hindu view of language makes clear that it is the "vibrating" spoken word that has power, that is heard (*śruti*) and remembered (*smṛti*). Oral speech is not only a means of ordinary communication; in the scriptures it is the voice of God. While the traditional Hindu view understands this as the Divine Word (*Daivi Vāk*) descending and manifesting itself as the Veda, for the help of humans, modern scholars see Vedic Sanskrit as a sacred language evolved over a thousand years by the wandering Aryans who invaded India from the northwest.[45] Whichever view is adopted, it is clear that the oral form of the Veda is crucial for the Hindu. To preserve and safeguard the oral text against corruption, the ancillary disciplines of the Veda or *Prātiśākhyas* (phonetics, or *śiksā*; grammar or *Vyākaraṇa*; and definitions, or *Nirukta*) developed early in the tradition (i.e., before 600 B.C.E.). The *Prātiśākhyas* prescribed rules for prosody, phonetics, accentuation, and *sandhi* (combining of letters), and thereby ensured that the oral form of Vedas would be preserved and passed on with little loss or distortion.[46] In the Hindu tradition, language is thought to be truly and most fully experienced only in its oral form. The written word is a secondary thing developed only for heuristic teaching purposes and as an aid for those too dull to remember the important texts by heart. For the Indian, the form of language that is used as the criterion is not written but oral, and the *Prātiśākhyas* play the important role of keeping the oral form disciplined and pure in its presentation. Knowledge of the Vedas, therefore, is not simply the "book-learning" of contents or main ideas, which characterizes modern Western scholarship. In the Indian tradition, language is only fully alive when spoken. Thus knowledge of the Vedas includes its memorization and the ability to speak the text with correct accent and meter. The fact that the vast majority of the Vedic hymns are poems made attention to the details of form specified in the *Prātiśākhyas* even more important.

Stress on the oral or spoken form is central to the Hindu view of language.[47] Thinking is seen as internal speaking to which not enough *prāṇa*, or breath energy, has been added to make it overt.[48] Writing is merely a coded recording that can never perfectly represent all the nuances of the spoken word, and is therefore always secondary. With regard to the relationship between written and spoken language, the Hindu approach is opposite to that taken in modern Western scholarship. In modern biblical studies, for example, the aim of the scholar is to get back to the earliest available written manuscript and then to use that as a criterion against which to check the text that is in use today. The rationale is that errors that have crept in over the years would not be present in the earlier manuscript. In addition, the modern school of Form Criticism has argued that before many of the scriptures (such as the Gospels) were written down, there was a period of oral transmission during which time the text (for example, the original teaching of Jesus) was modified by the needs of the people and the particular conditions under which they lived. This period of oral transmission is judged to be unreliable due to its inability to carry forward the original sayings in a pure and unchanged form.[49]

The Hindu practice is the exact opposite of this. When India achieved independence in 1947, one of the first acts of the new government was to establish a commission of senior scholars to go from place to place and listen to the assembled *Brahmins* reciting the Vedas. They would listen for errors in meter, accent, and *sandhi* and for any loss or change in words. It was the rigorous practice of the *Prātiśākhyas* that was being checked by the senior scholars. They had mastered the *Prātiśākhyas* and pure presentation of the Vedas through many years of careful oral practice and checking with their teachers. And the teachers of the present senior scholars had acquired their expertise not from books but from oral practice with the best teachers of the generation before them, who in turn had been taught by the best teachers before them, and so on in an unbroken oral tradition back to the Vedas.

It is not the dead or entombed manuscript but the correct and clear speaking of the memorized word in the here and now that makes for a living language and scripture. Large numbers of copies of *The Living Bible* stacked in bookstores or reverently placed on personal bookshelves are not true language or living scripture according to the Hindu. Only when a passage is so well learned that it is with one wherever one goes is the word really known. In such a state the words become part of or, even more exactly, are one's consciousness in the act of speaking. Books and all written forms are not knowledge in this sense of the word; rather, for the Hindu, they represent a lower, inferior, second order of language suitable only for the dull or the uneducated. The *Prātiśākhyas* are the training rules for the oral learning of language and for the preservation of the Vedic word in its pure form.

From the Vedas up to the present, the study of grammar and the philosophy of language has occupied a central place in Hindu thought. In the earliest *Prātiśākhyas* or rules for speaking the Vedas, the first formulations of Sanskrit grammar may be found. Before the time of Buddha (before 600 B.C.E.), the *Prātiśākhyas* alongside the *Brāhmaṇas*, *Upaniṣads*, and *Niruktas* (etymologies) were being developed. From this early period up to 1000 C.E. Sanskrit dominated and rapidly became the national language of India.[50] As Sanskrit became standardized, a regular grammar developed. This grammar was not an artificial construct of the scholars but, rather, developed directly and naturally from the spoken language.[51]

The oldest etymology available is the *Nirukta* of Yāska. Pāṇini, the widely known Sanskrit grammarian, mentions a number of other grammarians who preceded him. Patanjali wrote the important commentary on Pāṇini's *Sūtras*, and many others have written glosses on Patanjali. In addition there have been rearrangements of the Pāṇini *Sūtras*, with other lines of interpretation arising (e.g., *Siddhanta-kaumudī* of Bhaṭṭoji Dīkṣita). The overall aim of the Sanskrit grammarians was not to standardize language artificially, but to bring out the intended meaning. As Yāska put it, it is to get to the real meaning of an uttered word (*arthānityaḥ parikṣeta*).[52] Sanskrit grammar was an attempt to discipline and explain the behavior of a spoken language, so that the inner meaning could shine forth unobstructed.

It was this latter aspect, the perceiving of the intended meaning, that commanded the attention of the Hindu philosophers of language (Maṇḍana Miśra, Kumārila, Kaundabhaṭṭa, Abhinavagupta, etc.) among whom Bhartṛhari (580 C.E.) consistently ranks as the most important.[53] In Bhartṛhari's major work, the *Vākypadīya*, the ways in which Indian philosophy conceives the outer word form to be united with its inner meanings are discussed. Bhartṛhari's own position has come to be known as the Sphoṭa Theory after the Sanskrit term *sphuṭ*, which means "to burst forth," and when applied to language, "a bursting forth of illumination or insight." V. S. Apte, in his *Sanskrit-English Dictionary*, defines *sphoṭa* as the idea that bursts out or flashes on the mind when a sound is uttered.

As all this makes clear, the purpose of all the ancillary disciplines is to keep the oral word or text pure and powerful. Rather than the Western notion of scripture as something written—the Latin *scriptura*, "writing," and *scribere*, "to write," are closely related—for the Hindu scripture is the pure spoken word, which is awesome in its power and eternality. Although securely fixed or canonized by the *Prātiśākhyas*, the oral *śruti* of the Vedas is yet constantly having its eternal revelations represented in the ever changing oral traditions of *smṛti*—the epics, *pūraṇas*, and *tantras* spoken in both Sanskrit and the regional languages. The Vedas are reserved for the hearing of the male of the twice- born classes, the upper three castes, and are not for the general public. *Sūdras* and women are prohibited from hearing the Vedas. The *smṛti* texts speak the revelation in an easier form that continually adapts itself to the conditions of class and the changing historical situation. As such its hearing is open to all. And, as we shall later see, in the *smṛti* texts writing plays a more important role in making the text open to all, and even in making the book into an object of worship.

In the classical Sanskrit tradition the rigorous oral discipline of the *Prātiśākhyas* function in the context of the *guru*-student relationship. But oral traditions are also present in the mass public experience of the *smṛti*. A good example is found in the oral experience of the *Rāmāyaṇa* of Tulsīdāsa as performed in Hindi in north India.[54] Tulsīdāsa's verses are quoted by millions of people ranging from the scholar to the illiterate villager, in towns and villages, regardless of caste distinctions. How do these millions, especially the illiterate, come to know not only the story but also the words of the text, and their meanings, by heart? By repeated hearing of the text being performed in a variety of forms from the *Rāma Līlā* folk dramas to the musical performance by folk singers and the oral textual exposition by traditional scholars. The *Rāma Līlā* takes place as formal drama at specified festival occasions in particular cities. But the retelling of the Rāma text goes on constantly in the singing of the folk singers around the village fire in the evenings, and by the oral exposition of the text in *kathā*, or storytelling style, by scholars. These three forms of oral transmission of the text are experienced by all from a very young age and result in the text being passed on most efficiently from generation to generation. Although texts such as the *Mahābhārata* and the *Bhāgavata Purāṇa* are also passed on in this way in north India, it is the *Rāmacaritmānasa* of Tulsīdāsa that is by far the most popular.

The *kathā* or oral textual exposition of the *Rāmāyaṇa* in many ways resembles the Western Christian tradition of preaching: *kathā* is done by trained professionals, *vyāsa*, who artfully elaborate a sacred text generally focusing upon a very small part of it in order to bring out its meaning. Such a performer is viewed as a spiritual descendant or temporary incarnation of the original author, and is privileged to speak from a *vyāsa-āsana*, or seat of honor and authority in the assembly of devotees.[55] An expounder, a *vyāsa*, may be hired by a wealthy patron or group to perform for a year or more in a set public place. The more successful *vyāsas* often become "traveling preachers" on regular circuits offering shorter periods of exposition (e.g., seven, fifteen, or thirty days) on selected passages of the text. A top *vyāsa* may receive as much as several thousand rupees per hour for his exposition of the epic. This money may be collected as a free offering at the end of each performance. Such *vyāsas* today rank among the highest paid and most famous performers in northern India—perhaps here is where the analogy to Western preachers fails!

The majority of contemporary *vyāsas* are Brahmin males who spend a great deal of time early in their careers committing all of the text to memory under the supervision of a teacher who is a successful exponent of the art. Recently a number of women have gained renown as *vyāsas*. Lutgendorf, who interviewed a number of *vyāsas*, reports that most described their choice of this vocation as the result of spiritual experience or a response to an inner summons to dedicate their lives to the propagation of the epic, and of the experience of *bhakti*, or devotion.[56] Although printed texts and notes from teachers may be used for study or preparation, the exposition or performance itself is always extemporaneous and done without notes. A printed version of the text will always be present, and may be open, or, more often, closed and ceremonially wrapped in rich cloths and garlanded with flowers on an ornate stand in front of the performer. *Vyāsas* emphasize the importance of spontaneity and inspiration, with some even going so far as to allow audience members or patrons to select the theme or passage for exposition. The style of exposition is such that members of the audience are actively involved—to begin with by joining the *vyāsa* in brief *kīrtana*, or melodious chant, of the name of Rāma. When the *vyāsa* begins he may often open by quoting lines from the text and pausing to allow the audience to complete the last word or phrase of the passage. The performer usually starts speaking softly and slowly, his voice gaining in strength and speed as he proceeds. A typical exposition lasts an hour, with the end of the discourse being signaled by a sudden resumption of the opening *kīrtana* in which the audience will join with particular fervor if the exposition was good. What the *vyāsa* aims at is not logical argument, but the creation of a devotional mood in his listeners (a *bhakti rasa*).[57]

The oral presentation and experience of the Hindi *Rāmāyaṇa* has been described in some detail in an attempt to convey the flavor and vitality that oral texts still enjoy in the Hindu tradition. It is through such oral exposition that the Hindu scriptures are transmitted from generation to generation. And it is in this way that the canonical Sanskrit *śruti* is made personal and relevant, through the *smṛti* engagement with daily lives. Such oral preaching provides for the dynamic grounding of the Hindu community in a sacred text, and the powerful use of that text to transform human lives.

WRITTEN TEXTS

Van Buitenen has argued that the oral transmission of Hindu scripture was so well organized, and its preservation so perfect, that the oral texts can legitimately be treated as a written text—from the Western perspective.[58] In India written texts are very unreliable and their status very low. In fact the very act of writing was held to be ritually polluting in a late Vedic text; the *Aitareya Āraṇyaka* 5.5.3 states that a pupil should not recite the Veda after he has eaten meat, seen blood or a dead body, had intercourse, or engaged in writing. The Hindu bias against writing probably does not belong to the earliest period of the Vedas (1500–700 B.C.E.) when it seems that writing was unknown to the community. Hostility toward writing may be due to writing being introduced from outside, perhaps from the Middle East around 600 B.C.E. The written images of an alphabet, far from giving visual access to the sacred Vedic words, were regarded as defilements of the sacred sound. In addition to its alien introduction, other reasons have been offered to explain the early Hindu rejection of the written. For example, learning from a book was discouraged because it removed the learning process from the presence of a teacher (*guru*). It is the *guru* who can instruct the student in the proper modulation and accentuation of the sacred words. The basic assumption underlying the Hindu bias against the written word is that what is of crucial importance in scripture is not only its content or meaning (*artha*), but also its sound (*śabda*). To learn the sounds and the Hindu lifestyle correctly, one needs to learn in the presence of a living *guru*. A written book is not enough.[59]

In contrast with Eastern countries such as China, scribes in India have had a very low social standing. The low-caste Indian scribes often could not read the text being copied. Basically they were simply trained to reproduce the letters and combinations of letters from one text on palm leaves to another.[60]

Due to the rigors of the Indian climate, palm leaves or paper lasted only a very short time, so texts had to be recopied frequently. The regular writing down of texts seems to have begun with Buddhist scholars around 200 B.C.E. The materials used for writing in India were very perishable—birchbark and palm leaf. The heat and high humidity resulted in rapid deterioration, in addition to which there was severe danger from vermin. It has been said that 90 percent of Indian written texts have been eaten by white ants. If interest in a manuscript dwindled so that it was no longer regularly copied, it would rapidly disappear. Although a handful of Indian texts may be as old as 1000 B.C.E., the majority we possess date from no earlier than the seventeenth century. This was a period when Sanskrit learning diminished and many texts were lost.[61]

In addition to the problems of climate and insects there is the difficulty of poorly trained scribes and copying errors. The result has been a plentitude of scribal errors of all the classical kinds (dittography, homoioteleuton, homoioarchton, etc.) so that the received texts of our day are riddled with mistakes requiring editors to spend most of their time on scribal concerns.[62] Further problems resulted from the way books were handled and treated in India. Users made remarks or notes in the margins, which would intrude upon the text and end up being copied into it. Because a book in India was most often the personal property of someone—either due to inheritance or to having paid a scribe a fee to have it copied—the owner would feel at liberty to make additions and corrections or to add inspirational verses. The next copyist would then have no way of knowing what was original or what was added and thus would copy everything.

The traditional Indian method of keeping the pages of a text together in a book was also fraught with problems. The use of birchbark or palm leaf did not allow for binding in the European style. It made interpolations and libraries like the *Mahābhārata* a natural outcome. Van Buitenen describes the situation:

> The best that could be done would be to cut the leaves to roughly the same size and tie a cord around them. To protect the first and last sheets a wooden board would sometimes be placed at both ends. If the possession was highly prized, the endboards might be made of metal or silver,

> encrusted with gems, illuminated with pictures. But in spite of decorations and care, boards and cord could never adequately keep the book together. A book was only as secure as the cord that tied it. For additional security a hole was sometimes pierced through the middle of the leaves of the book, and the cord run through that. But cords could break, and whole chapters be lost.[63]

Even today, with modern bookbinding present in India, the oral rather than the printed form is valued. Books are printed poorly on cheap paper, and still tend to fall apart just as they have done down through the years.

It is via modern Western scholars that the written text is slowly attaining a higher profile within Hinduism. From Max Müller on, Western scholars, bringing both a value of the written and a scholarly discipline focused on the written, have gradually made available the Hindu sacred texts in better and better editions. Textual techniques like "Higher and Lower Criticism" are today being taught to Indian *paṇḍits* so that they will be able to do more than traditional Indian copying of texts.[64] Even today, however, the well-trained Hindu scholar depends on the memorized texts learned in childhood rather than upon books. Even if a Hindu student uses a written version of a text, it will be studied not alone at one's desk, but with a teacher who will read it aloud and explain the text in dialogue. It is still the oral tradition, within the *guru*-student context, that gives real knowledge. At the popular level, it is through the folk singers, storytellers, and professional reciters that the majority of Hindus continue to experience their scriptures. Although written aids such as texts, commentaries, and notes may be used by these performers in their preparation, when it comes to the *bhakti*, or devotion itself, the books and paper are left behind. Hinduism is not really a "religion of the book"—at least not the way books are thought of today—it is a religion of the spoken word.

Within the *bhakti*, or devotional, tradition there developed one practice in which the written text itself was given high value. In the *Kūrma Purāṇa* (244124–26) a person who copies the text and gives it to a Brahmin is freed from all sins and attains various heavenly rewards. The *Agni Purāṇa* (21153–54) even goes so far as to say that a person who copies out a *purāṇa*, the *Bhārata*, or the Rāmāyaṇa and then gives it away attains *mukti*, or release. The act of writing prior to giving and the giving of the book are both seen as pious deeds in the *purāṇas*. But for the book to have spiritual power it still must be recited aloud. In some *purāṇas* women and *śudras* (low-caste persons) may give books but are disqualified from reading or reciting them themselves. The *purāṇas* also occasionally mention the practice of worshiping a written holy book—of placing it in a special box or wrapping and offering it *puja*, or worship. In this way the written text of a *purāṇa* is treated as a kind of talisman.[65]

TECHNIQUES OF EXEGESIS

Hindu exegesis, or interpretation, is premised upon the idea that the full revelation is given originally in the Veda. Later works, both *smṛtis* and commentaries, serve only to bring out more clearly meaning that is already present in the Veda. An earlier truth may be represented in a way that is easier for a later generation to understand, or hidden meanings implicitly present in the original revelation may be explicitly developed. Throughout, however, continuity is maintained. Already in the later portions of the Veda itself the exegetical process can be seen at work. The original Vedic hymns, the *Saṃhitās*, are poems that contain a variety of meanings. The *Brāhmaṇaic* commentaries bring out the outer ritual aspects, while the later *Upaniṣadic* dialogues focus on the deeper spiritual insight of the original poems, yet always there is continuity. The intuitive vision (*dhi*) of the Vedic *ṛṣi* is still very much present in the *Brāhmaṇas*. For example, in a series of *mantras*, Indra's visions (*dhiyaḥ*) are said to be yoked (*yuj-dhiyah*) or made use of for self-realization (*Taittirīya Brāhmaṇa* 2.5.3.2). On a lower level, the sacrificial ritual, which had been present to some degree in the Vedic hymns, was given greater development and importance in the *Brāhmaṇas*. This meant that the *ṛṣi* of the Vedic hymns, the inspired singer of truth, now tends to become the possessor of a revealed scripture and the repeater of a magical formula.[66] But while the majority of *Brāhmiṇs* during the period of the *Brāhmaṇas* may have concentrated on establishing an authoritative systematization of the ritual sacrificial aspects of the Vedic hymns, there were always some inspired teachers who resisted rigid formalizing and focused on the subjective spirituality of the Vedic visions. Due to their efforts, evidence may be found in the *Brāhmaṇas* of early struggles toward the formulation of many of the philosophic statements of the *Upaniṣadic* Seers.[67]

In continuity with this spiritual group of *Brāhmaṇical* thinkers, the *ṛṣi* of the *Upaniṣads* sought to recover the ancient spirit and knowledge of the Vedic Seers by philosophic meditation and spiritual experience. As Aurobindo puts it:

> . . . they [the *Upanisadic ṛṣis*] used the text of the ancient *mantras* as a prop or an authority for their own intuitions and perceptions; or else the Vedic Word was a seed of thought and vision by which they recovered old truths in new forms. What they found, they expressed in other terms more intelligible to the age in which they lived. In a certain sense their handling of the texts was not disinterested. . . . They were seekers of a higher than verbal truth and used words merely as suggestions for the illumination towards which they were striving.[68]

This quotation from Aurobindo highlights several exegetical approaches of the *Upaniṣadic* Seers, which we shall now examine.

First, they experienced and further clarified the vision of *Vāk* (the Divine Word), which had previously been seen by the Vedic *ṛṣis*. Gonda gives evidence for this in his study that shows that the *dhī* or vision of the Vedic Seers is also central to the approach of the *Upaniṣads*.[69] In the *Upaniṣads* the adjective *dhīra* characterizes the one who clearly sees the true and fundamental nature of reality. In keeping with their increasingly precise analysis, the *Upaniṣadic* Seers make clear that this supersensuous *dhī* is a function of the mind rather than the senses.[70] It is this psychic faculty *dhī* which enables the *ṛṣi* to penetrate into the world of the unseen reality—even to the ultimate vision of his own true self (*Ātman*).[71] The more exact expression of the nature of the real as seen via the *dhī* is the unique contribution of the *Upaniṣadic* Seers. Whereas the *Saṁhitās* of the *Ṛg Veda* give external, cosmic, poetic expression to this vision of the underlying unity of all reality,[72] the *Upaniṣadic* Seers adopt the approach of philosophic dialogue and "negative exclusion" to help the truth seeker attain inner vision of ultimate unity (*Ātman* = *Brahman*).

A second aspect of the *Upaniṣadic* approach is the characteristic focusing upon or reference to the Vedic word, or *mantra*, by the *ṛṣi*. For example, in discussing the nature of the creation of this world the *ṛṣi* of the *Bṛhadāraṇyaka Upaniṣad* refers back to envisioned words, "I was Manu and the sun"[73] by the Vedic Seer Vāmadeva as the basis and authority for his contention, "This is so now also. Whoever thus knows 'I am Brahma' becomes this All; even the gods have not power to prevent his becoming thus, for he becomes their self (*ātman*)."[74] By focusing on the Vedic intuition of the underlying unity between the *ṛṣi*, the gods, and the real, the *Upaniṣadic* Seer brings out clearly the philosophic and religious implications of the vision, namely, creation consists of *Brahman* becoming the All (including gods, seers, men, etc.), and whenever one awakens to this truth one immediately realizes that one's essence or self is identical with *Brahman*—therefore, to worship God as some divinity other than one self is ignorance.

A third aspect of the *Upaniṣadic* approach is also illustrated in the example above. Whereas in the Vedic hymns and the *Brāhmaṇas*, the vision is usually verbalized in external mythical symbols (such as Manu and the sun), the *Upaniṣadic* seers adopt increasingly abstract ("this All") and internal (*Ātman*, or self, is *Brahma*) symbols in their verbalization of the Divine.[75] This process of increasing philosophic abstraction and internalization reaches its peak, in one sense, with the "negative exclusion" teaching of "not this, not that" (*neti, neti*). By this *via negativa* philosophic approach, the *Upaniṣadic ṛṣis* force their students beyond all possible conceptualizations to the realization of a higher than speakable truth, which is symbolized by the *turīya* level of AUM in the *Māṇḍūkya Upaniṣad*. As one *ṛṣi* puts it, *neti, neti* leads us to the understanding that there is nothing higher than the realization that one is *not this*—but the underlying Reality ("the Real of the real") upon which all particularization as "this" or "that" depends.[76]

A fourth aspect of the *Upaniṣadic* approach relates to the context naturally fostered by the philosophic method outlined above. Whereas the Vedic Seer spoke his vision in the form of a solitary hymn (evoking responses at the varying levels of ritual sacrifice, worshipful devotion or, for some, mystical self-realization), the *Upaniṣadic ṛṣi* spoke his vision within the context of the teacher-pupil relationship (the word "upaniṣad" comes from *upa-ni-sad*, "sitting down near" the teacher to receive instruction).[77] Consequently, the common form is one of philosophic probing toward the Divine by question and answer. A good example of this approach occurs in the *Bṛihad-Āraṇyaka*

Upaniṣad 2.4.5, which relates a dialogue between the sage Yājñavalkya and his wife Maitreyī as he leads her toward the realization that "it is the *Ātman* that should be seen . . . and that with the understanding of the *Ātman*, this world-all is known."[78] The goal of this teaching relationship is repeatedly described by the *Upaniṣadic ṛṣis* as the student's intuitive vision of the identity between himself and the Divine (between *Ātman* and *Brahman*). This is the essence of the Four Great Teachings, or *Mahāvākyas*: *tat tvam asi*, "that thou art"; *aham Brahma asmi*, "I am Brahman"; *ayam atmā Brahma*, "This *Ātman* is *Brahman*"; and *prajnānam Brahma*,"Consciousness is Brahman." The purpose of the philosophic dialogue preceding the statement of the *Mahāvākya* by the *ṛṣi* is to remove systematically the obstructions (*avidyā*) in the mind of the student, which are preventing him or her from directly perceiving the Divine (*Brahman*). The systematic use of *anumāna*, or reasoning, in removing defects such as contrary notions so that the unshakable immediate experience of *Brahman* can arise is characteristic of the *Upaniṣadic* approach to the Divine.[79] Various exegetical tactics are adopted by the *ṛṣi* in his use of reasoning. One tactic is to seek to identify the essence of the empirical world with its subjective underlying unity.[80] In such approaches the common method is to start with the gross and then reason toward the subtle.[81] Another tactic used by the *ṛṣi* is to approach the ultimate questions that seek to lay bare the reality underlying all change and suffering.[82] However, perhaps the most difficult of all these methods is the wisdom required for the admission that one's own intellectual prowess and system-building achievements do not attain for one the Truth:[83] The use of the intellect will help by removing the obstructions of wrong ideas, but in the end all pride, even in such a meritorious achievement as knowledge of the Veda itself, must be overcome by spiritual and mental discipline (*Yoga*) so that the intuition of the Divine can occur.[84] And in this direct vision, the Divine is found to be the overflowing of peace and bliss, or *ānanada*, upon which all life depends.[85]

This brief survey has shown that for the *ṛṣis* of the *Saṁhitās*, the *Brāhmaṇas* and the *Upaniṣads* alike, the supersensuous vision of *Vāk* is the ultimate exegesis of or approach to the Divine. As indicated in passages like *Māṇḍūkya* 3.33, this vision is seen to be a function of the mind in its capacity for direct intuition. Also for the *Upaniṣadic ṛṣis*, the intuition of the Divine has an internal rather than external focus in its symbolic expression. This exegetical approach depends for its validity upon the presupposition that the Divine is a given truth that requires only to be discovered or revealed. At the same time, especially in the *Upaniṣads*, an interiorizing tendency presupposes that the Divine is within each person. Consequently, for the *ṛṣis*, the revealed word (*śruti*) is not the Divine Truth in itself, but serves the necessary function of enabling one to see the Divine Truth—both within and without—through penultimate scriptural verbalizations such as the *Māhāvakyas*. For the Buddhist, all of these approaches are rejected: no scripture is necessary; only one's reason is required; unifying and interiorizing tendencies must be overcome by focusing on the discrete and momentary elements of reality. For both, however, the direct face-to-face vision or intuition of the Divine or Real is ultimate—although the two views are in complete opposition as to the nature of what is seen.

As we move from the exegesis within the Veda itself to the commentaries written within the classical and medieval periods, we find that the same basic pattern continues. Older commentaries add nothing new but simply bring out insights present in seed form in the original Vedas, and only partially or incompletely made present by earlier authors. Thus it is a process of commentaries written upon commentaries. Following the *Upaniṣads*, the next major works were in *sūtra* style—pithy aphorisms that summarized a great deal of content in "shorthand" form, and designed for the oral instruction of students by a teacher. Each of the major schools of Hindu thought claims to be based upon the Veda but really begins from a *sūtra* composed by a founding master. For example, the Saṅkhya-Yoga schools depend upon the *sūtras* of Patanjali,[86] the Pūrva-Mīmāṁsā school on the *sūtras* of Jaimini,[87] the Vedanta school on the *sūtras* of Bādarāyaṇa,[88] the *Nyāya* on the *sūtras* by Gautama and the Vaiśeṣikas on the *sūtras* of Kaṇāda.[89] Because of their absolute economy and conciseness, these *sūtras* are not intelligible without a prose commentary, called a *Bhaṣya*. In the teacher-student context, this *Bhaṣya* would ordinarily be given orally. Later it may have been written down and attached to the *sūtras* by a senior student. As the generations passed, a need may have been felt within the teacher-student lineage of the school for more commentaries to be added in order better to bring out the intended meaning of the earlier commentary, the *sūtra*, and so on back to the Veda. Thus the process of commentaries being written upon commentaries continues open-ended, yet with a thread of continuity running right back to the Veda. In this way the classical commentaries are able to update the exegesis of the texts, just as the *smṛti* represents in a fresh way the original *śruti* through new versions of epic, story, and drama.

Perhaps a sample of the kind of exegesis provided by the classical *sūtra*-commentary tradition would be helpful. *Yoga Sūtra* 1:24–25 can be taken as an example. The question at issue is: "How is it that the scriptural words of the Veda, invoked by the *ṛṣis* and sages, reveal reality? Since the objects of scriptural words are metaphysical (i.e., they cannot be seen or inferred), how can such words be trusted as valid verbal knowledge (*āgama*)?"

In *Yoga Sūtra* 1:24 the so-called Original Speaker of the Veda, Īśvara, is defined as a special kind of person (*puruṣa*) who is beginninglessly untouched by the taints of previous actions (*karmas*), or their fruition, or their latent impulses (*vāsanā*). The taints or hindrances, of which Īśvara is free, include ignorance, ego-sense, desire, hatred, and clinging to life. Īśvara has never been touched by any such experiences and thus is a unique being, or *puruṣa*. While all other *puruṣas* have to break their bonds with such experiences to realize release, Īśvara has always been and always will be free. Yet he is at the same time in the world (in *prakṛti*), because, as Vyāsa, the writer of the first *Bhaṣya*, or commentary, on the *sūtra* puts it, he has assumed a body of pure transparency (*sattva*). This pure *sattva* body enables Īśvara to function as a mind in the world. Vachaspati Misŕa, the writer of the *Tīkā*, or second commentary, notes that Īśvara takes on this pure *sattva* body due to this wish to help those *puruṣas* still in bondage. Unlike others whose pure personality (*sattva*) is tainted by admixtures of emotion (*rajas*) and dullness (*tamas*), Īśvara's *sattva* is free of the other qualities (*guṇas*), and this enables him to be in the world, yet untouched by it. Vachaspati offers the analogy of the actor who takes on the role of Rāmā and yet does not confuse his identity with that of Rāmā. Just so, Īśvara enters into the world to help others, but never confuses his identity as *puruṣa* with that of the worldly *prakṛti.* In answer to the question as to what causes Īśvara to take on this pure transparent *sattva* body, the answer is given by Vachaspati that at the end of each cycle of creation Īśvara thinks to himself, "After this period of latency finishes I must again assume a pure *sattva* body so as to continue to help the world." This thought lays down a seed, or memory trace, which causes Īśvara to take on a *sattva* body at the start of the next creation cycle. Again Vachaspati offers an analogy. Īśvara's action between the cycles of creation is like that of Chaitra who contemplates, "Tomorrow I must get up at day-break" and then having slept gets up at the very time because of a *vāsanā*, or memory trace, laid down by his contemplation.[90]

In answer to the question "What is the function of this *sattva* body that Īśvara takes on at the start of each new creation cycle?" Vyāsa replies that its function is to reveal the scriptures. Indeed, in response to an opponent who asks for proof of the existence of Īśvara's special *sattva* body, the existence of the scriptures is cited. Furthermore, the authority of the scriptures comes from the fact that they are a manifestation of Īśvara's *sattva*. Clearly this argument is circular and Vyāsa admits that there is a beginningless relation between the scriptures (with their authority on spiritual matters) and Īśvara's *sattva* body. This is the presupposition upon which the *Yoga Sūtra* definition of the authority of scriptural knowledge (*āgama*), with regard to supersensuous matters, is grounded. Yet another commentator, Śaṅkara, takes the further step of arguing that all of this is established by inference as follows: because Īśvara's *sattva* body has never been tainted, it is unique and therefore it is unsurpassed by any other power (all others have been tainted). Thus the special *sattva* of Īśvara and the scriptures it reveals can never be equaled. "Therefore this Lord is one whose power has none to equal or surpass it, and it is established that the Lord is a special *Puruṣa* apart from *pradhāna* and other *Puruṣas*."[91]

Having established the existence of Īśvara's special *sattva* body on the basis of scriptural testimony and inference, *Yoga Sūtra* 1:25 goes on to examine its special quality of omniscience. Unlike our minds in which the proportion of heavy obstruction (*tamas*) present prevents us from knowing supersensuous things and thus restricts our use of word knowledge to words based on inference and sensuous perception, Īśvara's pure *sattva* reflects all reality, the sensuous and the supersensuous. "All certain knowledge, of past or future or present or a combination of them, or from extra-sensory perception, whether that knowledge be small or great, is the seed of [Īśvara's] omniscience."[92]

The characterization of this omniscient knowledge in Īśvara's *sattva* as a "seed" (*bīja*) is consistent with the idea that it "sprouts" or manifests itself anew in the Vedas at the start of each cycle of creation. Out of all the beings or *puruṣas*, only Īśvara has the power to fulfill this crucial role beginninglessly, since only he has a *sattva* that has never been tainted by *karma*. The great saints such as the Buddhas or Jinas were all at one stage immersed in *karma*, and due to that limitation do not have the same fullness of omniscience as Īśvara, since he has never been limited by *karma*. Thus, as Patanjali's *Sūtra* says, Īśvara is the most perfect *puruṣa* in whom the seed of omniscience is at its utmost limit or excellence (*Yoga Sūtra* 1:25).

The sample above gives the flavor of the style of exegesis encountered in the classical Sanskit commentarial tradition. There is careful and often skillful use of reason in regard to scripture: (1) to remove doubts and (2) to remove contradictions. In Hindu exegesis, reason and revelation are seen to serve complementary functions: reason removes doubts and obstructions, thus clearing the way for the spoken scriptural words to evoke immediate knowledge of the Divine.[93] Without the Vedic words, however, reason is seen to be empty and powerless when it comes to revealing metaphysical knowledge. The spoken scriptural word is essential for release (*mokṣa*).

THE VEDA IN RELATION TO OTHER SCRIPTURES

Brahmanical Hinduism teaches one divine truth of which the Veda is the authoritative earthly manifestation. When the universe is born anew after its cyclical destruction, the same Veda is spoken again by ṛṣis for the benefit of the next series of generations. Veda is "*śruti*—the ṛṣis' direct supersensuous "seeing" or "hearing" and then speaking the Divine Truth. The Vedic word (*śruti*) is not the Divine Truth in itself, but serves the *necessary* function of enabling one to "see" ultimate truth through its penultimate verbalizations. Other scriptures are allowed as revelation, but they are judged to be secondary, *smṛti*—that which has been remembered, the *pūraṇas* and the *Bhagavad Gītā*. Such secondary revelation adds nothing new to the Veda. It serves only to re-present the original Vedic revelation in a way more suited to those whose minds are heavily obscured by *karma*—who need a personification of Divine Truth in the form of Krishna or Rāma. It is an easy and commonly made move by the modern Hindu simply to extend this ancient idea of secondary personifications of the Divine Truth so as to include Moses, Jesus, Muhammad, and Buddha—along with their respective scriptures. While at first glance this may seem tolerant, it is really the statement of a firmly based downgrading of all other scriptures. While such scriptures are definitely useful in raising one's spiritual status (and thus to be applauded), alone they are insufficient for the attainment of salvation or release. For that, one must progress spiritually to the point where in the next life one is reborn a Hindu able to study the Veda, by which means alone release can be finally realized. Thus, although all other scriptures may be welcomed by the Hindu, it is a very special and intolerant kind of welcome—that of the superior for the inferior.

Throughout its long history, Hinduism's attitude toward other religions has remained constant. There is one Divine Reality that manifests itself in many forms. The various religions and their scriptures are simply different secondary revelations of the one Divine Reality—*Brahman*.[94] Because it asserts that the Vedas are the most perfect revelation of *Brahman*, Hinduism sees its scripture as providing the criterion against which all other scriptures must be tested. Thus the Hindu tolerance of other religions is directly proportionate to their congruence with the Vedas. There is no doubt that for the Hindu there is only one Divine, as revealed by the Hindu scriptures, and that any other revelation (e.g., the Torah, New Testament, or Qur'an) is seen as a secondary manifestation to be verified against the Hindu Veda.

Hinduism is able to appear tolerant toward other scriptures by seeing them as secondary, as a form of *smṛti*, and their founders such as Moses, Jesus, and Muhammad, as *avatāras*, or incarnations, of Brahman. In this way all other scriptures are absorbed as secondary manifestations of the Veda. The Hindu approach to other religions is to absolutize the relativism implied in the viewpoint that the various religions are simply different submanifestations of the one Divine. The Hindu refusal to recognize claims to exclusive truth, as in the Bible or the Qur'an, that differ from the revelation of the Veda indicates the limited nature of Hindu tolerance. In this, of course, Hindus are no different from the believers of other religions who seek to impose their scripture upon others.

5

SCRIPTURE IN SIKHISM

THE PLACE OF SCRIPTURE IN THE SIKH TRADITION

While most religions have scriptures, the place and function of Sikh scripture seems unique. In no other religion can one find a human Guru founder, followed by a series of human Gurus living parallel with a collection of scripture, ending in a breaking of the human succession and the scripture attaining full authority as Guru.[1] Both the Gurus and the scripture are respected within the tradition because of God's word, which they express. This has opened the way for the error of idolatry of the Gurus and the scripture. Guru Nanak guarded against idolatry of the Guru by making a distinction between himself as God's mouthpiece, and the message he uttered: "I spoke only when you, O God, inspired me to speak" (Adi Granth 566).[2] Unlike Hinduism, pictures of the Gurus are not seen as suitable objects for devotion. Instead, the picture of the Gurus is said to be the *Gurbani* (God's word spoken by the Guru). Although first spoken as oral revelations, the words were memorized and written down. The fourth Guru, Arjun, compiled these utterances into the canonical collection, the Adi Granth. Gobind Singh, the tenth Guru, prepared the final recension of the Adi Granth and, when he was dying, installed the Adi Granth as Guru. As both Guru and God's word, the physical text of the Adi Granth became a very tempting object for idolatry. The Adi Granth is housed in its own building or room, the Gurdwara. It is placed on a cushion, covered by a canopy and wrapped in special cloths. It is physically located so that it will be in the most elevated position, and when being moved it is carried on the head—all of this to indicate its exalted status as Guru. Just as one would bow before the Lord, so one bows before the Adi Granth and is careful not to turn one's back to it. The book is ritually put to bed and awakened. Before entering a Gurdwara one must have bathed and removed one's shoes. Offerings are placed before the enthroned book, and after worship a *prasad*, (a communion-like blessing of food from God) is received. For many Sikhs the very sight of the scripture is a means of receiving grace.[3]

These practices surrounding the Adi Granth have a great deal in common with the way images of Siva or Krishna are treated in the Hindu tradition. These devotional practices can deteriorate into mere magic, the very kind of idolatry Guru Nanak was protesting against in the Hinduism of his day. But with the right motivation and understanding, which never confuses the physical symbol (the printed book) with that which it evokes (God's word), these practices can powerfully serve to separate the spiritual from the ordinary and not degenerate into idolatry.[4] They prepare the worshiper to hear the word of the Lord, which, through the Gurus, has been recorded in human language. This word, the voice of the eternal Guru, is numinously experienced as "vibrating in the pages of the Adi Granth."[5] In terms of its relationship with the Khalsa (the Sikh spiritual community), the Khalsa may be taken as the body and the Adi Granth as the soul. Without the divine word of the Adi Granth, the Khalsa would be but an empty shell. With regard to the other religions, the words of the Adi Granth speak of one Lord who also speaks through the Hindu Vedas and Qur'an of Islam. The Adi Granth proclaims God's path, which lies beyond the religions, though Guru Nanak does not deny that it may be reached through them.[6] Mullahs, brahmans, and yogis are censured because they proclaim their path, their guruship rather than God's, and so lead the people into sectarian dispute. Following the spirit of the Adi Granth, Sikhism understands itself not as another sectarian religion, but as a witness to the truth contained in, but transcending, all religions. The direct voice of this truth is the Adi Granth speaking as Guru to the world. Empirical evidence for the universal claim is seen in the fact that Hindu and Muslim hymns are included in the Sikh scripture.

THE EXPERIENCE OF SCRIPTURE AS GURU

A Guru is the channel through which the divine is revealed in a way specially suited to the time, place, and condition of the devotee. Within Hinduism, for example, God takes the human form of *ṛṣi*, or Guru, especially for this purpose—to speak the divine truth in a way that is suited to the needs (*karma*) of the devotee. Without the Guru to individualize it, the divine word is in danger of remaining an abstract universal truth passing far above the life experience of the devotee. The Guru engages the divine word in worldly life. When Nanak and the Gurus were alive, Sikhism was not unlike Hindu experience—the word was experienced as personalized through the Guru. The uniqueness of Sikhism appears when, after Gobind Singh, the written book, in addition to being the divine word, takes on the function of personal Guru, to Sikhs both in congregational worship and in personal devotion. The relation of the ten historical Gurus to the written book is nicely summarized by Reverend Pashaura Singh of the Calgary Guru Nanak Gurdwara: "There were not ten different Gurus. Guru is the one and the same spirit, and that's the spirit of Nanak. It is manifested in ten different historical persons. Finally, it resides in the word of God, in Guru Granth Sahib."[7]

VAK LAO—TAKING THE ADVICE OF THE WORD

Just as one would look to a living Guru for advice, so Sikhs look to their scripture. The procedure for doing this is called *vak lao*. In individual and congregation settings, the process of *vak lao* functions as follows.

In congregational worship there is no lectionary of readings that is followed; rather, the reader in a ritualized fashion opens the Adi Granth at random and begins reading from the first verse on the top left page. Just as a Guru through divine knowledge of the *karma* of the congregation would choose the right portion of God's truth to speak to that karmic condition, so divine inspiration operates through the process of random selection to choose the needed word appropriate to the situation. This word, when spoken, is received by the devotees as God's will or command for that moment or situation in life. This process of "taking God's word" (*vak lao*) occurs in every service of worship, in individual daily devotions, in the *Amrit* (initiation ceremony), and in the naming of one's child, in marriage, and in death. An example as to how effective *vak lao* is in Sikh experience is described as follows. During the 1920s large groups of Punjabi Hindu outcastes were becoming Sikhs or Christians in the hope of improving social status. While the Sikh tradition clearly held that any Sikh could share in offering *prasad* to the congregation, the question was raised to the suitability of untouchable converts doing this, since most Sikhs had been of a higher status. Traditionalists wished to refuse these untouchable converts the honor of offering *prasad* at the Golden Temple in Amritsan. The Singh Sabha reform movement, however, pressed the case of the outcaste converts. It was agreed that advice should be taken from Guru Granth Sahib and a copy was opened at random. The passage that turned up read:

> Upon the worthless he bestows his grace, brother, if they will serve the True Guru. Exalted is the service of the True Guru, brother, to hold in remembrance the divine name. God himself offers grace and mystic union. We are worthless sinners, brother, yet the True Guru has drawn us to that blissful union [A.G. 638:3].[8]

With the hearing of these words it was clear to all that Guru Granth Sahib had accepted the converts. The Sikhs all followed suit and accepted *prasad* from the hands of the untouchable converts. This event typifies the Sikh experience of God's commandment given through *vak lao* as always speaking with power and truth to the situation at hand.

The experience of taking *vak lao* during initiation (*Amrit*) is not different from that of congregational worship. In the experience of one devotee being initiated, the three scripture passages chosen at random at specific points in the ceremony all spoke of *Amrit* in the most appropriate ways. This led those being initiated to "all exclaim the wonder of the Lord." This divine correlation of God's word to human events is the self-validating aspect of the Sikh experience of the scripture as living Guru. From the purely human perspective the text is being opened at random and the fitness of the verse is a mere chance coincidence. From the Sikh perspective, the ritualized random choosing of the page to read functions to remove sinful human ego from the process so as to allow God to do the choosing. As Reverend Pashaura Singh puts it, "That *vak* will reveal the spirit of the event."[9] The wisdom in God's choice confirms the function of the scripture as Guru.

In individual daily devotion, *vak lao* (God's word) is taken first thing in the morning before beginning the day's activities. This revelation of God's will (*hokum*) serves as a verse for personal meditation throughout the day, just as in Hinduism a Guru gives the student a personally selected *mantra* for meditation. Again during evening prayers, *vak lao* is taken as the Guru's word upon which to conclude the day with its particular joys or sorrows. It is through these personalized experiences in daily devotion plus the congregational experiences of *vak lao* that God's grace is understood in such a way as to break the bonds of *karma.*[10]

Although the Adi Granth functions as a Guru giving specific advice for life, it also has the more general and perhaps more important function of providing the *banis* (required daily prayers) and *kirtans* (hymns for congregations singing the *bani*, or word of God). God's word as sung individually in the required five daily prayers or as hymns in congregational worship is the heart of Sikh devotional experience. Through such *kirtan* (singing) the individual attunes himself to vibrate in harmony with the divine word, just as the violin string is made one with the sound of the tuning fork. For the Sikh, as for the Hindu, participation in the divine word has power to transform and unify one's consciousness.[11] The purifying power of the sacred scripture is understood as a combing of negative thoughts from one's heart and mind that occurs as a regular part of one's daily discipline:

> Comb your hair early in the morning and at the time of going to bed. As you remove dead hair, the broken hair with the comb, similarly you comb your heart, remove the negative thoughts, evil thoughts. So you have two types of combs: the one a wooden comb, the other the comb of *Gurbani*, of sacred Scripture.[12]

As the hair is combed morning and evening, prayers are chanted to comb the heart. The outer symbols of the five K's—*kesh* (long hair), *kachh* (underwear), *kara* (iron bracelet), *kangah* (wooden comb), and *kirpan* (sword)—are understood as outer symbols of God's word. When one puts them on, with prayer, one is dressed in the word of God.[13] Through this daily ritual, then, the mind is purified and inspired and the body girded to do battle with the day's temptations.

In this Sikh experience of the Adi Granth, as providing both *vak lao* (advice on everyday problems, daily purification of body and mind) and *bani kirtan* (devotional inspiration), what are the respective roles of the written text and the spoken word? To begin with, the hymns of the Gurus were spoken or sung and then memorized and written down. The collection of the written hymns by Arjun in the first instance may have been his response to spurious hymns being circulated by heretical Sikh movements of the day. It also functioned to give the Sikhs a sacred book alongside the Hindu Veda, the Qur'an of Islam, and the Christian Bible. Gobind Singh's final recension not only filled the foregoing functions, but also took on the functions filled to that point by Nanak and the nine Gurus. For all of these purposes an official written text was essential. But what role does the written word play in Sikh devotional experience?

The presentation of the divine word in the form of a book with pages is obviously necessary for the "random consultation" mechanism of *vak lao* to function. And it is from the written copy in the Gurdwara that most Sikhs memorized their prayers and hymns. The presence of the written text in the Gurdwara and in the home also provides what a living Guru would provide—the physical manifestation of God. But the written words of the Adi Granth function quite differently from the written words of ordinary books or even of other scriptures. In Sikh devotion, the written words fulfill the same function as that of a musical score in relation to the performed music. Just as written music has no value until it is performed, so the written text of the Adi Granth has spiritual power only as it is sung. This is evident in the very structure of the written text. It is poetry, and at the top of each hymn the name of the raga and rhythm to be used in its singing are clearly stated. This is why the devotional experience of scripture cannot be had from translations—just as it is impossible to translate a Bach fugue into some other form. As is the case with the learning of music, if it is learned by heart in childhood it will never be forgotten. One may not bother with it for awhile, but it will always be there in the unconscious and later in life one will likely come back to it. But if music is not learned in childhood, it is very difficult to learn it (especially by heart) later in life. As *kirtan*, or sung words, the Sikh experience of scripture is very similar. Its music and poetry, when learned in youth, has a formative influence throughout life. Once learned, the constant singing and chanting of the scripture is described by one devotee as "vibrating into you . . . clearing and opening your mind to God's grace."[14] Ultimately it enables one to "dwell within the house of the Guru's Word." In village India, where most adult Alberta (Canada) Sikhs grew up, this kind of devotional immersing of oneself in scripture happened quite naturally and without great self-effort.

> I knew people in the village where I grew up as a child. . . . Those people had a very simple life. You get up in the morning and do prayers [together, as a family or community] and then go and do your work. In the evening you sit and there would be prayers and a wise man or priest who would interpret the *gurbani* [scripture], and people would sit there for two or three hours with no temptations to get away from it.[15]

In this rural traditional environment, with no television, radio, or other modern distractions, the divine music of the Adi Granth surrounded one and was naturally absorbed into one's consciousness.

The quotation above highlights a second aspect of the experience of scripture, namely, interpretation. In addition to losing oneself in the devotional singing of the word, the Adi Granth is to be studied and the meanings of its poetic words understood. Unlike the Hindu experience, a strong scholarly tradition of scripture interpretation did not develop early. In fact, the first full commentary was written by Sahib Singh only forty years ago. Instead of copying traditional Hindu commentarial methods, Sahib Singh takes his influence from the West and applies modern form criticism to the written text of the Adi Granth.[16] While the study of the text is deemed useful so as to obtain insights regarding the meaning of life, understanding gained in this fashion is clearly secondary to the wisdom gained from the devotional use of scripture in *vak lao* and *kirtan*. Copies of the text edited with commentaries for intellectual study are not the real Adi Granth. Rather, they are of the same status as translations, namely, the presentation of the scripture at a totally different level—the level of the study of the written score as opposed to the playing of the music. The former is simply preparatory for the latter, which is the real thing.

CHANGES IN THE SIKH EXPERIENCE OF SCRIPTURE FROM LIVING IN CANADA

Living in Alberta, Canada, or perhaps more correctly, living in modern Western society, is introducing changes in both the devotional and the intellectual experience of the Adi Granth by Sikhs. Modern society has many distractions and pressures that militate against the natural and simple experience of village India. The individualistic and rationalistic nature of modern society tends to emphasize the study of, as opposed to the devotional approach to, scripture. The crucial importance of one's being immersed in learning the singing of the scripture as a child poses a major challenge to Sikh parents in Canada. Let us examine each of these problems.

A modern Alberta Sikh describes the pressure he finds in the push for more and more material possessions, the social pressures to drink and to eat meat, and the lack of time for the daily discipline of saying morning and evening prayers (which usually takes two hours):

> I think we need to go back to more devotion. Living in the Western context, you are torn apart by these things. So many Sikhs, even those who have taken *Amrit*, have betrayed the religion. . . . I can easily opt out of so many things, accept only twenty percent of Sikhism, and live the other life for eighty percent of the time.[17]

He feels himself pulled apart by the pressures toward egoism, selfishness, and competition. All of these tendencies go directly against Guru Granth Sahib. In this situation many are moving to see the full commitment to scripture required by *Amrit* as the only solution. This seems very hard at first, but once the discipline has begun and *Amrit* taken, the practice seems quite possible and the obvious solution to the problem. Thus there may turn out to be a greater stress on the need for *Amrit*, for Sikhs living in modern society, if they are to have the full experience of scripture. In Canada, television, not the Adi Granth, is what one naturally absorbs. Special discipline is therefore essential if the scripture experience of village India is to be had in the modern West. Saying prayers morning and evening is not something that happens "naturally" in Canadian life; it requires considerable self-discipline.

The rational emphasis of the modern West is another influence that produces differences from the Sikh experience of village India. Congregational services in the Gurdwara in Canada (following the Protestant example) give more emphasis to sermon and rational interpretation than is the case in India.[18] In their Canadian homes, Sikhs are more tempted to spend their valuable time in study and interpretation of the text rather than in oral devotional practice.[19] In addition there is the problem that children in Western schools and society are being trained to be critical and rational. Unless the family and Gurdwara make a strong effort against the flow, the devotional approach to scripture will not be given value or development in the child's experience. In this connection a fundamental prerequisite is the teaching of the Punjabi language to the children—something that is being done with vigor both in the Gurdwara and in the families studied.

In the absence of grandparents, parents, or priest from whom one can learn how to "sing" the scripture by joining in, modern practice has introduced the use of cassette tapes. One family extensively uses tapes of the sung or chanted Adi Granth to provide leadership during morning and evening prayers, to play in the car while driving to work (as a way of "getting in" the last half-hour of the morning prayer), and to provide a general atmosphere in the house during the day.[20] The family reports that their young child likes these tapes of the Adi Granth so much that she chooses them herself and puts them on to play in preference to other, English children's stories and songs. In this way the voice of Guru Granth Sahib is modernizing by "speaking" through the new communications technology—a form of "computer-assisted Guru instruction." All these tapes are in the original Indian languages of Punjabi, Hindi, or Urdu rather than English. Only in these languages is the "spiritual vibration" of the Guru "present." In this way they provide a dynamic structuring of consciousness for the modern spiritual Sikh. As one respondent put it, "Hearing the tapes [of the Adi Granth] makes you feel light, clears your mind, leaves worries to God."[21]

It may be concluded that living in Canada has not significantly changed the formative role played by scripture in Sikh life. The difference is that the added challenges and obstructions that a modern technological society puts in the way of the spirituality of the Sikh tradition (as formulated in village India). Perhaps more successfully than other Indian religious believers, Canadian Sikhs are responding to these challenges. The significance and need for the full commitment of *Amrit* is receiving new recognition, especially by young adults. The daily discipline of dressing oneself in scripture (as symbolized by the five K's) and living in the house of the Guru's word is the focal point of the life being lived by many Canadian Sikhs. An interesting and innovative feature in this regard is the use of tapes of the Adi Granth to replace some of the functions filled by the spiritual environment of the Indian village. A danger, which may prove more difficult to handle, is the emphasis of the modern rational mindset to study the scripture for its meaning. While this can be an enrichment of the Sikh tradition, an addition of a valuable component not common in village India, it must not be allowed to overbalance the devotional or meditative practice of the word. It is the latter that is the heart of traditional Sikh spiritual experience. Should meditation in the word be overcome by rational study of the word, Sikh practice will have fallen prey to the barren rationalism that results when modernity robs religion of its soul.

6

SCRIPTURE IN BUDDHISM

> Through a regulated life in accordance wth *Vinaya* rules, to study doctrinal statements attributed to the Buddha as presented in the *sūtras*, to practise the teaching and to reflect on some of the points in the light of the commentaries are the consistent directives in Buddhist tradition. It is only through this threefold effort, the religious goal of Buddhahood, or *Nirvāṇa* might be attainable.[1]

In spite of the fact that Buddhism is one of the few world religions to reject the notion of "revealed scripture," the foregoing quotation makes clear that the Buddhist life is lived from within the Buddhist texts. Indeed, of all the religions, Buddhism has the largest scripture in many different languages—Pali, Sanskrit, Chinese, and Tibetan. Not only is the Buddhist scripture enormous in terms of the number of titles it contains, many of them are extremely long, for example, texts such as the *Mahāvibhāṣa*, which cover more than a thousand printed pages in Chinese, are not unusual. The Chinese Buddhist canon, if translated, would require more than a half-million pages of print to include it all. Thus when we speak of the Buddhist scriptures, we should have in mind a whole library rather than a single book such as the Torah, the Bible or the Qur'an. In addition to their huge size, Buddhist scriptures are also unique in having not just one but several separate canons or authoritative collections.[2]

Perhaps Buddhists have more scripture than others because, in their view, scriptural words do not have a special status such as the *qur'ans* of Islam or the *vāk* of Hinduism. For the Buddhist, words, even most scriptural words, are not divine but merely conventional—created by humans for the purpose of solving practical problems in everyday life. While words are necessary for the conduct of our day-to-day affairs, words function by imposing distinctions or categories where ultimately none exists. While this should not cause problems in practical transactions, words can easily get in the way and be more of a hindrance than a help. This is especially true in the realm of religion where

"God," "the good," or "the right" cannot be empirically grounded. Words about such topics can easily fall into creating artificial concepts that do not really exist. When this happens words, even scriptural words, become an obstruction. Even so, there is one problem that the words of Buddhist scripture help us to solve: "How do I get from ordinary life (*samsara*) to enlightenment (*Nirvāṇa*)?" Only if the words of scripture prove able to help one solve this problem have they any value. For the Buddhist, therefore, the worth of scriptural words is instrumental not intrinsic. From the sixth century B.C., the time of the Jewish prophets, millions of people spread over one-half the world have found the words of the Buddha useful in leading one to realize enlightenment.

In studying Buddhist scripture we shall examine (1) Buddha, the founder of the scripture; (2) the canon and the monastic communities; (3) the oral texts; (4) the written texts; (5) Buddhist exegesis; and (6) the *Tripiṭaka* in relation to other scriptures.

BUDDHA, THE FOUNDER OF THE SCRIPTURE

Unlike the cases of Muhammad or Guru Nanak, we do not have good historical evidence for the life of Gautama the Buddha. The extant versions of Buddha's life were all composed many years after his death. Even though legend was added to the historical elements, the intent of the early writers was to celebrate his deeds—they were poets rather than historians. Still, Aśhvaghoṣa, in his first-century *Acts of the Buddha*, saw Gautama as a real human being—experiencing conflicts and temptations, and exercising his own choices motivated by compassion for suffering human beings.[3] This image of Gautama is likely as close to the historical person as Aśhvaghoṣa could make it. As is the case for Jesus, here too we cannot get back behind the portraits developed of the founder by the early community. "But though the Community (*Saṇgha*) created the image of Buddha, the Buddha created the Community and in so doing impressed upon it his personality."[4] In imitating him, they transmitted an image of him along with his teaching for later generations. Although distortion undoubtedly creeps into this process, the purpose and dedication of those involved also introduces a good deal of fidelity into the process.

Gautama was born (ca. 560 B.C.E.) a *kṣatriya*, or warrior caste, to a princely family living on the edge of the foothills of the Himalayas in northern India. Growing up as an educated young man in Hindu culture, he would likely have had instruction in the Vedas. A study of the *sūtras*, or sayings of Buddha, indicates that he had definite views in regard to Vedic revelation.[5] In Buddha's view none of the teachers of the Vedic tradition, not even the original *ṛṣis*, have experienced a direct vision of Brahman. Thus, the Vedic claim to scriptural knowledge of Brahman is not trustworthy because it is not founded on direct experience of Brahman by one of the *ṛṣis*. The Veda, therefore, cannot be accepted as a revelation. Buddha does not seem to be denying the possibility of scriptural revelation altogether, although the admission of the possibility of such a revelation in a theistic form would be incompatible with the nontheistic character of Buddhism. In further discussing the Vedic tradition, Buddha observes that even if the original *ṛṣi* really did directly see Brahman (which the Buddha does not believe), we have no way of knowing that what might have originally been a true report has been faithfully handed down without allowing errors to creep in. These two possibilities cause a "double bind"—a true revelation might be misremembered, a false "revelation" might be correctly remembered. For these reasons, claimed the Buddha, the Vedas cannot be accepted as trustworthy revelation.

In his own religious experience, Gautama rejected a faith acceptance of the Veda and went out in search of a personal direct experience of reality. The words he spoke, which became the Buddhist scriptures, were a description of his experience of striving for and finally achieving the state of *Nirvāṇa*—the final goal of knowing reality and experiencing release from all suffering. Having had the direct personal experience face to face as it were, the Buddha had none of the doubts that had worried him regarding the experience of the Hindu *ṛṣis*. The words he spoke (e.g., "The Four Noble Truths") were intended to exhort and instruct others to enter this same path (*mārga*) and also to realize release (*Nirvāṇa*). These words were new, different from the handed-down doctrines of the Vedas:

> That this was the noble truth concerning sorrow, was not, O Bhikkus, among the doctrines handed down [i.e., the Vedas], but there arose within me the eye (to perceive it), there arose the knowledge (of its nature), there arose the understanding (of its cause),there arose wisdom (to guide in the path of tranquility), there arose the (light to dispel darkness from it).[6]

This passage is repeated twelve times to emphasize the newness of Buddha's enlightenment experience, and its discontinuity with the Veda.

Buddha's followers judged him to speak with an authority that arose from his own enlightenment experience, yet there seemed to be no thought that his words represented divine revelation or that they were dictated by a God. Lewis Lancaster puts it well:

> While the followers of the Buddha considered that his words possessed special power, the idea that the teaching arose from insights achieved in a special state of yogic development, a state open and available to all who have the ability and the desire to exert the tremendous effort needed to achieve it, meant that the words based on the experience need not be considered as unique or limited to one person in one time. Indeed, the Buddhists held that Sākyamuni was but one of a line of Buddhas who have appeared in this world system to expound the Dharma, and that there will be others to follow.[7]

For Buddhism, as was the case for Hinduism, the truth taught by the scriptures is beginningless, eternal. Like the *ṛṣis* (as they are understood within Hinduism), Gautama acts to clear away the obstructions that obscure the eternal truth. Other Buddhas have done this before him, and will do it again after him. But always it is the same truth that is revealed. Revelation in this Buddhist sense is *parivartina*—turning something over, explaining it, making plain the hidden. This is the role of the Buddhas: to make visible the timeless truth to the unenlightened; to point out the path to *Nirvāṇa* and guide the way. In the Buddhist view each of us is a potential buddha obscured in karmic ignorance, but with the possibility for enlightenment in us.[8]

Concern for the survival of his teaching is shown by Gautama just before his death. The *Mahā-Parinibbāna-Sutta* reports that Gautama's disciple Ānanda feared that the death of his teacher would mean the end of the teaching (*Dharma*), and thus the end of the opportunity for release from *saṁsāra*. Gautama reassures Ānanda and directs his followers that henceforth his words or teachings would be their leader: "The truths and the rules of the order which I have set forth and laid down for you all, let them, after I am gone, be the Teacher to you."[9] In this way Gautama took the lead in establishing the basis for the canon of Buddhist scripture.

THE CANON AND THE MONASTIC COMMUNITIES

Buddha was one of the first religious founders to establish monastic communities, and it was within these communities that the Buddhist canon was given shape. The different monastic groups tended to give the canon a different shape, and these diversities became more pronounced as the religion spread over a wide geographical area and into many cultures. Controversy developed among the various groups regarding the substance and the character of the scriptures. Some limited the canon to those words of the Buddha remembered by his closest follower and relative, Ānanda. Apparently none of these had been written down during the Buddha's years of teaching, which covered four decades. Tradition records that within the year that Buddha died (perhaps 483 B.C.E.), five hundred monks gathered together at Rājagṛha (the capital of the Magadha Kingdom) to agree on Buddha's teachings and to codify the Rule of the Monastic Order.[10] Ānanda is reported to have recited all the "remembered words," which were then approved by the whole community (*Saṅgha*). These words were passed on orally for several centuries until they were finally compiled and codified into treatises called *sūtras* (Buddha's teachings). Along with these *sūtras* the rules of conduct for the monastic community (*vinaya*) were also recorded and included as a part of the canon, since they were also considered to be the words of Buddha. Ānanda is said to have recited in order each of the five *Nikāyas* (also called *Āgamas*) in the *Sūtra Piṭaka*, or the "Basket of Discourses." The *sūtras* written on palm leaves were actually kept in a basket—thus the name. Each *sūtra* begins with the words, "Thus I have heard at one time. The Lord dwelt at . . . "[11] with the "I" here referring to Ānanda, the reciter of Buddha's words. These texts are chiefly in prose. Robinson comments:

> In the prose texts the early disciples seem to have been more concerned with the substantive content rather than the exact words. Everyone was allowed to recite the scriptures in his own dialect. . . . Sectarian bias undoubtedly has occasioned distortions, additions, and omissions. Nevertheless, a large fund is common to all versions, and the Sangha seems from the first to have striven to exclude spurious texts and to maintain purity of transmission. Strictness in preserving the essential kernel, and liberty to expand, vary, and embellish the expression, characterize Buddhist attitudes through the ages toward not only texts but art, ritual, discipline, and doctrine. The perennial difficulty lies in distinguishing the kernel from its embodiment. The Buddha is said to have told Ānanda that if the Sangha wished it might revoke the minor rules; but Ānanda forgot to ask which rules were minor, so the First Council, it is said, decided to retain everything in the Vinaya.[12]

Many Buddhists felt that only these memorized and transmitted sayings of the Buddha could be part of scripture; others took a much more flexible approach to the canon. One school formed around the *arhant* monks and called themselves the School of Elders (*Theravāda*). They took a conservative approach to the canon and argued that only the "remembered words" of the Buddha in the *sūtras* should be included. In these "remembered words" would be found the "seeds" of the *Dharma*, or Buddhist teaching, which could then be amplified and developed. They considered their philosophic treatises expanding on the "seed words" of the Buddha to be also part of the *Dharma*. These expanded texts (*Abhidharma*), although composed by teachers other than the Buddha, were judged to be necessary for a full exposition of the *Dharma*, or teaching. Thus they came to be a third "basket" (*piṭaka*) of the canon alongside the *sūtra piṭaka* and the *vinaya piṭaka*. Consequently the word for this tripartite canon was the *tripiṭaka* or "three baskets of scripture"—*sūtra* (Buddha's sayings), *vinaya* (monastic rules), and *Abhidharma* (philosophic treatises, *śāstras*). In the Buddhist canon transmitted in the Pali language, the language of the Theravāda school, the *Abhidharma* "basket" contains seven scholastic works that are particular to the Theravādins. Other Buddhist schools accepted the same general *sūtra* and *vinaya* collections but developed their own *Abidharma* or *śāstra* (philosophic) literatures. None of these words are attributed to the Buddha; they are all compositions of later Buddhist teachers and attempt to draw out and systematize the intended meaning of Buddha's *sūtras*. In this sense there is continuity from the *sūtra* through the *Abidharma śāstras*.

The Theravāda monks tended to form an elite community insisting that they alone knew the true *Dharma* and were thus in a position to pass judgment on the views of others. Some opposed this by arguing that a householder could become an *arhant* (Buddhist "saint") and keep his or her lay status. During the second century after Buddha's death, the community split into two groups, the *Sthaviras* (Pali, *Thera*, "Elders") and the *Mahāsanghikas* ("Great Assembly-ites"). The Elders (*Theravāda*) in their desire to be conservative seem to have distorted the original teaching somewhat by aggrandizing themselves and the Buddha. The *Mahāsanghikas* admitted laypeople and non-*arhant* monks to their meetings and were more open to popular religious values.[13] They were the religious innovators and formed the main basis out of which Mahāyāna Buddhism arose. They maintained the open approach of the Buddha, but they carried the transfiguration of the Buddha much further than the Theravāda in maintaining that "His body is infinite, his power is boundless, and his life is endless. He educates living beings tirelessly, awakening pure faith in them."[14] Between 100 B.C.E., and 100 C.E., the Mahāyāna movement arose from within the *Mahāsanghika* groups.

Like the Theravādins, the Mahāyanists accept the authenticity of all the *Nikāyas* remembered by Ānanda but they also add many new *sūtras,* such as *The Prajñāpāramitā Sūtras* and the *Lotus Sūtra*. These new *sūtras* were written from 100 B.C.E., until 400 C.E. Often these *sūtras* expressed hostility toward the Theravāda school.[15] The Mahāyāna action of calling these new books *sūtras*, that is, "sayings of Buddha" was greeted with incredulity by the established schools of Buddhism. Lancaster comments:

> To counteract the opposition arising from the other schools, the anonymously written *sūtras* maintained that when the disciples of the Buddha have trained in the teaching and realize its true nature, then they teach nothing which contradicts the Dharma. With this defense, they proceeded to invest the texts with all the authority of the "remembered words" and went even further in enhancing the prestige of the works by relegating the traditional *sūtras* to a lower degree of importance, asserting that those narrations were only elementary discourses. It is, said the first Mahāyāna *sūtras*, only in the Mahāyāna texts that one can find the full and complete teachings of the Dharma.[16]

Although these Mahāyāna texts were filled with claims about their own authenticity, there seems to have been no move to establish a new enlarged canon. Rather, each text was given the authoritative title "*sūtra*" and was opened with the *sūtra* formula "Thus I have heard. . . ." This had the result of enabling the canon to be augmented with new "remembered words" in a rather open-ended fashion. Thus it is no surprise that the Mahāyāna scriptures compose a massive library, which made it impossible to have large numbers of copies of the total corpus. "While the Buddhist monasteries were as zealous in promoting the copying of sacred texts as their counterparts in Europe, their diligence had to be directed toward the formidable problem of preserving the ever increasing profusion of folios. Distribution of large numbers of copies was a secondary concern."[17]

In the second century C.E., Mahāyāna authors began writing *śāstras*, or philosophic treatises, in their own names. They continued to begin from a *sūtra* as the basis, but began to rely more on inference and perception. The aim of these *śāstras* was to argue the Mahāyāna Buddhist position to non-Buddhists, who rejected the authority of the *sūtras*, and to the Theravādins, who denied the authenticity of the Mahāyāna *Sūtras*. Shortly after this period the Mahāyāna Buddhists stopped producing *sūtras*, and, following the lead of the Hindus, began composing *Tantras* which fostered a devotional approach. According to tradition these *Tantras* are the Buddha's word. This was justified by the Mahāyānist idea of the "Buddha's inspiration or charisma (*adhiṣṭana, anubhāva*) through which he infuses thoughts into the minds of men, and sustains the advocates of his Dharma."[18] Since the Buddha for the Mahāyāna is eternal and omniscient, it is thus quite logical to hold that his thoughts could pervade human minds in any age and that their inspirations would have the value of scripture. Mahāyāna Buddhism flourished in Southern India (e.g., Amaravati, Kanci) and particularly in northwest India. From there it spread successfully north to Tibet and Central Asia and east to China and Japan.

After the First Council of monks in 483 B.C.E., at which Ānanda had recited the "remembered words," and first established the canon, a Second Council met at Vaiśāli (in modern Bihar) under less harmonious circumstances. The schism between the Theravādins and the Mahāyānists was beginning to appear: The minority group, claiming to uphold traditional views, withdrew and eventually evolved into the Theravāda school. Because they were the smaller group, the name Hīnayāna, or "The Lesser Vehicle," was given to them by their opponents. The majority group, which remained in the council, designated themselves as the Mahāsaṅgha, or "Great Recitation," and evolved into the Mahāyāna or "The Greater Vehicle."

The Third Council of monks is said to have been called by King Aśoka at Patna in the mid-third century B.C.E. By then there were apparently already some eighteen interrelated schools within the Hīnayāna and likely a similar proliferation within the Mahāyāna.[19] There is good reason to believe that Aśoka was disturbed by the division within the monastic orders, and that he may have attempted to promote internal unity.[20] Aśoka clearly played a major role in making Buddhism a world religion. He mounted major educational initiatives and sent out "Ministers of Dharma" who combined political, judicial, and religious functions. In helping to spread Buddhism throughout the world of his day, Aśoka fostered the translation of the Buddhist canon into the three great language collections (Pali, Chinese, and Tibetan) in which we find it today:[21]

I. The Pali Tripitaka
   This contains the scriptures of one of the Hīnyāna schools, the Theravādins. The scriptures of the other Hīnyāna schools are partly preserved in Sanskrit and Chinese.

II. The Chinese Tripitaka

Its composition is less rigidly fixed, and it has varied in the course of time. The Japanese edition, the *Taisho Issaikyo*, 1924–29, gives 2,184 works in 55 volumes of ca. 1,000 pages each. It is composed of 21 volumes of *Sūtras*, 3 volumes of *Vinaya*, and 8 volumes of *Abhidharma* plus other items.

III. The Tibetan *Kanjur* and *Tanjur*

The *Kanjur* is a collection of *sūtras* comprising either 100 or 108 volumes. Of these, 13 deal with *Vinaya*; 21 with *Prajñāpāramita*; 45 with other *sūtras*; and 21 with Tantric texts.

The *Tanjur*, in 225 volumes, contains the commentaries and *śāstras*. Works belonging to the Hīnayāna scholars are included along with commentaries on Tantric texts as well as the regular Mahāyāna *Śāstras* on the Madhyamika and the Yogācāra schools. There are also commentaries on the *Prajñāpāramita Sūtras*.

It should be noted that as is the case in Hinduism, Buddhist scriptures contain many devotional texts. A good example are the personal verses of the monks and nuns in *The Theragāthā*, "Songs of the Elders," and *The Therigāthā*, "Songs of the Nuns," which show the appeal that Buddhism had for its early converts. Also devotional, but of a quite different character, are the "Birth Stories of the Buddha," *The Jatakas*, in which popular stories or fables are used to describe incidents in Buddha's previous lives. There are about five hundred such episodes,[22] which relate how Gautama in his former lives accomplished the perfections of the *bodhisattva*. These popular tales urged the listener to imitate a *bodhisattva*.

To be a scholar of Buddhist scripture requires considerable linguistic ability, endurance, and a long life. As can be seen above, the languages of the canon are many and difficult, and the quantity of the scriptures is enormous. For a nonrevelation tradition, Buddhism has produced a prodigious amount of scripture.

THE ORAL TEXTS

Unlike the Sanskrit texts of the Vedas, the Prakrit, or common language scriptures of Buddhism, have not been carefully preserved orally. Buddha's attitude seems to have been very open and flexible. Everyone was allowed to recite the scriptures in his or her own dialect—which did not make for a standardized oral form. We do not know the exact language the Buddha spoke; however, it was likely an early version of the Magadhī dialect in which most of King Aśoka's inscriptions are written. The complete canon of the Theravāda school has been preserved in Pali, a vernacular descended from Sanskrit and probably spoken in west India before being taken to Sri Lanka. Tradition maintains that the oral Pali canon was written down in Sri Lanka during the first century B.C.E.[23] A Sinhalese chronicle records this event:

> The text of the Three Pitakas and the commentary thereon did the most wise Bikkhus hand down in former times orally, but since they saw that people were falling away (from the orthodox teaching), the bikkhus met together, and in order that the true doctrines might endure, they wrote them down in books.[24]

Indian Buddhism shared with Hinduism an emphasis upon the oral as more basic than the written. Indian culture had developed systems to preserve "remembered texts"—a system that, given the Indian climate, was often more successful than attempts to preserve texts in written or printed forms. The oral system depended upon a regular succession of teachers and students as the means for passing on the "remembered words." The Buddhist monastic system was ideally designed to foster this teacher-student succession. Study, in this approach, consisted in hearing and repeating texts to oneself, not in the more passive reading of books. Ānanda's feat of being able to say by heart the whole of the Buddhist canon of his day is not unusual for those trained in this tradition. Group listening to check for errors is still an accepted method of verification in rural India today. This was the major purpose of the three Buddhist councils; they were entirely affairs of recitation of the "remembered words" by various groups of monks.[25] It was the living memory of Buddha's words in their hearts and minds that was judged to be crucial. Even the very sound of the words, as spoken or chanted, was judged to have spiritual power.

The mere memorization of the text is not judged to be the most important aspect of the oral tradition. Kitagawa has observed that the oral tradition represents a different mode of religious perception and meaning. By chanting or listening to the rhythmic words of a sacred text, the teaching and inspiration in the words becomes renewed and reinforced. In this sense the oral recitation of a text is a sacramental act.[26] In Tibetan Buddhism, for example, the chanting of *mantras* was refined into a highly skilled technique. Chanting was done together with set ritual gestures in such a way that the monks "felt" and expressed the word in addition to saying it. And the saying of it was not a simple speaking, but a chanting that involved the "singing" of a D-major chord by each monk individually. Each monk actually chants D-F#-A simultaneously. This seems to evoke overtones of the interdependence of the universe—the point of Buddha's enlightenment experience.[27] In this way the oral word is experienced as being much more powerful than a mere reading of the written text. Here Buddhism is very much at one with the Hindu emphasis upon the transforming power of chanted *vāk*.[28]

The felt aspect of Buddha's word as oral chant has been observed in modern Jodo Shinshu Buddhist experience in Canada.[29] Since coming to Canada from Japan there has been a shift away from the traditional emphasis upon ritual chanting of the texts to the more Protestant Christian style of listening to sermons and reading books. Goa and Coward report that this marked turn in the use of sacred language from the ritual-poetic to the discursive-rational is causing concern. The psychological effect of the shift from the ritual-poetic to the discursive-rational use of scripture is highlighted in the funeral service. The service begins and ends with chanting, while the middle focuses on the sermon. The sermon typically talks about the life of the deceased, explains Buddha's compassion and one's rebirth in Amida's Pure Land, and stresses that the relatives and the deceased are one in *nembutsu*, the ritual chant. The sermon attempts to communicate a sense of oneness with the deceased, on the basis of Buddha's teaching that after death all are reborn in Amida's Pure Land. While such discursive teaching undoubtedly has some effect, it is not the cognitive functions of the psyche that are dominant in the experience of bereavement. Simply telling a wife that she will join her departed husband when she is reborn in the Pure Land and that they are one when she chants the *nembutsu* is of little help. In the crisis of bereavement it is the nonrational—the emotional and intuitive—aspects of the psyche that dominate. These are precisely the psychological processes that seem to be actualized in the oral chanting of scripture. Although the discursive meaning of *Namu Amida Buddha* may be "I surrender myself to Amida Buddha," it is through the emotional, intuitive, and memory-laden processes of chanting that the existential experience of oneness is realized. A shift of emphasis in the funeral from the chant to the sermon has the effect of removing the power of the oral experience—the spiritual psychological mechanism by which the wife can identify with Amida and with her dead husband.

Buddhist priest the Rev. S. K. Ikuta of Calgary presents the following introspection into the psychology of the oral experience of scripture as chant:

> When you identify with the chant it has the function of structuring spiritual space: the sound of the chant, the smell of the incense, and the action of putting hands together—all this through repeated experience becomes predictable and induces the spiritual.
>
> When I chant it brings memories of my father, of gatherings with other ministers . . . it sets your mind psychologically to hear the Buddha's teaching. It [the mind] opens . . . like flower buds being opened to receive the sun.
>
> Chanting out loud is also quite important. Shinran says rather than recite the *nembutsu* quietly within yourself, say it out loud; bring it out and listen. Although I am chanting:
>
> Amida speaks it,
> Amida hears it,
> And I am the union.[30]

Another function of the oral chanting of scripture is as a mnemonic device. The Buddhist tradition, following the Hindu practice, has always used chanting as a device for embedding scripture in the budding consciousness of the young child. Raised within the tradition, the Rev. Y. Kawamura reports: "My father taught me scripture. I would repeat after him. After ten years he taught me how to read and what it meant. Later on in the University I studied these texts."[31] The order indicated has psychological importance. First the oral texts are learned by chanting; then comes the reading of the text, and finally study through rational analysis. The later stages are dependent on the earlier. The ritual chanting not only provides the mechanism for memorization, but also etches the sound of the sacred words ever more deeply within consciousness. Another devotee describes the oral experience this way: "To me [the chant] is meditative. It induces peace from the hustle and bustle of life. It is very comfortable. It has seeped in . . . it is part of my consciousness."[32] As such, the oral experience of scripture becomes the foundation from which rational analysis can proceed. More important, however, it is constantly available for immediate guidance, inspiration, and solace in the crises of life.

The analysis above strongly suggests that the modern tendency, within Canadian Buddhist experience at least, to turn from the oral chant toward the rational presentation of scripture through sermon and book may have the effect of gradually cutting off the Buddhist consciousness from its spiritual root. If Buddhist scripture is not learned in childhood through ritual repetition, if the oral teachings are not nourished and reinforced in adulthood by private and public repetition of the texts, then the psychological foundation will be missing and sermons and study of books may become empty exercises. Group chanting also helps to keep the community together in harmony. As one layperson observed, priests in their use of words in sermons and teachings conflict with one another. But the chanted texts, memorized in childhood and communally repeated, do not change. In all Jodo Shinshu festivals chanting has occupied an important place. It is reported that the unity and harmony found within a congregation can be measured by monitoring its chanting.

From Ānanda's first repeating of all Buddha's teaching right up to the modern-day chanting of the *nembutsu* by Canadian Japanese Buddhists, the oral text has continued as the dominant force in Buddhist spiritual life. Although the written Buddhist scripture is enormous, its function remains secondary to the experience of the oral text. As was the case for Hindus, Buddhists experience the spoken word as the locus of spiritual power, even though such words should not be blindly received as revealed truth.

THE WRITTEN TEXTS

For about four hundred years Buddhist scripture was transmitted only orally, by schools of reciters. Some characteristics of the older scriptures such as many repetitions, fondness for verse, and frequent numerical lists are typical of oral texts. Due to this long oral period, dates, places, and names of authors cannot easily be identified. The early Buddhists shared with the Hindus the Indian indifference to historical details. Historical events surrounding a text are judged to be unimportant in relation to the unchanging truth the text contains. The Buddhists also preserved few records of authorship, since it was bad form for a monk to make a name for himself by writing. It did not matter to them *who* said something, but whether it was true and helpful. Originality in writing was not encouraged; anonymity was taken as a sign of sanctity.[33] Even when names are mentioned they cannot be taken at face value, since the names of great teachers such as Ashvaghosa, Nagarjuna, and Vasubandhu were often attached to later works to give them added prestige. For all of those reasons, modern textual criticism has a hard time with the oldest Indian Buddhist texts. Chinese translations of the Buddhist texts are of considerable help, since they carefully record the date of the translation, thus allowing the date the Indian original had to be in existence to be inferred.[34] In many cases, however, evidence suggests that the written composition of a work may spread over a long period. For example, a work like the *Lalitavistara* may contain materials ranging from 200 B.C.E. to 600 C.E.[35]

Although the Buddhist monasteries, like their European counterparts, provided dedicated labor to copy the sacred texts, the ravages of the Indian climate made the task of preservation most difficult. The favorite writing material was the dried leaf of the palm tree. While it was a tough, long-lasting fiber under good conditions, it was susceptible to the destructive action of water, mildew and insects, all of which were prevalent in India. During the first ten centuries C.E., Buddhism gradually dwindled in strength in India. As the number of monasteries decreased, the activity of recopying texts also diminished with the result that hundreds of texts crumbled away and were permanently lost.[36] The oldest Buddhist manuscripts discovered so far were found in a jar in Afghanistan—birch bark scrolls dated to the first century C.E.

The written texts are also complicated by the variety of languages in which they are found. Within India alone the manuscripts of Buddhist texts are found in four languages: (1) Pali; (2) Prakrit (found in the old manuscript of the *Dhammapāda*); (3) Classical Sanskrit; and (4) Buddhist Hybrid Sanskrit (as for example is found in the *Mahavastu*). Thus editors attempting to get back to the earliest text cannot be sure which was the original language. Lancaster observes, "No editor can now escape from the fact that the changes made to achieve the 'best' reading may create a false view of the original, imposing a Classical Sanskrit form where none ever existed."[37] Today, editors of Buddhist texts have consulted many of the extant Sanskrit and Prakrit manuscripts so that better published editions are available for study. The complete Pali canon has been edited and translated by the Pali Text Society in London, although this version is based only on manuscripts from Sri Lanka. Hundreds of other Pali manuscripts providing alternate readings to the ones used by the Pali Text Society in London are to be found throughout Southeast Asia, especially Burma. This is to say nothing yet of the Buddhist canons that exist in other cultures beyond India. Lancaster summarizes them as follows:[38]

Type I The Buddhist Canons of India
 (1) Pali
 (2) Sanskrit (also Prakrit) (see Type V [1])

Type II The Translated Buddhist Canons
(1) Chinese (Sanskrit [also Prakrit])
(2) Tibetan (Sanskrit)

Type III The Secondary Translated Buddhist Canons
(1) Mongolian (Tibetan)
(2) Manchu (Chinese)

Type IV The Transliterated Script Canons of Buddhism
(1) Script Canons based on Pali
(2) The Tangut Canon (from the Chinese)

Type V Scriptural Texts (not belonging to a canon)
(1) Sanskrit (also Prakrit)
(2) Central Asian Languages (Sanskrit [also Prakrit])

Unfortunately Types II to V use very little material also used in Type I. Attempts to match up titles in any two canons are relatively unsuccessful, with the location of hardly any common titles. Thus the notion that Type I is the seed form for Type II canons can be misleading.[39]

A parallel kind of problem exists in the Mahāyāna texts of Tibet and China where the old Sanskrit manuscripts that have survived are often treated as the *textus receptus* and called the "original." Yet these are not the original forms of the Mahāyāna texts, nor are they the "originals" used by the Chinese or Tibetans for making their translations. Thus there is no guarantee that the Sanskrit text is more accurate than is the Chinese or Tibetan version.[40]

In India there are scattered palm leaf and paper manuscripts with the oldest dating to the ninth century. But the largest collection of Buddhist texts in the Indian subcontinent comes from Nepal with the copies dating from the eighteenth and nineteenth centuries. None of these copies is old in terms of Indian Buddhism, and thus all carry the doctrinal imprint of a time far separated from the original text—which was already separated from the Buddha by some four hundred years of oral tradition. In the Chinese canon, however, there are versions of texts translated as early as the second century C.E. that have been preserved along with colophons giving the date, name of translator, and title.[41] Although the Chinese texts are much more helpful with historical information, they have not been found useful when it comes to editorial problems of content. Because Chinese language has no inflections for case, number, tense, mood, or voice, past editors of Sanskrit texts have found little help in solving problems in the Sanskrit texts, which are replete with distinctions of numbers, tenses, moods, and the like. Lancaster, however, has recently argued that "The proof . . . is becoming more formidable every year that in the Chinese canon we have an invaluable source of evidence for making new editions with some assurance that those translators knew their craft and practiced it with vigor and accuracy."[42] Whereas the transmission via regular recopying of the palm leaf texts in India has produced a constantly increasing number of scribal errors, the Chinese scribal procedures have been highly accurate, producing few variant readings. This is partly due to the Chinese development of printing at an early date. "By the 10th century, the Chinese had carved a complete set of blocks for printing the canon, blocks which represented most of the available texts that had been translated from Sanskrit or other Indic languages."[43] Thus a standard Chinese text was established early that has continued unchanged to the present and must have been a close approximation to the texts of the first translations. From China the tradition of block printing of the canon spread to Tibet. In both China and Tibet, therefore, the early printing of the Buddhist scriptures put the scribe in a much different position from the scribe in India and South Asia, where a tradition of printing never developed. The Chinese and Tibetan scribe-printers were highly skilled craftsmen called upon to prepare on paper or silk the copy that was transferred to the wooden block in preparation for carving. The tremendous effort required to carve out the intricate wood letters put considerable pressure on the scribe to produce accuracy.

In Tibet from the seventh to the ninth centuries C.E. Buddhist texts arrived not only from India, but also from China, Khotan, and other surrounding Buddhist countries.[44] But this new religion arriving in Tibet was not adopted in unchanged form. Eva Dargyay points out that after Buddhism had secured royal patronage in Tibet, the missionary effort had to be widened to include the views of the lower classes. By this process the *Bon*-religion and popular belief were incorporated into Buddhism.[45] In addition Tibetan thought had to digest the many differing systems of Buddhism that had been brought into Tibet during the first missionary period. In translating the texts, synthesizing them, and integrating the native Tibetan materials, new statements of Buddhism were produced which, as Leslie Kawamura has argued, cannot be seen simply as a translation from old Sanskrit texts or as a transplanted religion from India.[46] The Tibetan Buddhist texts have an authenticity that is unique and cannot be reduced back to being mere copies of Indian Sanskrit texts.

The written texts of Buddhism thus present us with a vast variety and quantity of material for study. Any attempt by historical critical methods to remove conflations, additions, or doctrinal expansions in the hope of getting back to an original text would erase from the texts the crucial aspects that have characterized its development in cultures like China and Tibet over the years. After his detailed study of the written texts, Lewis Lancaster concludes "that for the Buddhists the Dharma is always potentially available, and the verbalization of it by Sākyamuni was not its only possible expression."[47] It is the dynamic unfolding of Buddhist understanding, rather than the recovery of an original static text, that is the important knowledge the written texts convey.

BUDDHIST EXEGESIS

It has been said that all of Buddhism is exegesis, or interpretation, of Buddha's First Sermon, "The Four Noble Truths." The Four Noble Truths proclaim "The Middle Path" in which the bodily and sensual appetites are fed sufficiently for health but not indulged or starved. Yet it is much more than merely a parallel statement to the Greek or Chinese Golden Mean. The Fourth Noble Truth is really a commentary explaining how to actualize the teachings of the first three truths. After showing that our ordinary or *saṁsāra* experience of life is one of suffering or frustration (*dukkha*), that the cause of this suffering is desire or ego-selfishness, and that this ego-selfishness can be got rid of, Buddha goes on in the Fourth Truth to outline the means to achieve this—the Eightfold Path. "The Eightfold Path is equivalent to a shorter formula, the Threefold Training, namely morality (right speech, action, and livelihood), wisdom (right views and intention), and concentration (right effort, mindfulness, and concentration)."[48] Morality goes beyond mere self-mortification because it focuses on the effects of one's acts on others. Wisdom is the understanding of the teaching that results from hard study and meditation upon the scripture. Study of the scripture is more demanding than just the physical yogas of controlling one's breath or posture; it requires a discipline of the intellect. Concentration (*samādhi*) is achieved by the cultivation of specific psychic skills that Gautama learned from his teachers. The Middle Path resulting from this Threefold Training is a *yoga,* or stringent discipline, which engages the whole person and causes one to go against worldly life.[49]

Since scripture provides both the Four Noble Truths and its initial exegesis, the Eightfold Path (or Threefold Training), scripture may be said to provide the link and pathway between *saṁsāra* and *Nirvāṇa*, or release. Scripture both points to the revelation experience of the Buddha and provides a pathway by which others may realize enlightenment. Buddhist scripture expresses in conventional terms the intuition of reality experienced by the Buddha. Scholars differ as to what degree the scriptural descriptions can be taken as adequate verbalizations of reality or the divine. Schmithausen, for one, maintains that "In the case of Early Buddhism, most of the sources referring to Liberating Insight or Enlightenment . . . do not seem to indicate that there was any problem in verbalizing experience. Therefore, these sources would seem to refer either to experiences not felt to be in conflict with concepts or to theories of Liberating Insight or Enlightenment."[50] Robinson adds that although later Mahāyāna doctrine elaborates the idea of the silence of the Buddha and maintains that *Nirvāṇa* is indescribable, "nowhere does the early Canon say that the content of the Enlightenment is nonintellectual, or that it is inexpressible."[51] For the early canon of the Theravāda, then, Buddha's enlightenment consisted in the discovery of ideas that could be communicated via scripture, and commented upon. Yet when a wanderer approached the Buddha and asked a series of questions about ultimate truth—for example, "Are the world and souls eternal, noneternal, both or neither?"—the Buddha, in some scriptures, is said to remain silent (although explaining his silence afterward to a disciple). Buddha's point would seem to have been that categories of existence or nonexistence do not obtain at the level of *Nirvāṇa*—it is not so much a question whether such ideas are true or false but, rather, that *Nirvāṇa*, the Absolute, transcends them.[52] Cessation of suffering (*dukkha*) is not annihilation or emptiness but the overflowing of transcendence.

Buddha's parable of the poisoned arrow provides a helpful illustration. A man has been struck by a poisoned arrow and a physician has been brought to the scene. But before the man will allow the physician to remove the arrow he wants to know: who shot the arrow, to what clan he belongs, what wood the bow and the arrow shaft were made from, what kind of feathers were used on the arrow, and what kind of tip the arrow had (on which the poison had been smeared). Just as this man would die, said the Buddha, before his questions were answered, so also a person wishing to know the nature of the Absolute in words will die before the Buddha would be able to elucidate it to him (*Majjhimaa-Nikāya, Sutta* 63).

Winston King puts a helpful slant on it when he observes that Buddha shunted aside the philosophical questions so as to emphasize the getting on with the spiritual discipline that alone can lead to release. "Philosophical-ontological truth is here directly converted into practical existential procedure."[53] King observes, "Buddhist negativity concerning the final goal (*Nirvāṇa*) was intended as a methodological device rather than an ontological statement; later on in the growth of the tradition and its conflict with other traditions, such statements were ontologized into 'descriptions' of the Supreme Reality."[54] In the *Majjhima Nikāya* I.431, Buddha responds to the Absolute philosophical questions by bringing the consideration to the level of existential experience: " 'there is birth . . . aging . . . dying . . . grief, sorrow, suffering, lamentation and despair' and their 'suppression . . . here and now.' These matters he *does* explain, and only these, 'because it is concerned with the goal, is fundamental to Brahma-faring, and conduces to turning away . . . to dispassion, stopping, calming, superknowledge, awakening and *nibbāna*.' "[55] As King concludes, theorizing about metaphysical ultimates has no place in this original or core Buddhism. What predominates "is the pure existentialism of dispassionate detachment from the space-time world which results in *nibbāna*—which is elsewhere defined simply as the absence of greed, hatred and delusion."[56] Rather than wrinkled-browed philosophers, the canon pictures the Buddha and his liberated followers as calm, cheerful, spontaneous, humorous, free from strife, and humane:

> Let us live happily, hating none in the midst of men who hate.
> Let us live happily then, free from disease.
> Let us live happily then, free from care.
> Let us live happily, then, we who possess nothing.
> Let us dwell feeding on joy like the Radiant Gods.[57]

The style of exegesis of Buddha and his immediate followers was that of preaching in the dialects of the people. In contrast to the restrictive Hinduism of his day in which the Vedas were available only to the elite, the upper three castes, Buddha's teaching was for all in their common tongue. Females as well as males were accepted as disciples, and special communities were created for the laypeople. The narrative techniques of story and parable played a major role in his preaching that constitutes the *sūtras*.

Modern scholars of Buddhism have paid more attention to the *śāstras*, or systematic philosophic works written by the followers of the Buddha, than to his own *sūtras*.[58] The *śāstras*, like the *Upaniṣads* of Hinduism, tended to be systematic developments based on the seed ideas present in the earlier scriptures. For example, the ideas of no-self (*anātman*), momentary elements (*dharmas*) and dependent origination (*pratītya-samutpāda*) are taken from the *sūtras* and then given full philosophic formulation in the *Theravāda Śāstras*. Although attractive to scholars because of their systematic nature, the disadvantage of focusing too much on the *śāstra* literature is that it has dealt with only certain limited aspects of the Buddhist tradition. The danger is that Buddhism is seen to be, at best, an esoteric means of salvation or release for but a few intellectuals.[59] Exegesis for the masses came through the simple power of the *sūtras* preached in the language of the masses, or structured into formula phrases like the *nembutsu*, which the masses could chant both in private devotions and in public worship.

In his analysis of the *śāstras*, Y.-H. Jan finds them classifiable into three types: (1) those that condensed excessively large portions of *sūtras*; (2) those that give analysis of the *sūtras'* deeper meaning; and (3) systematically arranging that which in the *sūtras* is in disorder.[60] In addition to these exegetical treatises, *sūtras* were written for other purposes such as criticizing other schools. Vasubandhu's *Abhidharmakośa Śāstra*, for example, is a Vibhāṣā Hinyāna work that attacks some Mahāyāna concepts. The *Abhidharma-nyāyānusāra* by the Vibhāṣā scholar Sanghabhadra is a *śāstra* written as a reply to Vasubandhu's criticism. In this fashion a *śāstra* written to bring out the meaning of the *sūtras* may then generate other *śāstras* in an ongoing and open-ended series of scholarly statements and counterstatements. Other *śāstras* were designed for the technical training of students rather than the elucidating of the Absolute. The *Vigraha-vyavartanī* ("For Refuting the Challenges of Antagonists"), a work attributed to Nāgārjuna, is cited as an example of this kind of *śāstra*.[61] The numbers of these scholarly commentaries rapidly expanded, putting a high demand on the students of the tradition. The Chinese pilgrim Hsüan-tsang reports of his visit to Nālandā University in northern India that in attendance were ten thousand monks who studied both Hinyāna and Mahāyāna *śāstras* as well as worldly books. Of these "more than a thousand could master twenty scriptures and commentaries, more than 500 were expert in thirty books, and ten, including the master, were thoroughly learned in fifty books."[62] We should understand that to be "learned in a book" entailed knowing it by heart and being able to exegete it fully line by line.

An important point often missed by modern scholars is that Buddhist exegesis was not aimed at abstract intellectual knowledge. *Śāstric* learning was aimed at the training of teachers, and *śāstric* knowledge "is valid only when the intellectual work is based on religious practice and virtue."[63] In line with Buddha's criticism of the otherworldly abstract knowledge of Hinduism and his insistence on the compassionate living of religion as one's first priority, the *śāstras* were seen only as a part of the scripture. The aim of Buddhist scripture was to help the devotees to live the Buddha's teaching, not just to understand intellectually. To accomplish this, emphasis upon the *sūtras* and *vinaya* were as important, if not more important, than mastery of the *śāstras*. Perhaps this is why some *sūtras* warn the disciple against the danger of too much learning (*bahuśruta*).[64] Another Chinese pilgrim to Nālandā observed that the most important texts for the monks were not the *śāstras*, but the *vinaya*:

> After the lapse of five summers from the time that the pupil masters the Vinaya, he is allowed to live apart from his Upādhyāya teacher. He can then go about among the people and proceed to pursue some other aim. Yet he must put himself under the care *of some teacher wherever* he goes. This will cease after the lapse of ten summers, i.e., *after he is able to understand the Vinaya.*
>
> . . . If a priest does not understand the Vinaya, he will have to be under another's care the whole of his lifetime.[65]

In addition to mastering the *vinaya*, the monks would meet their *guru* in the mornings and be taught the *Tripiṭaka* in relation to the moral conduct of life. They were also taught to chant devotional hymns. This emphasis on the existential side of Buddhist exegesis is clearly reflected in Bu-ston's medieval *History of Buddhism*:

> By study and analysis only, without the practice of meditation, one is unable to get a firm stand in the Doctrine. Likewise is this impossible, if one merely practices meditation and does not take recourse to study and investigation. But if both parts (study on one side and analysis and meditation on the other) are resorted to and accepted as a foundation, one gets a firm standing in the Doctrine.[66]

Only as one behaves morally with others and practices profound meditation is one in a position to engage seriously in study of the philosophy of the *śāstras*.

The *sūtras* also warn against the temptation of the pernicious sin of pride in one's *śāstric* knowledge, which so quickly leads to moral impurity.[67] All of this squares with the reports of the behavior at Nālandā where all the various schools of *śāstras* of Buddhism were taught on the same campus. Although the monks held different *śāstric* viewpoints, they lived together and were uniform in religious life.[68] The intention of the *śāstras*, then, was the systematic exegesis of the certain points originally taught in the *sūtras*, or the removal of wrong ideas found in other intellectual viewpoints, for example, nihilism. But this *śāstric* knowledge was valid only when it was based in the religious practice and virtue of the *sūtras* and *vinaya*. For this reason, says Y.-H. Jan, modern students of Buddhism must not repeat the error of their predecessors and overemphasize the philosophic or *śāstric* aspects of Buddhism.[69] More attention must be given to the *sūtras* and the experience of the *sūtras* by devotees at all levels of intellectual knowledge, all over the world.

A balanced position in this regard was set forth by Kamalaśīla who, along with his teacher Sāntarakṣitā, is credited with the establishment of the Yogācāra-Mādhyamaka school of Buddhism in Tibet. In his *Bhāvanākrama*, Kamalaśīla states that knowledge (*prajñā*) alone is insufficient for enlightenment; compassion also is an essential ingredient. "To accept knowledge (*prajñā*) alone," says Kamalaśīla, "would contradict the teaching of the Buddha; in fact such a theory as that knowledge alone leads to Enlightenment disagrees with what we read in the Holy texts."[70] Enlightenment results from three things: study (*śrutamayī*), investigation (*cintāmayī*), and contemplation (*bhāvanāmayī*). By means of *śrutamayī*, or study, one learns the meaning of the truths revealed by the Buddha in the *sūtras*. *Cintāmayi*, or investigation, draws out the implicit as well as the explicit meaning of the *sūtras* by means of logic (*yukti*) and authority (*āgama*). *Bhāvanāmayī*, or concentration, completes the process by making immediate in experience the intellectual truth.[71] One begins the process where one is, with an ordinary everyday experience of language—in particular the language of the *sūtras*, which provides one with the pathway to release. Although the words of scripture are merely conventional words, they are still useful in removing the obstacles of ordinary experience. The *sūtras* teach us "that the only reality is the non-production of things, all the rest is unreal; from the absolute point of view we cannot speak either of origination or non-origination, because both notions imply a duality, and reality is beyond all sorts of relative notions; whatever we say or predicate is a non-entity."[72] Following Kamalaśīla's exegetical procedure, the truth of this *sūtra* must then be confirmed by reasoning (*yukti*). Reason supports the *sūtra* by demonstrating that only from the conventional point of view can we speak of the origination of things. The third and most essential step of Buddhist exegesis is that through meditational technique the truth of this *sūtra* must be directly experienced—meditation must take one beyond the level of subject-object discrimination.

While sophisticated exegetical techniques such as Kamalaśīla's above can help one to realize enlightenment, they are practiced by only a small minority of intellectual Buddhists. By far the vast majority trust to a *bodhisattva* or to faith in the simple chanting of scripture to accomplish the same goal. Exegesis for the Jodo Shinshu, for example, is nothing more than sincere chanting of the *nembutsu* although the requirement for chanting to be "sincere" is indeed stringent.[73] For Zen Buddhism, the meditation taught by the *sūtra* is the sum total of the exegesis. All forms of Buddhist exegesis, however, have one thing in common—the requirement that the teachings of the text be fully manifested in one's life.

THE *TRIPIṬAKA* IN RELATION TO OTHER SCRIPTURES

The attitude of the Tripiṭaka toward the scriptures of other religions is one of critical tolerance. Critical in the sense that any removal of moral freedom and responsibility in these scriptures will be rejected. Tolerant in that so long as moral responsibility is safeguarded, other teachings contained in these scriptures such as, for example, belief in God—teachings that the *Tripiṭaka* rejects—will be put up with. The approach of the Buddha to other scriptures is to superimpose his teaching over the other scripture. So long as the main points of the Buddhist teaching, or *Dharma*, can be found (i.e., belief in survival after death, moral values, freedom, responsibility, and the noninevitability of salvation or release) then other unacceptable aspects such as free grace from God can be tolerated.[74]

The teachings of the *Tripiṭaka* are clearly different from the Christianity of St. Paul, the devotional Hinduism of the *Bhagavad-Gītā*, or the Qur'an. The scriptures of these last three teach that it is God's grace that makes possible religious attainment, whereas, for the Buddhist *Tripiṭaka* it is human effort, not supernatural intervention, that is effective. But it is the goal of salvation or release that ultimately concerns the Buddhist. Consequently if following their scriptures the Jew, Christian, Muslim, or Hindu finds that it is necessary to believe in a God to reach salvation, that may be quite acceptable. The danger of such a devotional tactic (i.e., of believing in a supernatural god who gives grace) is that it may become a hindrance to one's own sense of moral responsibility and one's own efforts toward release. But if the theistic beliefs taught by these scriptures do not get in the way, then there is no objection. Indeed Mahāyāna Buddhism itself employs just such "spiritual devices" as aids to release.

The kind of theism that the *Tripiṭaka* flatly opposes is typified by the views of Makkhali Gosāla, who believed that God had predestined salvation for all. Gosāla's view was that everything had been preplanned and takes place according to the will of God. Such fatalistic and deterministic theism was repulsive to the Buddha because it denied free will and moral responsibility and militated against human effort. In the *Tripiṭaka* two arguments offered against this kind of theism are (1) if God designs the life of the entire world—the glory and the misery, the good and the evil acts—then man is but an instrument of his will and God is responsible (*Jātaka* 5.238); (2) some evils are inexplicable if the truth of such a theism is granted (e.g., if a good God is omnipotent why does that God create injustice?) (*Jātaka* 6.208).[75] Both arguments attack the moral irresponsibility that a theism such as Gosāla's produces. But in his conversations with Hindu Brahmins, Buddha also made it clear that so long as theism allowed for individual freedom and moral responsibility and produced compassionate behavior, then, on pragmatic grounds, belief in God is not to be discouraged.[76]

A contemporary example of such an open approach to religions, including theistic religions, is found in the Theravāda Bhikku, Buddhadāsa of Bangkok.

Stressing nonattachment and compassionate action, he declares that to the extent these are found in all religions, all religions are the same.[77] If belief in God in other religions achieves such ends, then God as world savior may be judged as equivalent to Dharma as world savior—but he does urge that God be understood in impersonal terms. In a comparative analysis of Christian and Buddhist teachings regarding sin, death, and nonattachment, he finds little significant difference between the two.[78] It seems clear that for early Buddhism and for contemporary Theravāda thinkers like Buddhadāsa, religion, including theistic belief, is to be judged according to its instrumental value for the realization of truth and the compassionate life.

7

SCRIPTURE AND THE FUTURE OF RELIGIONS

> Early man had a true, if at the same time confused, sense of the mystery, power, and holiness of the word. . . . Today the oral word, the original word, is still with us, as it will be for good. But to know it for what it is, we must deliberately reflect on it. The spoken word, center of human life, is overgrown with its own excrescences—script, print, electronic verbalism—valuable in themselves but, as is generally the case with human accomplishments, not unmixed blessings. One of the reasons for reflection on the spoken word, the word as sound, is of course not to reject the later media but to understand them, too, better.[1]

Ong's suggestion that the original spoken word has become "overgrown with its own excrescences" is indeed a provocative observation that connects with points made by great thinkers down through the ages. Plato in the *Phaedrus* recounts Socrates' discussion of the implications of shifting from the spoken to the written word.[2] Socrates argues that contrary to expectations, writing does not improve one's memory and wisdom but in fact accomplishes the reverse: memory will suffer because people will begin to rely on writing; writing will not impart wisdom to the mind but, rather, will serve only as reminder; by learning things through writing people seem to know much, while for the most part they know nothing; using writing is not real teaching, for the students become filled, not with wisdom, but with the conceit of wisdom, and as such they will be a burden to their fellows.[3] Socrates also objects to writing because of the way it objectifies wisdom, and the negative possibilities that open up: "Once a thing is put in writing, the composition . . . drifts all over the place, getting into the hands not only of those who understand it, but equally of those who have no business with it. And when it is ill-treated and unfairly abused, it always needs its parent to come to its help, being unable to defend or help itself."[4] Here Socrates certainly reflects the experience of all of the religions studied, namely, that the oral word is not only the parent of the written, but must constantly be pressed into service to interpret and defend the written scripture. Thus the necessity of studying written texts within the *guru-śiṣya*, or oral teacher-disciple, relationship in Hinduism, Buddhism, rabbinic Judaism, Islam, and perhaps in the first few decades of Christianity.

In his Seventh Letter, Plato says that the most sacred and serious things are not to be put in writing. Rather, they are to be entrusted to the rhetoric or oratorical skills of one who is a true lover of wisdom. The *Phaedrus* makes clear that the art of the spoken word can be used for either good or evil, but not left objectively neutral. While the evil orator uses words for selfish and base ends, the good orator uses the forces of the spoken word to evoke truth. In his recent novel *The Portage to San Cristóbal of A.H.*, George Steiner highlights this dual potentiality of language. As one of the novel's characters remarks, "When he made the Word, God made possible also its contrary." Steiner adds, "My whole work is devoted to language, to the central fact that we can use words to pray, to bless, to heal, to kill, to cripple, to torture. Man creates—and he uncreates—by language."[5] Either the oral or the written word can be made to serve demonic ends. Thus the requirement of Socrates that the most sacred things are to be entrusted to an orator who is a true lover of wisdom, and not put into writing. Presumably, written words may fall into the hands of someone who does not love wisdom and used for selfish or evil ends. Paul sees himself to be waging battle against evil rhetoricians in his second letter to the Corinthians. Paul's battle-cry to the members of the congregation is striking: " . . . show that you are a letter from Christ delivered by us, written not with ink, but with the Spirit of the living God, not on tablets of stone, but on tablets of the human heart" (2 Corinthians 3:3). What Paul seems to be emphasizing is that the oral character essential to the word is found in an event of personal relationship—"written . . . with the Spirit of the living God . . . on tablets of thc human heart." It is in the interacting power of the Spirit between human hearts that the "goodness" of the word seems most present. And it is this interactive power of the word that seems most in danger when the word is left as an "ownerless writing." Paul's words provide an apt example. They are the words of a letter, but words that are not left ownerless. Paul entrusts them to his emissary who delivers them in the spiritual context of the Corinthian congregation.

Another way in which the original holy and powerful word can be "overgrown with its own excrescences" is by allowing language—either oral or written—to develop into a closed system or ideology. The modern structuralist and poststructuralist thinkers have shown how language can be an alien system weighing upon human consciousness. Feminists turn away from traditional hierarchical approaches as typical of the masculine use of language and seek instead to construct a genuinely feminine linguistic practice. Nāgārjuna, a second-century C.E. Buddhist monk in India, was fully aware of this imprisoning quality of language. Nāgārjuna taught that words ensnare us when we make them into a philosophical or theological system and then become ego-attached to that system.[6] Rather than experiencing reality, we construct our own philosophy, theology, or way of describing reality as absolute and these word-systems then become obstacles to a clear experience of what is true. This is why Buddhism does not accept any scripture as divine revelation, and in most cases stresses meditation on *sūnya*, or emptiness, rather than meditation upon words. Words, then, even oral or written scriptural words, can become Nietzsche's "prison-house of language."[7]

Yet the claim of scripture, even Buddhist scripture when held provisionally, is that it reveals truth. Rather than a "prison-house" the scriptural word has the power to realize release from ignorance (the *mokṣa* of Hinduism, the *Nirvāṇa* of Buddhism) or to bring one into a saving experience of God's living word (Judaism, Christianity, and Islam). In attempting to see how scripture does or does not make good on this claim, we shall look first at the spiritual power of oral and written scripture, and shall then examine the future of scripture in our educational and devotional experience. Throughout this chapter we shall attempt to draw our discussion from the data provided by our previous study of the way scripture functions in each of the world religions.

ORAL AND WRITTEN SCRIPTURE

Contrary to the modern tendency to think of "scripture" in terms of a printed book, we have seen that in all of the world religions the oral experience of scripture is at least as strong, and in some instances stronger, than the written. To arrive at a correct understanding of how scripture functions in religious experience requires that the narrow identification of scripture with the written book be broken. This is crucial for us both as scholars of religions and as religious practitioners. In either capacity our understanding of scripture will be severely crippled if we do not enlarge our modern awareness until a recovery of sensitivity to the oral/aural word is accomplished. Only then will our experience and understanding of the written word be complete. Our study of how scripture functions in each religion has identified common themes: (1) the primacy of the oral; (2) the need for the written; and (3) the spiritual power of oral and written scripture. Let us examine each of these points in detail.

The Primacy of the Oral

In the modern West when we think of scripture, it is the notion of written sacred books that comes to mind. For modern Christians and for some Jews, it is frequently the written Bible that evokes awe, rather than the power of a memorized and recited scriptural word that is "lived with" orally in liturgical practice as well as in everyday life. This dominance of the written text for modern Westerners is partly a result of the impact of modern, print-dominated culture on religious experience. But it is quite out of line with the traditional experience of scripture as found in the five world religions. In each religion the scripture began orally and to varying degrees has remained a basically oral phenomenon.

The primacy of the oral is perhaps clearest in Hinduism. There the revealed word is spoken by the *ṛṣis*, heard by the people, and passed on by word of mouth through traditions of highly trained teachers and students right up to the present day. The written is introduced as an aid to those too dull to remember the texts, and the written is always corrected by the oral. In Islam, too, the word is fundamentally oral. God speaks the revelation through the angel Gabriel, and Muhammad is instructed to listen and recite what has been conveyed to him word for word. His followers hear, remember, and recite for others, and so the revealed words are transmitted orally from one generation to the next. The written text is maintained as a safeguard against the loss of the oral, and the oral Qur'an judges the written. Indian Buddhism shared with Hinduism an emphasis upon the oral as more basic than the written. From the time of Buddha (c.a. 500 B.C.E.) until the first century B.C.E. the Tripiṭaka or Buddhist scripture, was handed down orally. Even then it was put into written form only as a safeguard against possible loss. The Buddhist monastic community continued to learn and debate the scripture orally.

In Judaism and Christianity the situation is less clear-cut. However, if we rely on the words of the texts themselves, there appears to be a stronger emphasis upon the oral. Although both religions begin with a basic written text, the Hebrew Bible, or Old Testament, its first presentation is often described as being oral. At Mount Sinai, for example, the Lord speaks to his people using Moses as a mediator (Exodus 19–20). Moses is called to the top of the mountain where the covenant agreement and the Ten Commandments are given by the Lord speaking with Moses. Only after God has uttered them does he write the commandments on tablets of stone (Deuteronomy 5:22). In the other major section of the Hebrew Bible, the prophets, the revelation also usually comes first in the form of the Lord speaking to the prophets who in turn speak God's word to the people (Ezekiel is perhaps an exception). Only later is the prophecy written down and collected into book form. Critical scholars, while allowing for an increasing emphasis upon the oral, point out that the oral narration of the Lord's voice is presented in written form. What we encounter are two different attitudes: one sees written scripture as more sacred than the oral; the other sees written scripture as an echo of the sacred oral word. But even in its written form the Hebrew Bible functions orally. It is read aloud in the synagogue and chanted in daily prayers like the shema. And for rabbinic Judaism the written Bible is only one-half of the Torah. The other half, the oral Torah, is held by tradition to have also been given by God to Moses at Sinai, and then to have been passed down by word of mouth through the prophets to the rabbis. The rabbis then systematized this oral Torah into the Mishnah, which functions to interpret the written Torah, the Hebrew Bible. For rabbinic Judaism the oral experience of the Torah is primary.[8]

Jesus and his followers adopted the oral approach of the rabbis in their use of the Hebrew Bible. But of greater importance is the fact that Jesus did not write down his teachings but gave them in the oral forms of stories, parables, and wise sayings. Jesus' teachings and his actions were not written down by his disciples, but were passed on orally. Even when the teachings and acts of Jesus were collected and written down as Gospels, these written Gospels were not intended for silent reading but for oral performance before a congregation. Even the letters of Paul, although initially written, were delivered in public narration before the congregations by a skilled orator. The early Christians understood such orated letters to be vehicles through which the Holy Spirit was speaking rather than the compositions of individual human authors.

This stress on the primacy of the oral experience of scripture in Christianity continued even after the New Testament became a written document. The inspiration of the Holy Spirit, which Judaism judged may have been closed off after the last of the Old Testament prophets at the time of Ezra, Christians saw to have been reopened in Jesus and to be continually available to each generation through the preaching of his gospel. Thus for Luther and the Protestant Reformers, it was the spoken or preached word of scripture that manifested Christ's living Spirit. Similarly in Judaism, the functioning of the oral Torah through the teachings of the rabbis enabled the "closed-off" inspiration of the law and the prophets to be brought to life and made relevant to each new generation.

In addition to the oral scripture being experienced as prior to and more fundamental than the written, the spoken word is understood as having creative power. In Genesis it is through speaking that God creates the heavens and the earth and all that is therein. In the New Testament, Jesus himself is identified with the divine *logos* which is God in action creating and redeeming: "In the beginning was the Word, and the Word was with God, and the Word was God . . . all things were made through him, and without him was not anything made that was made" (John 1:1–3).

Islam sees all scriptures as having been created by a single "Mother Book" in heaven. (Qur'an, *Sūra* 43:14; 13:39). The fact that the various earthly scriptures, which originated from the same Mother Book conflict with each other is due to the corrupting activities of the various religions in their transmission of the divine words. Only Islam has kept the revelation pure in the form of the oral Qur'an.

Perhaps more than any other religion, Hinduism develops the doctrine of the spoken word as being the creative and sustaining source of the universe and of individual spirituality. In the Vedas, speech (*Vāk*) is described as the creative power of gods and people (*Ṛg Veda* X:125). As was the case in the Gospel of John, the Vedas directly identify speech with the Divine. Even in the *Āraṇyakas* and *Upaniṣads* there is a continued equating of speech and Brahman (e.g., *Bṛhadāranyaka Upaniṣad* 4:1:2). The first progeny of the Divine Word (*Daivī Vāk*), of Spirit descending and embodying itself in phenomena, are the words of scripture uttered by the great *ṛṣis* or prophets of Hinduism. The *ṛṣi*, having purged off his ignorance through yogic meditation, directly sees the Divine Word in its full reality and speaks it forth as scripture. This suprahuman origin is judged to give the *ṛṣis*'s words a healing power and to make them into a deed of salvation. It is this understanding of the creative power of spoken scriptural words (*mantras*) that lies behind the Hindu practice of *mantra* chanting. Such chanting is seen as having the power to remove ignorance (*avidyā*), reveal truth (*dharma*), and realize release (*mokṣa*) (*Vākyapadīya* 1:5). It is this understanding of spoken scriptural words (*mantras*) as being inherently powerful and creative that is so difficult for the modern mind to comprehend.

For many Hindus the creative power of *Vāk* (speech) is not limited to its first-born scripture (the Veda), but indeed extends to all use of language. Bhartṝhari, in his *Vākyapadīya*, declares that Brahman creates all objects of the world and that it is through his divine essence, the word (*śabda*), that all objects are known (*Vākyapadīya* 1:1). Thus we may conclude that for many Hindus the word, in its naming and determinative function, is co-creator with God (*Śabdabrahman*).

The creative effort of the poet *ṛṣi*, the "seer" of the word, however, is not to manufacture something new out of imagination but to relate ordinary things to their forgotten eternal truth.[9] And the activity of the literary critic in the technical analysis of the use of language is seen by the Indian as intellectual "brush-clearing" activity, which opens the way for a rediscovery of eternal truth in relation to everyday objects and events. Because of the power inherent in words for both human inference and divine truth, great care must be taken to ensure correct usage. This is the special role of the grammarian and philosopher of language in the Hindu tradition —and this role is virtually completely focused on the oral use of language. Panini's great Sanskrit grammar, the *Aṣṭadhyāyī,* for example, is based on phonetics and is taught orally even today.[10]

In Vedic practice careful attention is given to the correct speaking of the scripture verses. If the eternal meaning is to be revealed, distortions of oral delivery or corruptions of content must be avoided. Since the Vedic verse or *mantra* is seen as the sonic reverberation of divine power, it is hardly surprising that the quality control of its components cannot be left to the caprices of the individual reciter.[11] In the Hindu approach the art of rhetoric is to be taken with utmost seriousness for, as a manifestation of divine power, it can evoke either evil or good. In Indian aesthetics all of this concern for correct speaking is applied equally to performers of poetry, drama, or fiction.[12] They, too, are either removing ignorance and thus forwarding the Divine Good, or else, by the misuse of the spoken word, are keeping people in ignorance and fostering evil. From Bhartṛhari's Hindu perspective the spoken word must be controlled and kept pure so that its creative powers will not be wasted or misused.[13] Proper grammatical usage, correct pronunciation and use of gesture, and so forth, are crucial not only for the success of the ritual use of Vedic words, but also for the other branches of knowledge.

In Buddhism the creative power of the word is most often seen as working in a negative direction, of obscuring the direct experience of truth (*dharma*). Thus Buddha counsels his followers not to accept on blind faith any words claiming to be scripture or the words of any teacher who claims them to be revelation. All words, oral and written, including even the Buddha's own words, are to be tested out in the personal experience of each individual. Only then, if they prove to lead to the direct experience of truth are such words to be accepted as useful instruments. We note, however, that even when found to be useful, such words, like the boat used to cross the river, should be discarded and left behind. To become attached to even the good words of scripture, would, in the end, prevent them from evoking the direct experience of *dharma*, the goal to be achieved. Perhaps Zen Buddhism provides the paradigm case of the Buddhist worry that words end up being obstacles rather than creative resources. In one form of Zen, Soto, only silent meditation (*Zazen*) is allowed with no word use. The other form of Zen, Rinzai, does make use of words, but only in a negative way.[14] *Kōan* practice (such as meditation upon "What is the sound of one hand clapping?") is prescribed for the purpose of convincing one, once and for all, that the use of words to reach truth or reality (*dharma*) is a futile and mind-breaking exercise that must be given up. Only then, when all word use is released, is the mind capable of the direct intuition of *dharma*, or truth. The Zen rejection of all word use (oral and written) is the logical extrapolation of Nāgārjuna's philosophic critique of words when they are used to create philosophical or theological systems that claim to define reality. However, as we shall see later, some forms of Buddhism do make positive use of words in their meditation practice. Indeed, for *Jodo Shinshu*, or Pure Land Buddhism, one sincere chanting of the scriptural *nembutsu* is sufficient for the realization of *Nirvāṇa*. As was the case for Hindus, when Pure Land Buddhists do experience their scripture as a positive aid, it is the spoken word that is the locus of creative power.

The oral word of scripture is also usually experienced as eternal. The *dharma*, or teaching, of Gautama the Buddha was not invented by him, but, according to some Buddhist traditions was learned in a previous birth from another teacher or enlightened one, who in turn had learned it from his teacher, and so on backward in an infinite regress.[15] The *dharma* thus being passed down has always existed, and in each age an enlightened one, a Buddha, would make known the *dharma* teachings to the world. Until it is manifested in spoken teaching, the *dharma* is the eternal void or fullness (*sunya*), and for the teaching words to be effective they must eventually return to *sunya* in the experience of the hearer. For the Hindu the scriptural word that is spoken by the *ṛṣi* at the beginning of each cycle of creation is a verbalization of the eternal Divine Word that has existed beginninglessly. Some Hindus take the eternal word itself as the source of all scripture. For others, God (*Brahman*) and the word co-exist eternally and together are the source of the Vedas. In Judaism the word is thought of as being beginninglessly present in Heaven and as providing the divine blueprint from which God created the world. Torah is the eternal word of God dictated or revealed to Moses at Sinai. Johannine Christianity, like Hinduism, sees the word as divinely co-existing with God: "In the beginning was the Word, and the Word was with God, and the Word was God" (John 1:1). In Islam, as we have already seen, the "Mother Book" exists eternally with God in Heaven and is thus the source from which comes all created scriptures. In all religions, then, there is some notion of an eternal and uncreated *logos* (void or *sūnya* in the Buddhist case) of which the earthly scriptures may be taken as manifestations.

Not only is Scripture seen to be primarily oral, eternal and creative, but its exegesis is also often presented as being necessarily oral in nature. Before the modern period, all religions, including Buddhism, existed in dominantly oral cultures and passed on the primary oral scripture through living chains of teachers and students. Validity checks were built-in to this system of oral teaching. It was in the oral context of the teacher-student relationship that exegesis of the scripture took place. The student first memorized the scripture itself, by repeating it after the teacher, and was then introduced to oral commentary on the rehearsed verses. Various interpretations could be examined in this oral context. Its special dynamic was that it allowed the student to raise questions out of life experience and allowed the teacher to interpret the scripture so as to meet the specific questions of the individual student. In this way the exegesis assumed the living quality of a dialogue between the oral word itself and the existential situation of the student, with the teacher as mediator. Following this approach the scripture had the opportunity to remain dynamic, relevant, and immediate to changing times and was experienced as giving wisdom.

In addition to the individual teacher-student exegesis, some traditions such as Judaism and Christianity stressed exegesis of the word in preaching before a congregation. Synagogue practice followed the oral reading of scripture with a closing of the scroll and then a spontaneous oral interpretation of the meaning of the passage. Jesus, himself, followed this pattern when he read in the synagogue (Luke 4:16–30). The early Christians adopted the same practice, and it continues to this day in the sermons preached during services of worship. A key principle here is the Christian belief that it is predominantly through oral preaching rather than written interpretation that the living presence of the Holy Spirit functions. It is the preached gospel, say Christians, that transforms hearts and creates congregational fellowship. This belief follows directly from Paul's admonition to the Corinthians that they are to be living letters "written not with ink, but with the Spirit of the living God" (2 Corinthians 3:3). As Philo reported, spontaneous exegesis was the norm in early worship.[16] Luther, for all his concern to have a printed German Bible in the hands of every peasant, still maintained that to be alive, the word had to be proclaimed. As Luther put it, Christ did not write but only spoke. He called his teaching "gospel," which means good news or proclamation. "That is why it must not be described with the pen but with the mouth."[17]

In addition to synagogue preaching, Judaism has the strong tradition of the oral Torah, which is basically exegetical in nature. As systematized in the Mishnah, the oral Torah consists of questions and answers dealing with specific topics often arising from an interpretation of the written Torah. The Talmud, even though written, still continues to be studied orally, that is, memorized and then discussed, in traditional Jewish yeshivas or seminaries. One Jewish scholar, Jacob Neusner, even goes so far as to find that the internal oral pattern of the Mishnah itself is the embodiment of divine wisdom. The mnemonic patterns of the Mishnah, argues Neusner, express a mode of thought attuned to abstract relationships rather than concrete and substantive forms.

> The formulaic, not the formal, character of Mishnaic rhetoric yields a picture of a subculture which speaks of immaterial and not material things. In this subculture the relationship, rather than the thing or person which is related, is primary and constitutes the principles of reality.[18]

The Mishnah teaches that relationship is all-important implicitly, through the structures of consciousness created by the very pattern of the oral mnemonic forms employed. The oral patterns of the Mishnah, suggest Neusner, actualize what Chomsky would call inherent deep structures of the mind,[19] in such a way that mnemonic discipline of the Mishnah superimposes its own deeper level of meaning upon everything that is said.[20] Thus the oral patterns and contents of the Mishnah exegete the deeper meaning by engaging the deep structures of consciousness already present. While agreeing with Chomsky's suggestion that our minds contain innate deep structures of language, what Neusner maintains is that when the memorized form of the oral scripture is added to the inherent deep structure of the mind, a metaphysical meaning results.

The above Jewish perspective is very similar to the Hindu Sphoṭa theory of Bhartṛhari according to which the "seed-form" of word meaning is divinely given in the very nature of consciousness itself. The hearing, memorizing, and repeating of the externally presented words of scripture enable that seed-meaning within to "blossom" into a full-blown "ah-ha!" experience of insight—a direct intuition of the nature of reality. The Sanskrit word *sphoṭa* actually means a bursting forth or disclosure—an idea which bursts out or flashes on the mind when a sound is heard.[21] Because it is the divine meaning that is already inherently present in our consciousness, the scriptural word has the greatest power to assist in its realization. Words of poetry and fiction, if well formulated by the author out of the author's own clear experience, can also powerfully realize or make present a similar experience in the consciousness of the hearer. For example consider the way Shakespeare's Sonnet 116, on love, is able to bring forth the fullness of that idea in the experience of the listener. The reader of the written sonnet can also have the same experience by hearing the printed words in one's mind as if they were spoken. Bhartṛhari's presupposition is that the idea of love, for example, is inherently present in the consciousness of the hearer and what the successful poem (play, parable, or story) does is to call it forth in a flash of insight. However, the scriptural traditions maintain that when it comes to metaphysical truth, the special words of scripture accomplish this "making present" of insight in a way that other words cannot. As to how far nonscriptural words of poetry and story can take us in the direction of spiritual experience, there is great debate. Some Indian schools of literary criticism, for example, maintain that poetic and dramatic words can bring forth within us not only experiences of the more ordinary human emotions but also the ultimate experience of spiritual serenity (*śānta rasa*).

Augustine's analysis of how scriptural words functioned in his own personal conversion is relevant here. It is offered in books VIII–X of *The Confessions*, framed in terms of an interplay between scripture and memory. The memory of God within, an active memory which elsewhere Augustine identifies with the Holy Spirit,[22] continually pricks at Augustine from within. Added to this innate memory of God are memories from childhood of the chanting of prayers and scriptures with his mother and in church. Such early memories engrave themselves deeply upon one's childhood consciousness and, like the poem learned by heart in grade 4 or 5, remain with one for life always capable of bubbling up with meaning and power from the subconscious. We are also told that during this period Augustine is immersing himself in scripture—especially the Apostle Paul's writings. The demand for personal decision coming from both within and without so provokes Augustine that he rushes in upon his friend Alypius and cries out:

> What is wrong with us? What does this mean, this story you heard? Unlearned men are raising up and storming heaven, while we with our teachings which have no heart in them, are tumbling about in flesh and blood. Is it because they have led the way that we are ashamed to follow . . . ?[23]

In an agitated state they go out into the garden and Augustine bursts into tears over the internal conflict going on within himself. He urges himself to make a decision feeling the two parts of himself to be locked in conflict.[24] He hears a voice chanting over and over, "Take it, read it!" He stops his tears, takes up the scriptures, opens them and reads the first passage that he finds, "Not in revelry and drunkenness, not in debauchery and wantonness, not in strife and jealousy; but put on the Lord Jesus Christ . . . immediately . . . all the darknesses of doubt were dispersed, as if by a light of peace flooding into my heart."[25]

Two things seem to have come together in this moment to have caused the conversion experience of Augustine: memory and scripture. The memory of God within, that had been gaining power, and the words of scripture from without. How these two could come together so powerfully is given psychological explanation by Augustine as follows. First there is Augustine's presupposition that the mind, even though it has become impaired and disfigured by loss of participation in God, still retains an image of God in memory.[26] Thus, says Augustine, "I should but hide Thee from myself, not myself from Thee."[27] The problem is how to bring that *a priori* image of God in memory into conscious awareness—how is God to be remembered? Augustine's answer is deceptively simple and one that we can all verify from our own experience. The way we "remember God" is just like the kind of exercise we all go through when we are trying to recall someone's name which we say is "on the tip of our tongue." We ask that various names be presented to us aloud, "John," "George," "Jim," etc., for, we say, when the right name is said we will recognize it immediately as the name for which we are searching. This presumes, of course, that we already have the person's name present in our subconscious. As Plato points out in *Meno*, we cannot look for anything absolutely new for how would we recognize it when we found it unless it were already present in memory.[28] The image of God, said Augustine, is already present in our memory. Augustine's search for the name of God, prompted by its *a priori* presence in memory, had led him to try the names embodied in the teachings of Cicero, Mani, and Plotinus but without success. No transforming flash of recognition had occurred. Only when, at the right moment, the New Testament is opened and the name of the Lord Jesus Christ is spoken does it "click" or "fit" with his inner subconscious memory of God and his conversion takes place. The "outer" expression of God's word in scripture powerfully joins with the "inner" expression of God in memory and the perfect fit triggers a transformation of Augustine's consciousness. It is the joining together of scripture with memory that makes Augustine's conversion possible. Scripture alone without the image of God in memory would not result in recognition or verification. And the innate name of God in memory, without the revealing word of scripture, would have no way of being made present to conscious experience. We would be left unable to discover the name "on the tip of our tongue" because no one would be in possession of the name of Jesus Christ to present to us and so trigger recognition, remembrance and revelation. In *De Trinitate* Augustine identifies the will as having the function of bringing together name and memory so that recognition occurs.[29] The other side of the coin to the discovery or remembrance of God is the discovery of oneself as being in relation to God.

This explanation, however, presents us with a problem. Why was there no remembrance of God when the scriptures were previously experienced by Augustine as an adolescent? The answer is given in *De Trinitate*, Book XI. It is the function of the will to bring together and unite sense perceptions with the corresponding likenesses to be found in memory.[30] Indeed, this is exactly what happened in Augustine's conversion. The sense perception of the words of scripture were united with the memory of God. The will played an active role in this uniting process in that it was actively seeking a resolution to the conflict in which Augustine was embroiled. Why did this not happen earlier when after reading *Hortensius* and being disappointed in not finding the name of Christ there, Augustine actively turned back to the scriptures? The answer is found in the *Confessions*. Augustine reports that in matters of style he found the scriptures unable to measure up to the standards of Cicero[31] and so he turned away from the scriptures. At this point in his life Augustine is more interested in matters of style than decisions of the heart. Thus his will is directed to other things and consequently remembrance of God does not occur.

A psychological analysis of such a situation is offered in *De Trinitate* where

Augustine points out that as well as uniting sense perceptions with memory the will also has the power to divide and separate them.

> The will turns away the memory from the sense when it is intent on something else, and does not allow things that are present to cling to it. This can easily be established; for, when someone is speaking to us and we are thinking of something else, it often appears as if we had not heard him. But this is not true; we did hear, but we did not remember, because the speaker's words slipped immediately away from the perception of our ears, being diverted elsewhere by a command of the will which is wont to fix them in memory. And therefore, when something of the kind occurs, it would be more correct to say, "We did not remember," rather than "We did not hear."[32]

Augustine did not remember God in his adolescence because the attention of his will was not centered on memory but was directed elsewhere. Rather than attending to the voice of God in the scripture and its corresponding resonance in memory, Augustine's will was directed to a comparison of the literary style of the scriptures with the style of Cicero's *Hortensious*. Consequently no remembrance or conversion took place.

It might be remarked in passing that this is exactly what seems to take place in much contemporary study of scripture. Attention is focused on an intellectual analysis of the literary structure of scripture and this results in the will separating the hearing of God's word from the memory of God within. No remembrance takes place, no transforming power is experienced. The problem is not with scripture, for it still contains the name of Christ, nor with memory, for the memory of God is still innate within us. The problem with us, as it was with the adolescent Augustine, is that our wills are directed elsewhere to matters of analysis rather than direct sensing, and so obstruct the uniting of scripture with memory. And memory is more typically embedded in the oral rather than the written experience of the word.

Oral exegesis also enables the oral scripture to retain its relevancy to changing times and circumstances. The oral form of the parable that was used by Buddha, Jesus, and the rabbis is an especially good example of how oral scripture blends into exegesis that changes with changing times and places. The metaphorical structure of the parables suggests but withholds meaning. This open-endedness makes parables particularly dependent on the oral context. The parable, when told, engages the hearer to complete the process begun by the story. This may not happen as effectively when the parable is frozen in a written text and read in the abstract. Even in a modern literate culture, a living context of speakers and hearers that allows for the functioning of gesture, facial contact, and a shared environment are crucial aids in helping the parable to convey its meaning without explicitly saying it—and in this transcending of what is literally said resides its spiritual power. With changing times and circumstances, the parable remains new and relevant when it is told or preached in this oral way. As such the parable may be described as an open-ended speech act which lacks both an original form and an original meaning. Each new oral context provides the opportunity for a fresh experience of the revelation to which the parable points. As long as the oral context is maintained, the parable never loses its ability to grasp and change the psyches of its hearers in new and unexpected ways. But when a parable is written down and removed from the oral setting, its power and freshness vanish.[33]

A somewhat parallel notion of the open-ended nature of the primary oral revelation is found in the Shi'ite Muslim notion of *ta'wil.* According to this view the oral text of the Qur'an has two meanings: the outer, or *tanzil,* which does not change, is open to everyone who knows Arabic; and *ta'wil*, or the inner meaning made available through the succession of *imāms* whose inspired interpretations of the Qur'an keep it relevant to current situations.[34] Shi'ites believe that through the mediation of the *imāms* Muhammad's revelation remains dynamic and relevant to every new situation. The Sufis, another branch of Islam, also use the idea of inner meaning in their interpretation of the Qur'an. The Sufi method of exegesis is both oral and mystical in nature. While listening to the oral recital of the Qur'an, the Sufi master becomes inspired by the hearing of a certain keynote phrase or word and breaks into ecstatic utterance, which is copied down by a disciple.[35] The Sufi approach seems to have been influenced by the Hindu idea of being sensitive to the vibrating energies contained in the speaking of the divine word. This is exemplified in the *kathā* or oral exegesis of the Hindu *Rāmāyaṇa* by a *vyāsa* or professional expounder. Members of the audience join the *vyāsa* in chanting a verse of the scripture. Then the *vyāsa* offers a spontaneous, inspired exposition of the verse speaking softly and slowly at first but then with his voice gaining in strength and speed as he proceeds. A typical exposition lasts for an hour and ends with the audience joining in the rechanting of the verse on which the exposition was based.[36] Rather than logical argument, the creation of a devotional mood is the aim. For his exegesis to be effective, the *vyāsa* depends on the fact that all of his listeners know the text by heart. Such oral exposition of the canonical scriptures keeps them alive and relevant for each generation through engagement with their daily lives.

The Need for the Written

Although the world religions begin with oral scripture as primary, all at some point experience the need for a written text. But even then the written text dominantly functions as a script for oral performance. Paul's letters and the New Testament book of Revelation were written to be read aloud before the congregation. The Torah was written to be read aloud, as was the Mishnah. The special merit of the King James Version of the Bible is that it was written with an "ear" to how it would sound when read aloud in public worship. It is only in modern times that translators of scripture have focused on philological or analytical meaning and existential relevancy at the expense of the oral power of the text when used in liturgy.

Perhaps the most frequent explanation given as to why the oral text becomes written is the fear of loss of the oral. Often the writing down of the oral occurs when the religious culture itself is felt to be threatened. A Sinhalese chronicle from the first century B.C.E. records that the Buddhist scriptures and commentaries that had been handed down orally for four hundred years were recorded in written Pali because people were falling away from the orthodox teaching and there was fear that it would be lost.[37] Similarly in Islam it was the death of Muhammad along with the death in battle a few months later of a large number of persons who knew the Qur'an by heart that led to the worry that portions of the scripture might ultimately be lost. In response to this concern Caliph Abū Bakr gathered together all the written fragments of the Qur'an and compiled an authoritative written text. The acceptance of a standard written text was also used as a way of controlling disputes that arose during the expansion of Islam over which community had the true text or reading of Muhammad. In Christianity, too, the formation of the canon of the Bible was prompted by challenges from Gnosticism. Although the oral materials of the teachings and acts of Jesus had been written down in the form of Gospels between 70 and 100 C.E. following the deaths of some of the original apostles, these written Gospels, along with the letters of Paul and others were circulated and read freely in the early Christian congregations in addition to the Hebrew Bible. But in the middle of the second century C.E., Marcion, due to his Gnostic attitudes, taught that the Hebrew Bible was inferior and proceeded to create a new Christian scripture composed of the Gospel of Luke and the letters of Paul. His action and popularity forced the other Christian churches to develop their own canon of Christian scripture.[38] The same concerns to safeguard the revelation and to control potential heresies may also have prompted the first appearance of the scroll found by Hilkiah, the high priest, in the Temple during the reign of King Josiah in 621 B.C.E. (2 Kings 22). Worry over dissipation of the tradition seems to have motivated Ezra's bringing of the written "book of the law of Moses" from Babylon in 458 B.C.E. to use as a basis for renewing the weak and scattered Jewish community in Jerusalem (Ezra 7:6–10, 14). The final canonization of the written Hebrew text may well have been spurred on by the destruction of the Temple in Jerusalem (70 C.E.) and its cultic ritual as the center point of Judaism.

While fear of loss or the challenge of heresy may have been a strong impetus in the writing down of the Hebrew and Christian scriptures, Kelber has recently suggested that there were other reasons for adopting the written form. In the case of Jesus, for example, the oral tradition by its very nature did not allow for a synoptic and complete presentation of Jesus' life. The author of the Gospel of Mark, argues Kelber, used the power of the written form to organize the scattered oral reports of healings, exorcisms, teaching stories, and parables into a unified whole with its own particular perspective or theological thrust.[39] Other authors of the Gospels of Matthew, Luke, and John made different selections from the same source collection or oral traditions in writing their synopses so as to present different theological perspectives. Kelber's point is that the written form of the Gospel made it possible to do things that the oral forms could not accomplish—the presentation of a unified life of Jesus from a specific theological perspective. Whether or not oral forms do lack the power to provide larger unifying frameworks is a suggestion that needs careful study in a comparative context. The Indian tradition, for example, seems to have had no difficulty in constructing oral synthetic overviews of a very high order including complex Sanskrit grammars (e.g., Panini's *Aṣṭādhyāyī*, still the object of doctoral dissertations in modern Linguistics Departments). The Indian evidence would seem to call into question Kelber's thesis that written forms are needed to handle more complex intellectual tasks of systematic organization, which the oral forms are not capable of sustaining.[40]

Hinduism seems to be the one religion that has experienced little need to establish standardized and authoritative written forms of its oral scriptures. Perhaps this is because the Hindu culture in India has not felt itself to be seriously threatened either by loss of its traditions or by challenges from heresies or other religions. Indeed it has been the arrival of modern scholars from the West, with their reliance upon the written text, that has initiated the process of establishing trustworthy critical editions of the Hindu scriptures. While such written texts may make possible the application of modern textual techniques of analysis to the Hindu scriptures, the religious and traditional use of these scriptures within Hinduism still remains strongly oral in nature.

Brown has recently pointed out that even though the Hindu *purāṇas* developed a tradition of written scripture, "So strong, indeed, that, despite a supplemental manuscript tradition existing perhaps since the early centuries of the Christian era, the written transmission history is scarcely noticed by the Purāṇas themselves, which give extended accounts of their oral transmission, often from some deity down to Vyāsa and to his disciples."[41] One account in the Hindu tradition of the writing down of a scripture appears in the *Mahābhārata* (1:1.53ab). The passage tells how Vyāsa, having composed the great epic, wonders how he might teach it to his disciples. The god Brahmā, the teacher of the world, approaches Vyāsa:

> After the appropriate ceremonies of greeting, Vyāsa complains to Brahmā that, despite the great honor the epic has received, no writer (*lekhaka*) for the work can be found on earth. Brahmā then recommends Gaṇeśa to be the scribe, who indeed soon fulfills the task of transcription.[42]

The story does suggest a motivation for writing down the epic—to make it available to all people regardless of caste or sex. Brown argues that the writing down of the *Purāṇas* effectively freed that class of the priestly class.[43] It democratized the texts and made the scripture widely available to all in a way perhaps parallel to Luther's translation of the Bible into German so as to take it away from the control of the priests and make it widely accessible to the German common people. But even though encompassing a written textual tradition, it is still the oral telling of the story that has remained primary, as can be seen in the *kathā* tradition. Now, however, the story can be read and told by anyone, not just a priest.

The continued strength of the oral within the Indian Sanskrit tradition may be due to its scholarly sophistication. Oral forms of technical grammars and dictionaries were developed very early along with a high-quality oral corpus of poetry, prose, and drama. Complex philosophical commentaries on the Vedas along with free philosophical speculations were composed orally and passed down through chains of teachers and students from the classical Hindu period 700–200 B.C.E. right up to the present day. Although writing was available very early in India and there were evidently large temple libraries—a few written Sanskrit texts are available which date back to 1000 B.C.E.—the rigors of the Indian climate (described in chapter 4, above) meant that few texts survived for long periods.

Today, as in the past, the well-trained Hindu scholar depends on memorized text learned early in life rather than upon books. Even if a written version of a text is used today, it will be studied not alone at one's desk, but with a teacher who will read it aloud and explain the text in dialogue. For Hinduism, it is still the oral tradition, with the *guru*-student context that gives real knowledge. At the popular level, it is through the folk singers, storytellers, and professional reciters that the majority of Hindus continue to experience their scriptures. For the modern well-off Hindu, espcially those living in diaspora in the modern West, audio and video cassettes of such oral performances of the favorite texts are increasingly being used as substitutes for the real thing.

The Spiritual Power of Oral and Written Scripture

In all religions studied, the scriptural word is seen as a means of reaching or realizing the transcendent. However, this spiritual power of the word is most often primarily located in the oral scriptural relationship rather than the written form of the text. It is the spoken sound in a relational context that effectively evokes the Divine. The written word, when read silently, may share in some of this power if the silent reading results in a relational mental hearing of the words being spoken. A reading of the words for intellectual analytical purposes, with little or no sense of oral reverberation in the mind, seems not to take one to the transcendent. Yet it is through union or communion with the transcendent that one's consciousness is transformed and the deepest religious experience realized.

Of the spoken words, some seem to have more evocative power than others. Poetic scripture is experienced as more powerful than prose scripture. In Hinduism, for example, the Vedic hymns, which take the form of poems spoken by the *ṛṣis*, or seers, are the primary scriptures. The later prose *Brahmanas* and *Upaniṣads* serve to exegete the fundamental insights contained in the Vedic poems. In ritual and devotional practice it is the poetic words of the Vedas that are chanted.[44] Of the secondary Hindu scripture, it is the epic poetry of the *Bhagavada Gītā* (sometimes the *Gītā* is also called primary) and the *Rāmāyana*, along with the poems of poet saints such as Manikkavacakar in the south and Kabir in the north, that are learned by heart in childhood and chanted devotionally throughout life. This oral performance of scriptural poetry can take the form of individual chanting as in morning and evening prayers, or group singing of the poems as hymns of *kathā*. Great emphasis is placed upon the correct use of accent, meter, and melody in the chanting, so that the spoken form will "match up with" or evoke the divine word of which it is an earthly resonance. It is because of this perceived resonance between the uttered sound and the transcendent, that Hindu practice prescribes the repeated chanting. A direct correspondence is seen as existing between the physical vibrations of the phenomenal chant and the noumenal vibrations of the transcendent. The more the physical vibrations of the uttered chant are repeated, the more transcendent power is evoked in experience until one's consciousness is purified and put into a harmonious relationship or even identity with the Divine. It is this principle that is behind the practice of the repeated chanting of *mantras* or scripture verses in both Hinduism and Buddhism. A technical description of this purification process is offered in *The Yoga Sutras of Patanjali*.[45] Special symbolic scriptural words, such as AUM, are judged to have particular power. They are said to be the "seed forms" or fundamental sounds out of which all others arise. Thus, chants such as AUM are taken as symbolically including within themselves, in potential form, all other scriptural sounds. The repetition of AUM, then, provides a "shorthand" technique of chanting all scripture in one syllable. The vibration produced by chanting AUM is seen to equate with the primal manifestation of *Daivi Vāk*, the divine word, in its descent from the noumenal into the phenomenal realm.

Some Buddhist schools share with Hinduism this notion of oral recitation of scripture as being a sanctifying and sacramental act.[46] The memorization of a text, although an important prerequisite, is not the most important aspect of oral practice. It is the different mode of perception involved in the oral performance of scripture that is crucial. By chanting or listening to the rhythmic words of a sacred text, the teaching and inspiration in the words is renewed and reinforced. In Tibetan Buddhism, for example, the chanting of the syllables OM MA NE PAD ME HUM accompanied by the performing of ritual gestures enables the monks to feel the evocation of overtones of the interdependence of the universe—a meaning that can be said symbolically in the chanted sounds and gestures, but not said explicitly. The evoking of the symbolic overtones was the more powerful by virtue of the fact that the monks chanted the Tantric syllables not in monotone but in chords—with each monk actually chanting a D-major chord, D-F#-A, simultaneously.[47] The felt experience of the resonance of the chanted chord within one's own voice box powerfully induces numinous sensations throughout one's whole being.

In Jodo Shinshu Buddhism also, ritual chanting is the major means of spiritual practice. Finding that rational study of Buddhist texts was not helpful, Shinran, the founder of Jodo Shinshu, taught his followers that one sincere chanting of the *nembutsu* ("Namu Amida Buddha") was instrumental in enabling one to respond in gratitude to the realization that one is already liberated or saved. Although the rational meaning of the chant may be "I surrender myself to Amida Buddha," it is through the power of the chant to evoke emotional, intuitive, and memory-laden processes that the existential experience of oneness with Amida Buddha is realized. Shinran urged his followers to chant the *nembutsu* aloud, rather than chanting the text quietly within if its full spiritual power was to be felt.

The Buddhist tradition, following Hindu practice, has always used oral chanting (both group and individual) as a device for embedding scripture in the budding consciousness of the young child. First the scripture is memorized by being repeated aloud after the teacher, and only after that is it studied analytically for its rational meaning. But discursive academic study is always of secondary importance, since knowledge of the transcendent can never be fully captured and communicated in words. Spiritual transformation takes place more through the continuous action of the memorized words, which have become a part of the very structure of consciousness, than through intellectual study. The poetic power of the words to point beyond themselves and resonate strongly with the transcendent is a major force in the religious tranformation of consciousness. In addition, the permanent presence of the memorized scripture within consciousness makes it constantly available for guidance, inspiration, and solace in the crisis moments of life.

Judaism also emphasizes the early learning of the scriptural words and then their ritual repetition throughout life. The *shema* is taught to the children at an early age and chanted by the whole family, morning and evening. Elementary schooling provided by the community to children was devoted largely to learning the sacred Hebrew language and to becoming capable of reading the written Torah in public. To do so virtually required that the text be known by heart, since in the synagogue the Torah is unpointed (i.e., lacking vowels and punctuation) and in the early texts the consonant letters were not even divided into words. Thus to read the text correctly prior knowledge of what the text was saying was required so that the letters could be divided into words and sentences and correctly voweled.[48] In addition to learning to read the written Torah in the Jewish elementary school, the students then went on to the advanced school where the oral Torah was taught. Even in the yeshivas or seminaries, study of the scripture traditionally proceeded by group chanting of the words in pairs so that they became deeply ingrained in one's consciousness. Once the basic memorization of both written and oral texts was completed, exegesis would be begun, but this too in the form of oral discourse between teacher and students.

A similar oral practice seems to have been followed by Jesus and his apostles, who grew up as Jews within functioning Jewish communities. Thus the early memorizing of the written Torah along with the oral traditions of the teachings and acts of Jesus was the norm for Christian practice for the first few decades. Even when the teachings of Jesus were written down in Gospels between 60 and

100 C.E., these Gospels were not primarily written to be read as books in individual study, as is usually done today, but as scripts for oral performance in worship.

Islam not only adopted the tradition of oral memorization and repeating of scripture, but if anything pursued the oral word with even greater rigor and intensity. Indeed, spiritual merit in Islam is said to be measured by the thoroughness of one's knowledge of the scripture. According to the tradition, on the day of resurrection everyone will be called upon to rise up and recite the Qur'an. For each verse that is correctly recited, the person rises up one station in heavenly merit. If the whole of the text can be recited, the devotee is said to be like a prophet, and to share in the rewards of everlasting life in paradise.[49] The memorization and later recitation of the Qur'an was what was required of Muhammad by God, and is likewise the expectation of every pious Muslim. The truth of the words is seen to be verified by the aesthetic beauty of the poetic form and sound of the musically chanted Arabic Qur'an—which, it is claimed, surpasses all other experiences of poetry, either secular or sacred. But to experience the beauty fully, it is essential that the listener already know the text—just as the full experience of a Bach fugue requires a complete familiarity of a kind that can be realized only from the repeated hearing and playing of the fugue by oneself. Just as such a performance of the fugue must be done without a musical score (so that there is nothing between the performer and the music, allowing a complete loss of oneself in the music, e.g., Glenn Gould playing Bach), so also the full experience of living life in scripture requires that the text be known by heart so that one can lose oneself in it.

Learning the scriptures by heart while one is young, and then repeatedly chanting them throughout the course of one's adult life, is a requirement built into all five of the major religions examined. It is a requirement that, when followed, gives to scriptural words the power of transforming lives. It is strange today that our pedagogy, within modern religion as well as within our school curricula, has moved in the opposite direction. While we agree with music teachers that our children need to learn their pieces by heart for full mastery of the music, yet, in the modern West, at least, we have given way to educational approaches that have given up the need for memorization and are content with the literary skills of being able to find the Bible in the library, use its table of contents, have some knowledge of its literary sources and the sociocultural background they reflect. Descriptive knowledge of the scripture rather than intimate acquaintance with the scripture has too often become the accepted standard for scriptural study.

In this modern context frequently more time is spent in reading about scripture than in the firsthand reading of scripture itself—let alone any expectation that the scripture should be memorized. As a result, for most moderns, scripture has ceased to be the guiding companion of life that resides in one's deepest layers of consciousness, influencing one even when one is not aware of its presence. Instead, scripture has become a literary object to be studied and analyzed along with the other literary texts that we possess. Not only is scripture lost to us as the grounding source of our individual thought and behavior, but no longer does it function as the baseline of our corporate or communal consciousness. We have recognized that it is important to train our children in the music of Bach, through hard hours of practice and often against their own wishes. As parents we have persisted with such training in the conviction that it is essential if our children are to participate in, enjoy, and value the music that we have received as a valued part of our culture. Yet as parents and teachers, we have given up the same requirements for the teaching of scripture to our children, even though down through the histories of our religious traditions, it is the deep immersion in scripture that has provided a foundational source of religious experience.

While the comments above apply most obviously to the modern Western Christian experience (especially Protestant), the same thing can be seen to be happening to the other religions as they encounter the challenge of having to live within the context of modernity. In Islamic Egypt, for example, Islamic teachers are alarmed at the decreasing memorization of the oral Qur'an by young children, and the falling off of good teachers and reciters. Similar worries have arisen in Hindu communities. Analysis of the experience in Hindu families that have emigrated to Canada suggests that the parents are ineffective in transmitting their oral experience of scripture to their children, and that even in the parents' own spiritual discipline shortcuts are sought to replace traditional morning and evening recitation of scripture. For many, instead of setting aside one or two hours morning and evening to chant passages from the scriptures in Sanskrit, all of this has been replaced by the chanting of the *guru's* name 108 times two or three times a day. The rationale for this practice is that it can be done successfully in the context of the fast pace of modern life—which, unlike the slower pace of India, leaves little leisure for lengthy devotional exercises. It also gets around the problem of having to maintain and pass on knowledge of Sanskrit to one's children. Since learning Sanskrit and the proper melodic forms of chanting verses seems to be out of the question in Canada, and since most agree that English translations do not "vibrate correctly," the solution adopted appears to be the use of a very simple chant in the original Sanskrit language—such as the repetition of the guru's Sanskrit name.[50] Adults who do engage in the serious study of scriptures are often led by modern scholarship to do so by using written texts in English that follow a literary-critical rather than a devotional approach.

Modern Buddhist communities in Canada also report a shift away from traditional oral chant and toward the rational presentation of scripture through sermon and printed book. The worry expressed by some Buddhists is that this shift may have the effect of cutting off the Buddhist consciousness from its spiritual root. If Buddhist scripture is not learned in childhood through ritual repetition, if the oral teachings are not nourished and reinforced in adulthood by private and public repetition, then the spiritual foundation they provide within the psyche will be missing, and sermons and the study of books may become empty exercises. In the Jodo Shinshu tradition it is held that the unity and harmony found within a congregation can be measured by monitoring its chanting.[51] In a Protestant context it may well be that a similar evaluation can be made based on the way the congregation sings its hymns.

The Buddhist analysis reported above makes an important point. It is not the case that written down and read scriptures and sermons are always empty of spiritual power. The point being made is that when scripture is learned and nourished *only* through written and read materials without an underlying oral foundation having been established and maintained, then the written scripture will be empty of spiritual power. Such scripture would be like a written poem that may be taken up and read from time to time but never becomes a part of a reader's consciousness in such a way that the written text is transcended. Until the poem takes shape and roots itself in one's consciousness, its words lack the power to move one. It is the contention of the oral traditions that for such "rooting within consciousness" to take place the words must shift from the visual sense (the objective perception of an external form) to the oral-aural sense (the subjective experience of a living word with which one can strongly identify).

This traditional contention has recently been supported by Jacques Ellul who finds the printed word to be of a nature entirely different from that of the spoken word. His thesis is that our modern experience biases us toward printed words that function as signs with fixed factual referents (information). Spoken words, on the other hand, function as symbols that cannot be reduced to factual information, but necessarily involve emotions that transcend reflexes and rationality and overflow into breadth of meaning, ambiguity, and paradox.[52] Ellul is not seeking to disparage the written word and its function but, rather, to point out that the written word belongs to a different realm of truth, and to refuse to reduce spoken language to the written realm. Ellul realizes that in reality the two realms of the written and the oral overlap. His complete separation of the two is only for the purposes of conceptual analysis. A protest similar to that of Ellul's was mounted by Paul in his contrast between the oral and the written word. In 2 Corinthians 3 it is the embodied word spoken in human relationship that manifests the living Spirit of God, as opposed to the unembodied word written with ink. Paul's point, like Ellul's, is that for the word to have transforming power it must be "written," not on paper or stone, but on the human heart. Paul, of course, does not originate this polarity but picks it up from the Hebrew Bible where the prophet Jeremiah reports God as saying that to redeem his people he must make a new covenant with them: "I will put my law within them, I will write it upon their hearts . . ." (Jeremiah 31:33).

Luther, in his turn, valued the written word to the extent of dedicating much of his life to translating the Bible into German so that it could be read aloud in services of worship and so orally enter the consciousness of German-speaking people. But for Luther it was the spoken and preached scripture that had power to transform lives, not the bare printed text. Even when orally encountered, however, it is the action of the Holy Spirit within one that allows the good news of the spoken word to take possession of a life and be understood.[53] Luther's great reforming plea to his age was that people put their ears where their eyes were; for faith is *ex auditu*. In the *Kirchenpostille* of 1522, Luther insists that the gospel is really oral preaching. Luther is not just asking that scripture be read aloud. He seems to be talking about what philosophers now call "speech act." It is a subtle point about the possibilities of language that relates to Luther's distinction between law and gospel. In the *Kirchenpostille* of 1521 Luther talks of the law written on tablets becoming a dead scripture, while the gospel is given from a live voice to the ears.[54] Luther's point would seem to be that the oral character essential to the word is that it be experienced *in the context of personal relationship*.

As we have already noted, the King James Version accomplished the same goal for the English-speaking people. The printed text was to serve only to provide for the powerful oral performance of the word in the congregation, which was to be followed by preaching. Indeed the King James translators were given the instruction that the ordinary Bible *read* in the church (i.e., the Bishops' Bible) should be altered as little as possible. Oral considerations frequently governed the final wording selected by the translators, who were scholars experienced in the conduct of public worship. "Their choice of the final wording of a passage was often determined by a marvelously sure instinct for what would sound well when read aloud"[55] and would thus have power to engage the congregation in worship.

The Puritans of England and North America gave further stress to Luther's emphasis upon the presence and action of the Holy Spirit in preaching. They saw printed and mechanically read sermons as obstructions that served to "kill" rather than proclaim the good news. In order for the scripture to speak through him, the preacher had to submit to the impulse of the Holy Spirit and allow it to lead him into fresh oral exposition. Preaching of the "lively word," as the Puritans called it, required freedom from a printed text so that the inspiration of the Holy Spirit within both the preacher and the hearers could take possession of the process.[56] The presence of large portions of memorized scripture in the consciousness of the preacher and the hearers paves the way for this spontaneous and inspiring functioning of the Holy Spirit. The lack of power in many modern sermons may well be due, at least in part, to the lack of this reservoir of scriptural knowledge as held in common by both the preacher and his congregation. Perhaps the reason one hears from the pulpit so many allusions to television programs, is because TV, rather than scripture, provides the pool of knowledge that is held in common today. Surely this must make it difficult for even the Holy Spirit to make such sermons into inspiring preaching. Jesus had the advantage in his teaching of sharing with his listeners the "oral pool" of the Hebrew scripture. It would seem then that for the scriptural word, whether spoken from memory or read aloud from a book, to be proclaimed with transforming power requires that to some degree it be already present in the consciousness of the hearer and the speaker.

With the exception of some forms of Buddhism (e.g., Soto Zen), the sacred words of scripture are experienced within all religions as having spiritual power. The recitation of the sacred word not only purifies the life of the individual devotee but is also often seen to be necessary for the well-being of the rest of humanity and the maintenance of order in nature. The recitation and preaching of the word evokes the truth of the Divine, which transcends all words. To this end the scriptural forms that seem to have the greatest power are those of poem, parable, and *via negativa* dialogue. But in all of these it is the oral in human relationship rather than the written word in which the full spiritual power is present. It is the oral word experienced within the context of Talmudic debate, preacher and listener, *guru* and student, and in chanted prayer or meditation that has been found to have the power to transform lives. By itself the written word seems largely empty of such power. But when it functions as a script for oral use, the written word through the oral joins in the production of spiritual power. In certain situations, the written word is seen to have made possible the production of oral experiences, which, without the use of the written, might never have occurred (e.g., the writing of the gospels for subsequent oral performance). Or the written may, to use a Christian context, be experienced as engaging the reader in dialogue with God or the Holy Spirit. In such cases, even though there may be only one person involved (i.e., the solitary reader of the Bible), the presence of God or the Holy Spirit creates a context of relationship of the sort that Luther said was required to transform the dead letter of the law into living gospel. The written, in effect, enters into the immediate oral relationship.

The written text also provides the basis for the investigation of past events as history and the abstract analysis and classification of scripture.[57] Except in classical Greece the writing down of a scriptural text has usually given it special authority and at times made it an object of veneration. Copies of sacred books (Bibles, Qur'ans, *Purāṇas* and Buddhist *Sūtras*) were popularly used for divination and as talismans possessing magical powers.[58] In earlier times, as van der Leeuw points out, writing also functioned as magic, as a way of gaining power over the living word. Committing the oral scripture to writing was an act of power in that it enabled humans to do what they wanted with the written word.[59] The great danger in modern life, with its strong bias toward the written and its lack of awe before the written copy of any text, is that the oral experience of scripture will be reduced to the written and the transforming power of the word will no longer be experienced.

With the notable exception of some branches of Hinduism, the awe and respect traditionally given to written scripture is well evidenced: in the pious copying and special ornamentation of the Bible, the exquisite beauty of Qur'an calligraphy, the elegant block-print collections of the Tibetan texts, Hindu *puja* before garlanded *Purāṇa* texts, and the special qualifications and purifications involved in the scribe's copying of the Torah. All of this has traditionally functioned to set written scripture apart from other writing and to highlight its special symbolic qualities. However, in our modern culture with its surfeit of written materials, the printing of the scripture in the latest paperback style leads to a familiarity that lessens any sense of a separateness or special quality. This loss of awe is reinforced when we study the scriptures by subjecting them to the same kinds of literary critical analysis that would be given to any other piece of writing.[60] As a result of all of this there is the strong danger that written scripture will be redefined as nothing but sign language referencing empirical objects, that its intimate relation to oral performance and relational experience will be lost sight of, and that its ability to act as an evocative symbol of the transcendent with power to transform lives will be lost.

THE FUTURE OF SCRIPTURE

Having studied the oral and written function of scripture in the world religions, let us now turn our attention to the future of scripture.

Paying closer attention to the total context of scriptural experience (i.e., Source-Message or Text-Receptor) has recently led biblical scholars to begin to focus on the text-reception side of the scriptural communication process.[61] Whereas in the past the main thrust of research was on the text-production and text-transmission side of the communication process, the recent shift in interest to the reception side opens the way to a greater sensitivity to the oral and relational dynamics that have traditionally characterized the experience of scripture. This shift also stimulates reflection on the reception processes involved in our current and future engagement of scripture in worship, education, and private devotions. While recent scholarship has tended to study text reception as "reader-response" (a focus that accepts and assumes the "printed text" as the form of the message), more reflection is needed on text reception as "hearer-response" (a focus that accepts and assumes the "oral/aural text" as the form of the message). The following comments represent a beginning into the study of text reception as "hearer-response" and are seen as being complementary to the study of text reception as "reader-response."

Approaching oral scriptural communication from the reader-response side makes clear its fundamental nature as symbol rather than sign. Rather than there being one correct meaning for a text, the hearing or reading of a Vedic poem or New Testament parable may convey many different meanings or insights depending on the listener, the time, and the place. Instead of a hermeneutics of reduction, based on the assumption that the text has only one correct meaning, the oral experience of scripture paves the way for a hermeneutics of unfolding (*Entfaltung*), an opening up of the richness of the word in terms of its symbolic potentialities.[62] Because the written word is, to a degree at least, fixed in a particular book in black and white, it has less flexibility than the oral word to respond to the hearer's existential context. Thus the retold story, parable or poem takes on new meaning or evocative power depending on the way it is spoken in different contexts. And this speaking of the word will change in response to the hearer's response as the passage unfolds. Every new hearer or group of hearers will bring a new inner spirit and experience to the moment, and this new hearer-response will cause the telling to be different.

Because the writer of the word and the typesetter of the printed text cannot interact with the reader in this free way, an element of symbolic power is lost. That is why an author's reading of a poem in public is usually more powerful than one's silent reading of it, and why a good preacher is needed to bring the printed Bible to life.[63] It is this more powerful hearer's response that makes the oral word effective in transforming human lives. What are the implications of all this for our future use of scripture in worship, education, and private devotion?

Worship

What are the respective roles of the oral and the written word if the goal of worship is taken to be the transformation of human lives? The aim of public worship has been described as making people aware of the presence of the transcendent.[64] Worship is not an exercise of asking the transcendent to be with us, for, in all the religions examined, there is no time when the transcendent is not with us. Nor is the aim to lead people into the presence of the transcendent, for, as all religions agree, there is no time when we are not in the presence of the transcendent. Speaking from a Christian context, William Barclay puts the point well: "What we are really trying to do in worship is to make [people] aware of the presence of God, to make them realize the presence of God."[65] Even in Buddhism and those forms of Hinduism in which there is ultimately no theistic conception, the goal of all spiritual discipline is the realization of the transcendent. Are oral words or written words more powerful in sensitizing people to the presence of the transcendent? Judging by the evidence presented in the preceding chapters, it is the oral word and its relational context that has the greater power to reveal the transcendent.[66] And once revealed, the transcendent has effectively demonstrated the power to transform lives.

What is the implication of this for our present and future experience of worship? It suggests that in worship the oral experience of the word should be predominant. Although this has historically been the case in all the religions, the impact of modernity, with its strong bias toward the written, is today tending to reduce the predominance of the oral. This tendency must be strongly combated if the word is to retain its transforming power in worship. We have noted the concern of North American Buddhist priests over the lessening use of the *nembutsu* chant in worship. We have also noted the "shortcutting" of oral practice among Hindus living in Canada. In Christian worship, some Protestant churches have introduced practices that emphasize the written at the expense of the oral. Under the guise of congregational participation, unison prayers and responses are printed to be read by the congregation. While this may be acceptable as the first step in a learning process in which prayers and responses are ultimately learned by heart, in many churches these prayers are changed so frequently (on the premise that change means freshness) that they never become well enough known to reach the heart. Prayers and responses remain at the level of print-eye-mind coordination, with an underlying anxiety produced by the fear of misreading or stumbling in one's pronouncing of the words. While such ever-new words may dazzle and engage the mind of some, even for them the experience evoked will most often be of mental fascination rather than a deep opening to the presence of God. For those worshipers who are not fascinated by new words the result will be a deadening of the Spirit brought on by having to once again struggle to see, pronounce, and think unfamiliar words—a psychological process that engages the surface rational-conceptual processes of the mind rather than the deeper nonconceptual emotions and intuitions. It is the latter that are the psycho-spiritual channels to awareness of the transcendent.[67]

The problem with all of the above is that the words of worship are spoken as they would be in the first reading of a dramatic script rather than a familiar and fully engaged speaking of the words. When the script is known by heart, cherished from repeated practice, and spoken as in the powerful performance of a play, then the written script does not get in the way. Earlier we used the example of the importance of music being memorized if it is to be fully experienced in its playing. The same is true for our prayers and responses in worship; they must be known by heart if the presence of God, of which they speak, is to be fully experienced by the worshiper. The devotee must feel comfortable and "at home" with the oral responses involved in worship. If as a Christian I have to come before God in such a way that there is always a printed page between us, my experience of God's presence will not likely be comfortable or powerful. Can we imagine ourselves in a deep life-transforming conversation with a friend in which we keep on having to read everything we say from an order of service, a looseleaf book or an ever changing bound text. Surely in such an encounter, if it is to have transforming power, the paper or book must be put down and the words come from the heart. The constant changing of prayers and liturgies, like a constant changing of a musical script, functions as an obstacle to the deep losing of oneself in an experience of worship.

Another problem introduced by our modern written rather than oral bias is that when "scripts" are written for worship in the form of prayers, responses, or scripture translations, the words are often not composed with an "ear" to their being read aloud for public hearing. One of the great strengths of the King James Version of the Bible was that it was translated to be read aloud in worship. The Anglican Book of Common Prayer had the same aural qualities as did the Latin Mass of the Roman Catholic Church. Not only were these "worship scripts" well composed for oral performance but also they were not changed from week to week or year to year. Heard in worship in one's childhood, these words of worship became deeply engraved on one's consciousness, and, like a poem learned in elementary school, remained with one for life. Being already deeply present in the consciousness of the worshiper, and carrying the memory traces of countless previous "speakings" and "hearings" in worship, these words are powerful potential evokers of the transcendent.[68] Once the worshiper enters the sanctuary and kneels or sits as tradition demands, all that is needed is the utterance of the familiar first word of the liturgy, and the powerful potentialities of past experience (conditioning or habit, to use modern psychological terminology) awaken sensitivity to the presence of the transcendent, and the aim or worship is achieved.

The power of the aural evocation of the transcendent not only requires a "script" composed for speaking (which remains constant from early childhood) but also "delivery" by a worship leader trained in rhetoric or oral performance. In Christian worship today, ministers, priests, and lay leaders frequently lack the training and aptitude required to provide powerful aural leadership. Instead, one increasingly experiences changing prayers, liturgies, and scripture translations (written for reading rather than hearing) delivered by a worship leader lacking in oral performance skills. Given these circumstances, all of which militate against the word's sensitizing us to the presence of the transcendent in worship, it is not surprising that many of the older people find worship somehow lacking, and younger people never do have their lives transformed. This weakness is not found where the world religions have not modernized their worship practice: for example, Orthodox Judaism, Hinduism in India, Buddhism in Ceylon, Islam in Arabia, and Christianity in the Eastern Orthodox Church, and, until recently, in much of the Anglican Church. "Modernization" in this sense means allowing the "written word" to obstruct the power of the oral word in the flow of worship. The obstructing power of the written word occurs when it ceases to function as a carefully composed script for oral performance and instead becomes a technique or technology for the human manipulation of worship. Then instead of evoking the worship relation between the divine and the human, what is evoked is the human relation of person with person—the transcendent is left out or at least not experienced. Here Ellul's critique of the dangers of technology directly apply to our experience of the oral and written word in worship.[69]

Our modern approach presupposes that if something is to be present in our experience, we have to create it. Thus our constant inventiveness in worship. We assume that anything that has become standardized and repetitive in worship has lost its power to evoke the transcendent.[70] Modernity asks, "How could the repeated chanting of a Hindu *mantra*, the Buddhist *nembutsu* or a Catholic rosary be anything but an empty mechanical repetition and as such incapable of evoking the transcendent?" Only the new and spontaneously creative use of words can have spiritual power—or so modernity seems to think. The mistake made by modernity is in the presupposition that if something is to be present, we have to create it. But in worship, the transcendent is already present. No new creation is called for from us. If anything, what is needed is a quieting of the restless creating activity of our minds so that we can experience the presence of the transcendent rather than the presence of ourselves. To accomplish this end, the familiar and oft-spoken prayers and words of scripture are an effective means of reawakening us to the abiding presence of the transcendent in worship.

Spontaneity does have a place in one aspect of worship, that of preaching. But even here spontaneity for its power depends on a store of deeply familiar word-use (prayer, scripture, and hymn) shared in common by preacher and listeners. The skillful and spontaneous use of such deeply rooted memories, associated with past word-use in worship, resonates strongly within our consciousness. Within this resonance there is transforming power. But, as demonstrated by the Hindu *Vyāsa* expositing the *Rāmāyana* or the Puritans preaching the "lively word," the preacher must be immersed in the word yet not tied to a written text. The spontaneity spoken of here comes not from human inventiveness but, rather, from the removal of the creative ego from the process so that speaker and hearers are transparent to the transcendent. Here written texts that do more than prompt one's memory serve as obstructions in the worship process.

Religious Education

For the worship described above to take place, certain basic requirements must be met. The words of scripture and prayer must be learned, by heart wherever possible, early in life. Such learning must begin in the home,[71] with parents and children joining in prayer and in the speaking of scripture. The form this activity takes varies slightly between religions. In Hinduism the children would rise early in the morning and join with parents in the chanting of scriptural passages and prayers. Family practice in Judaism requires that both parents teach the Torah to their children (Proverbs 1:8; 6:20), and formalizes family occasions for the oral repetition of the key prayers and scriptural passages. In post-Reformation Protestant Christianity, parents have read the Bible aloud to their children or, less formally, simply told them the Bible stories. The words of Deuteronomy 6:7 effectively summarize the responsibility of parents as encountered in many world religions: "You shall teach (these words) diligently to your children, and you shall discuss them in your family." This teaching cannot be done by sending the young child off to read quietly the Torah, Bible, Qur'an, Vedas, or Tripiṭaka. Rather, the scriptural words must be shared by the parents in oral interchange with their children.

It is in this hearing of scriptural words from the parents throughout the preschool years, when the child's mind is still open and uncluttered, that the firm foundation for all future religious practice is established. The temptation for modern and busy parents is to abdicate this responsibility and instead leave their children to watch cartoons and other programs on television. Television, like the spoken word, is oral and direct in nature and thus has a deep impact upon consciousness. This then, rather than prayer and scripture, becomes the content that is deeply absorbed into the innocent minds of our children. It is unlikely that such television content will sensitize them to the presence of the transcendent in their experience. The difficult but essential requirement for present and future parents is to exercise discipline over themselves and their children—to turn off the television, and to devote regular times to the telling of scripture and the saying of prayers.

School, either Sunday school or full-time schooling in a religious context, must build upon this home foundation. From ages six to twelve is the time for the learning of a sacred language, for example, Hebrew or Sanskrit, if one is needed, and the systematic memorization of text, prayers, and liturgies that are the essence of the tradition. Such memorization will root the key scriptures and prayers firmly within the consciousness of the child so that they will remain with him or her for life. During this period understanding of the meanings of the words is not the most important goal. Rather, it is the learning of the texts by heart. Then the remainder of life can be devoted to appropriating the meaning of the words, and throughout life an increasing depth of such understanding can be realized. The essential requirement is that the words be memorized early so that they become a fundamental part of the deep structure of the mind through which all the rest of one's life experiences will be filtered and interpreted.[72] Such scriptures and their inherent teachings remain in the unconscious of the individual and influence one's thinking and perception even when one is not consciously aware of such influence. In times of crisis, such words spring spontaneously to mind to help one cope and to give one guidance. However, this sustaining and guiding quality of scripture does not function strongly unless the texts are memorized in one's youth. At times of crisis one is not likely to take down the Bible or the Qur'an and look up its guidance. But if the word is already within one, already part of the structures of one's mind, it will automatically become a key element in one's response to moral and existential dilemmas. When the word is already there, it provides a responsive and fertile ground for evocation in the liturgy and preaching of public worship. As Carl Jung would put it, such words provide the forms through which the power of the transcendent can integrate and transform one's life.[73]

Once the basic scriptures are learned by heart in one's youth, later education (from about twelve years on) can benefit from the techniques of critical analysis, which for many will require the use of a written text. In some traditions, such as those of India and Tibet, even the processes of so-called Higher Criticism and exegesis go on in a fully oral format. But for those educated in the modern West, the use of the written texts will prove necessary and helpful for critical study. The teaching offered in university religious studies departments makes a valuable contribution at this point. The many excellent contributions made by modern biblical studies would not have been possible without a close reading of the written text. Superimposed upon an already existing knowledge of the texts by heart, the critical study of texts in their written form can be an enriching experience that further deepens the transforming power of the spoken word. But alone, and without the supporting structure of the text being already present in consciousness, the critical study of written texts often becomes an empty intellectual exercise bereft of life-transforming power. One ends up like the music critic who knows all that has been written about the score of Bach's Toccata and Fugue in D-minor, but cannot play or hear it so as to be deeply moved by the music. Critical study of the written text needs the firm foundation of oral exposure and memorization in one's youth and, in adulthood, must lead back in spiral fashion to renewed oral experiences of the word in public worship or private devotion. Oral experience of the word and the critical analysis of written text must inform one another in a mutually deepening way. While this complementary relationship has in the past been preserved in Judaism, Christianity, Islam, and Buddhism (Hinduism, alone, has not given the written text an important place), the impact of modernity has disturbed the traditional balance and threatens to have the written overwhelm the oral. If scripture is to have the power to transform lives in the future, this overbalancing of the oral must not be allowed to happen. It is in the processes of education, especially, that the functions of the oral must be maintained.

Private Devotion

All the religions studied agree that when scriptures are used in private devotion they should be used orally. Luther taught the laypeople reading his German translation of the Bible that they should read the word aloud. Eastern *mantra* practice requires that the meditative chanting be done aloud for maximum power. If the chanting can be done from memory, without the need for a supporting written script, so much the better. This of course depends on the key text and prayers having been learned by heart in one's youth. Having learned them by heart also means that the devotion can be done at any time and place, such as when one is very sick in a hospital bed, without need for the external text—one might not be available, and even if one is, physical disabilities or circumstances might make it too difficult for the written text to be used (e.g., suppose one is very ill in an intensive care unit). If one's scriptures and prayers have been learned by heart in youth, and have been reinforced by regular saying in later years, they will be easily available to one's mind and tongue and can be quietly or silently said and so evoke the transcendent presence in times of need.

In Eastern devotional practice, the meditative chanting of *mantras* or special scriptural syllables such as AUM or OM MA NE PAD ME HUM are used as a method of controlling worldly distractions (focus on the chanting excludes them from the mind) and of realizing unity or communion with the transcendent.[74] The Sufi masters use the spoken sounds of the Qur'an in a somewhat similar way. In Zen meditation *kōan* practice is used negatively to remove the ego fascination with humanly created words and thought-systems until they dissipate from the mind, leaving only unobstructed flow of the mind (*satori*). Even this use of words in a *via negativa* fashion (which is also found in the *Upaniṣads*[75]) has a positive goal—an experience in which the sense of separation of the ego-mind of the devotee from the transcendent is overcome. All such private devotional practice in the Eastern religions assumes the oral context of a teacher-student relationship. Grave warnings are entered against any attempt to follow such practices using only the written text for guidance.

The modern Western bias toward the written text and analysis of the written text via historical study has led many to adopt an academic textual approach even in periods set aside for private devotional study of the scriptures. Instead of opening the mind to the devotional experience of the word, the devotee surrounds himself or herself not only with the written text itself but also with various translations and commentaries. Instead of being open to resonate to the spiritual power of the spoken word, one's mind becomes enmeshed in the complexities of human discussion and debate about possible settings, speakers, and meanings of the text. Rather than devotionally hearing the word in one's heart, what has been entered into is a human discussion about the scriptural word. Human scholarly discussion has an important role to play in deepening and broadening our knowledge about scripture, and in this study written texts and writing itself play an important role—except perhaps in Hinduism. But academic study about scripture can never replace the direct devotional experience of the word. For many modern Christians (and for some Jews, Hindus, and Buddhists) this may necessitate a change in habits, if scripture is to be a transforming power in their lives. The temptation, fueled by the modern bias toward the written text and its academic study, will be to fill the time set aside for private devotional experience of the word with a scholarly study of the word. If the word is to have transforming power in future private devotions, new habits focusing on oral experience of the word itself will need to be developed. Listening to a tape cassette of a King James or Revised Standard Version of the Bible read with skill by someone like Sir Laurence Olivier, to take a Christian example, might prove a helpful beginning alternative to the private reading of a written text and commentaries. Better still would be the reading or saying aloud of the text by oneself repeatedly until the text becomes a part of one's own consciousness. Only then would the hours spent in private scripture study or devotion have the power to transform one's life.

In the three areas examined above, worship, education, and private devotion, both the written and the oral experience of scripture have been shown to have importance. The modern bias toward the written, however, has the tendency of shifting contemporary practice away from the traditional predominance of the oral word. Our analysis suggests that the traditional approach of emphasizing the oral experience of scripture in early education and then continuing to nourish that early experience through repeated oral practice in adult worship and devotion is essential if scripture is to continue to have transforming power in human lives.

NOTES

1. SCRIPTURE IN JUDAISM

1. "Torah," *Encyclopedia Judaica* (New York: Macmillan, 1971), p. 1235.

2. Jacob Neusner, *The Way of Torah: An Introduction to Judaism* (2nd ed., Belmont, Calif.: Dickenson, 1974), p. 12.

3. Jacob Neusner, *Torah: From Scroll to Symbol in Formative Judaism* (Philadelphia: Fortress Press, 1985), p. xi.

4. Ibid., p. xiii.

5. Jonathan Rosenbaum, "Judaism: Torah and Tradition" in *The Holy Book in Comparative Perspective*, ed. by F. M. Denny and R. L. Taylor (Columbia, S. C.: University of South Carolina Press, 1985), p. 22.

6. Neusner, *The Way of Torah,* p. 43. Scholars differ in the way the term *Judaism* is used. Some, notably Jewish scholars, see a continuity from ancient Israelite beginnings to the fully developed forms of Judaism, using this word to cover the entire history; for example, see Salo W. Baron, *A Social and Religious History of the Jews* (New York: Columbia University Press, 1952). This is the interpretation adopted in this book.

7. "Moses," *The Interpreter's Dictionary of the Bible* (Nashville: Abingdon Press, 1962), p. 448.

8. Neusner, *The Way of Torah,* p. 13. As Neusner notes, it is this open-ended redemptive element of the Mosaic proclamation that resolves the tension between what we are told to do in the covenant, and what we actually accomplish.

9. "Moses," *The Interpreter's Dictionary of the Bible*, p. 448.

10. Ibid.

11. George Foot Moore, *Judaism* (Cambridge, Mass.: Harvard University Press, 1958), vol. I, p. 239.

12. Ephraim E. Urbach, *The Sages* (Jerusalem: Magnes Press, 1975), p. 287.

13. Lou H. Silberman, "The Making of the Old Testament Canon," in *The Interpreter's One-Volume Commentary on the Bible* (Nashville: Abingdon Press, 1971), p. 1209. See also Bernard Childs, *Introduction to the Old Testament as Scripture* (Philadelphia: Fortress Press, 1979), p. 54.

14. Moore, *Judaism*, vol. I., p. 20.

15. Silberman, "The Making of the Old Testament Canon," p. 1210.

16. Ibid.

17. See H. Wheeler Robinson, *Inspiration and Revelation in the Old Testament* (Oxford, England: Clarendon Press, 1946), p. 75.

18. Michael Fishbane, *Biblical Interpretation in Ancient Israel* (Oxford, England: Clarendon Press, 1985), p. 528. See also S. W. Baron and J. L. Blau, *Judaism: Postbiblical and Talmudic Period* (New York: Bobbs-Merrill, 1954), p. 102.

19. Peter Craigie, *The Book of Deuteronomy* (Grand Rapids, Mich.: Wm. B. Eerdmans, 1976), p. 262.

20. Robinson, *Inspiration and Revelation in the Old Testament*, p. 209.

21. Moore, *Judaism*, vol. I, p. 239. However, it is also true that some ancient Israelites did perceive of a continuous revelation.

22. The following is based on the entry "Scribe," *Encyclopedia Judaica*, pp. 1043–44. Current practices differ slightly from this description.

23. Ibid.

24. Rosenbaum, "Judaism: Torah and Tradition," p. 26.

25. This and the following are based on the entry "Torah, Reading of," *Encyclopedia Judaica*, pp. 1246–54.

26. Moore, *Judaism*, vol. I., p. 291.

27. "Torah, Reading of," *Encyclopedia Judaica*, p. 1254.

28. "Music," *Encyclopedia Judaica*, p. 584.

29. Ibid., p. 585.

30. Eric Werner, *From Generation to Generation: Studies on Jewish Musical Tradition* (New York: American Conference of Cantors), 1958, p. 139.

31. *The Cantorial Art*, ed. Irene Heskes (New York: National Jewish Music Council, 1966), p. 7.

32. Moore, *Judaism*, vol. I, p. 320.

33. Ibid., p. 322.

34. "Judaism," *The Canadian Encyclopedia* (Edmonton: Hurtig Publishers, 1985), vol. 2, p. 926.

35. "Oral Law," *Encyclopedia Judaica*, p. 1439.

36. Ibid.

37. Ibid., p. 1441.

38. Urbach, *The Sages*, p. 300.

39. Jacob Neusner, "Scripture and Mishnah" in *Scripture in the Jewish and Christian Traditions*, ed. F. E. Greenspan (Nashville: Abingdon, 1982), pp. 73–74.

40. Ibid., p. 75.

41. Ibid., p. 76.

42. This and the following analysis is based on Michael Fishbane, "Jewish Biblical Exegesis: Presuppositions and Principles," in *Scripture in the Jewish and Christian Traditions*, pp. 94–102.

43. Ibid., p. 101.

44. Ibid., p. 96.

45. Hag 15b, as quoted by Fishbane, "Jewish Biblical Exegesis," p. 97.

46. Rosenbaum, "Judaism: Torah and Tradition," pp. 19–20.

47. Jacob Neusner, *The Memorized Torah: The Mnemonic System of the Mishnah* (Chico, Calif.: Scholars Press, 1985).

48. Ibid., p. 1.

49. Ibid., p. 5.

50. Saul Lieberman, "The Publication of the Mishnah," as quoted by Jacob Neusner, *The Memorized Torah,* p. 28.

51. Lieberman's theory is summarized by Neusner, *The Memorized Torah,* pp. 28, 112. This theory, however, needs further substantiation. Neusner's evidence is only a first step in verification.

52. Ibid., p. 67.

53. Ibid., p. 111.

54. Ibid., pp. 113–14.

55. Ibid., p. 114. Neusner attempts a description of the delicate psychological process at work: "What is repeated here is not form, but formulary pattern, a pattern effected through persistent grammatical or syntactical relationships and affecting an infinite range of diverse objects and topics" (p. 114). It is this open-ended and evocative character that suggests parallels between the oral Torah (in its apparently legal language) and poetry.

56. Ibid., p. 120.

57. Ibid., p. 125.

58. Ibid., p. 124.

59. Ibid., p. 128.

60. Ibid., p. 129.

61. Jacob Neusner, *Formative Judaism: Religious, Historical and Literary Studies.* Third Series: *Torah, Pharisees and Rabbis* (Chico, Calif.: Scholars Press, 1983), chap. 1.

62. Ibid., p. 8.

63. Ibid.

64. Jacob Neusner, *Torah: From Scroll to Symbol in Formative Judaism* (Philadelphia: Fortress Press, 1985), p. 17.

65. Ibid., p. 53.

66. Ibid., p. 61.

67. Ibid., pp. 74–79.

68. Ibid., p. 83.

69. Ibid., p. 87.

70. Ibid., p. 96.

71. Daniel Jeremy Silver, *A History of Judaism* (New York: Basic Books, 1974), vol. 1, pp. 224–45.

72. Urbach, *The Sages*, p. 299.

73. Fishbane, "Jewish Biblical Exegesis," p. 92. See also Baron and Blau, *Judaism*, pp. 107–8, for a description of Rabbi Ishmael's thirteen exegetical principles by which the Torah is expounded.

74. Neusner, *Torah: From Scroll to Symbol in Formative Judaism*, p. 65.

75. Ibid., p. 66.

76. Ibid., p. 79.

77. Ibid., p. 82.

78. Ibid., pp. 85, 87.

79. Ibid., p. 90.

80. Joel H. Zaiman, "The Traditional Study of the Mishnah," in *The Study of Ancient Judaism*, ed. Jacob Neusner (New York: Ktav Publishing House, 1981), p. 27.

81. Neusner, *Torah: From Scroll to Symbol in Formative Judaism*, p. 93.

82. Jacob Neusner, *Major Trends in Formative Judaism: Society and Symbol in Political Crisis* (Chico, Calif.: Scholars Press, 1983), p. 94. For modern historical and literary critical studies of the structure of the Babylonian Talmud, see *The Formation of the Babylonian Talmud*, ed. Jacob Neusner (Leiden: E. J. Brill, 1970).

83. Ibid., p. 95.

84. Ibid.

85. Paraphrased from the translation by Jacob Neusner, *Major Trends*, pp. 102–4.

86. Jacob Neusner, *Torah: From Scroll to Symbol in Formative Judaism*, pp. 99–127.

87. Michael Fishbane, "Jewish Biblical Exegesis," p. 99.

88. Jonathan Rosenbaum, "Judaism: Torah and Tradition," p. 20.

89. Maimonides, as summarized by Michael Fishbane, "Jewish Biblical Exegesis," p. 105.

90. Jonathan Rosenbaum, "Judaism: Torah and Tradition," p. 21.

91. This summary of the Kabbala is from Michael Fishbane, "Jewish Biblical Exegesis," pp. 107–8. A sense of the modern experience of the Kabbala can be found in Herbert Weiner, *9½ Mystics: The Kabbala Today* (New York: Collier, 1969).

92. Jonathan Rosenbaum, "Judaism: Torah and Tradition," p. 22.

93. Ibid.

94. Rabbi Freehof's many volumes of responsa have been published by the Hebrew Union College and Jewish Publication Society. The lectures of the intellectual founder of Reform Judaism, Abraham Geiger (1810–74), have recently been published in the "Brown Classics in Judaica" series: Abraham Geiger, *Judaism and Its History* (Maryland: University Press of America, 1985).

95. Jonathan Rosenbaum, "Judaism: Torah and Tradition," p. 28.

96. Ibid. In a bid to counter so-called modern interpretations, the English-speaking Orthodox began publishing a translation and commentary of the Bible in 1976—the Artscroll Series. This series, designed for all levels of readers, has produced rabbinic-based translation, and interpretation and exegesis, which combines the traditional sources of midrashim, talmudism, and targumim. As a result, many old and forgotten texts have been rediscovered. But throughout there is a regular challenging of modern biblical studies. See B. Barry Levy, "Our Torah, Your Torah, and Their Torah: An Evaluation of the Artscroll Phenomenon," in *Truth and Compassion*, ed. H. Joseph, J. Lightstone, and M. Oppenheim (Waterloo, Canada: Wilfred Laurier University Press, 1983), pp. 137ff.

97. *Franz Rosenzweig, His Life and Thought*, ed. N. Glatzer (New York: Schocken Books, 1953), pp. 257–58.

98. "Study," *Encyclopedia Judaica*, p. 453.

99. Jonathan Rosenbaum, "Judaism: Torah and Tradition," p. 24.

100. "Study," *Encyclopedia Judaica*, p. 454.

101. Ibid.

102. Ibid., p. 456.

103. The following is taken from the article on "Study" cited above, p. 456.

104. Ibid., p. 458.

105. Jacob Neusner, *Major Trends,* see chap. 7, "Torah Today: *Lernen* and Learning in Samuel C. Heilman's People of the Book," pp. 109–16.

106. Ibid., p. 113.

107. Ibid., p. 114.

108. Ibid.

109. Jacob Neusner, *The Way of Torah*, pp. 3–4.

110. Peter C. Craigie, *The Book of Deuteronomy*, p. 28.

111. Ibid., pp. 377–78.

112. Ibid., p. 379.

113. R. J. Zwi Werblowsky, "Judaism or the Religion of Israel," in *The Concise Encyclopedia of Living Faiths*, ed. R. C. Zaehner (New York: Hawthorn Books, 1959), p. 31.

114. Ibid.

115. J. Kenneth Kuntz, *The People of Ancient Israel* (New York: Harper & Row,

1974), p. 356. See also Lamentations 2:4, Psalm 137, and Ezekiel 1–24.

116. Ibid., p. 416.

117. As quoted by Leo Trepp, *Judaism: Development and Life* (Belmont, Calif.: Wadsworth Publishing Co., 1982), p. 160.

118. Moses Mendelssohn, *Jerusalem,* trans. Alfred Josepe (New York: Schocken Books, 1969).

119. Ibid., p. 66.

120. Ibid., p. 107.

121. Ibid., pp. 108–9.

122. Emil L. Fackenheim, *Encounters between Judaism and Modern Philosophy* (New York: Basic Books, 1973), p. 174. It should be noted, however, that the medieval Jewish rationalism was more concerned with the worry that contact with Christianity would result in apostasy rather than seeing Christianity as idolatry.

123. Ibid., p. 192.

124. Ibid., p. 197.

125. Abraham J. Heschel, *The Insecurity of Freedom: Essays in Applied Religion* (New York: Farrar, Straus and Giroux, 1966), 182. Other very open views have been expressed by the saintly chief rabbi of Israel, Abraham Isaac Kook (1865–1935), who declared that the mature human mind will recognize all expressions of spiritual life as one organic whole; and by Martin Buber, who proclaimed that Christianity and Judaism would be of aid to each other in ways that we can now hardly conceive. See Leo Trepp, *Judaism*, p. 161.

126. "Torah," *Encyclopedia Judaica*, p. 1239. However, it is also taught in the universalistic prophecies of Isaiah and Malachi that each nation has its own Torah, in its own language, and is not allowed to hold the Jewish Torah.

2. SCRIPTURE IN CHRISTIANITY

1. Harry Y. Gamble Jr., "Christianity: Scripture and Canon," in *The Holy Book in Comparative Perspective*, ed. F. M. Denny and R. L. Taylor (Columbia: University of South Carolina Press, 1985), p. 37. It should be noted that most early Christians used the Greek translation of the Hebrew Bible—the Septuagint.

2. Jacob Neusner, *Judaism in the Beginning of Christianity* (Philadelphia: Fortress Press, 1984), p. 11. It must be remembered that the Hebrew Bible was not closed until the end of the first century C.E., and it took a long time-period before the canon set at Jamnia was fully accepted. Jewish sacred scripture was a "fluid" entity, not a concrete concept in the first century C.E. See Brevard S. Childs, *Introduction to the Old Testament as Scripture* (Philadelphia: Fortress Press, 1979), pp. 62–68.

3. Gamble, "Christianity: Scripture and Canon," p. 38. In addition to the prefigurement emphasis, early Christian interpretation also employed other approaches such as allegory.

4. "Introduction to the New Testament," in *The Oxford Annotated Bible*, ed. H. G. May and B. M. Metzger (New York: Oxford University Press, 1962), p. 1167.

5. C. H. Dodd, *The Authority of the Bible* (London: Fontana, 1929), p. 269.

6. Henry J. Cadbury, "The New Testament and Early Christian Literature," *The Interpreter's Bible* (Nashville: Abingdon, 1951), vol. 7, p. 32. For the way in which Jesus related to and differed from the rabbis of his day, see Geza Vermes, *Jesus the Jew* (London: Collins, 1973). For an excellent study of the role of the "Torah of Moses" or the Tanak in relation to other contemporary writing that might also be regarded as

scripture or Torah, see Wayne O. McCready, "A Second Torah at Qumran?" *Studies in Religion* 14 (1985): 5–15.

7. See, eg., Jacob Neusner's analysis of the power and practice of the oral Torah in *The Memorized Torah: The Mnemonic System of the Mishnah* (Chico, Calif: Scholars Press, 1985). The stress on the oral here is not meant to imply that there were no writings. On the contrary, the popularity of the literature of the Pseudepigrapha (as well as the Apocrypha) argues for the presence of a considerable quantity of religious writing contemporary with the turn of the common era. See, eg., *The Other Bible*, ed. Willis Barnstone (New York: Harper & Row, 1984).

8. Cadbury, "The New Testament and Early Christian Literature," p. 32.

9. Ibid., pp. 32–33.

10. Amos N. Wilder, *Early Christian Rhetoric: The Language of the Gospel* (Cambridge, Mass.: Harvard University Press, 1978).

11. Ibid., p. 13.

12. Ibid., pp. 13–14.

13. Ibid., p. 14.

14. Robert C. Culley, *Studies in the Structure of Hebrew Narrative* (Missoula, Mont.: Scholars Press, 1976).

15. Robert C. Culley, "Oral Tradition and the Old Testament: Some Recent Discussion," *Semeia* 5 (1976): 21. See also in the same issue of *Semeia*, articles by A. B. Lord, W. J. Urbrock and John Van Seters on oral antecedents of various parts of the Old Testament.

16. Jacob Neusner, *Torah: From Scroll to Symbol in Formative Judaism* (Philadelphia: Fortress Press, 1985). See the detailed presentation of Neusner's argument in chap. 1, "Scripture in Judaism," above.

17. Roger Lapointe, "Tradition and Language: The Import of Oral Expression," in *Tradition and Theology in the Old Testament*, ed. D. A. Knight (Philadelphia: Fortress Press, 1977), p. 141.

18. See Birger Gerhardsson, *The Origins of the Gospel Traditions* (Philadelphia: Fortress Press, 1979); and Rainer Riesner, *Jesus der Lehrer: Eine Untersuchung zum Ursprung der Evangelien-Uberlieferung* (Tübingen: Mohr/Siebeck, 1984).

19. Wilder, *Early Christian Rhetoric*, p. 15.

20. As quoted by Wilder, *Early Christian Rhetoric*, p. 16.

21. C. H. Dodd, *The Apostolic Preaching and Its Developments* (London: Hodder & Stoughton, 1960), pp. 7–8.

22. Wilder, *Early Christian Rhetoric*, p. 20.

23. Ibid., p. 27.

24. Norman Perrin and Dennic C. Duling, *The New Testament, An Introduction* (2nd ed. New York: Harcourt, Brace, Jovanovich, 1982), p. 257.

25. Wilder, *Early Christian Rhetoric*, p. 29.

26. Norman Perrin and Dennis C. Duling, *The New Testament, An Introduction*, pp. 234–35.

27. Werner H. Kelber, *The Oral and the Written Gospel* (Philadelphia: Fortress Press, 1983).

28. The ten are Peter's mother-in-law (1:29–31), the leper (1:40–45a), the paralytic (2:1–12), the man with a withered hand (3:1–6), Jarius's daughter (5:21–24, 35–43), the woman with a hemorrhage (5:25–34), the Syrophoenician woman (7:24–30), the deaf mute (7:31–37), the blind man of Bethsaida (8:22–26), and the blind Bartimaeus (10:46–52).

29. Albert B. Lord, *The Singer of Tales* (Cambridge, Mass.: Harvard University Press, 1960).

30. Kelber, *The Oral and the Written Gospel*, p. 51.

31. Ibid., p. 52.

32. Ibid., pp. 52–55.

33. Ibid., pp. 55–57.

34. Joachim Jeremias, *The Parables of Jesus* (New York: Charles Scribner's Sons, 1963), p. 20.

35. C. H. Dodd, *The Parables of the Kingdom* (London: Fontana, 1961).

36. John Dominic Crossan, "The Good Samaritan: Towards a Generic Definition," *Semeia* 2 (1974): 96–98.

37. Paul Ricoeur, "Biblical Hermeneutics," *Semeia* 4 (1975), pp. 32, 118.

38. Kelber, *The Oral and Written Gospel*, p. 62.

39. As quoted by Kelber, *The Oral and the Written Gospel*, p. 76.

40. Ibid., p. 62, n. 68.

41. Ibid., p. 64.

42. Ibid., p. 66.

43. Ibid., p. 67.

44. Ibid., p. 71.

45. Walter J. Ong, *The Presence of the Word* (New Haven: Yale University Press, 1967), pp. 79–85.

46. Amos Wilder, *Early Christian Rhetoric*, p. 30.

47. Ibid., p. 31.

48. Ibid., p. 33.

49. See Kelber, *The Oral and the Written Gospel*, pp. 140–151.

50. Ibid., chap. 5.

51. Richard F. Ward, "The Apostle Paul and the Politics of Performance at Corinth." A paper read at the Annual Meeting, Society of Biblical Literature, Anaheim, Calif., Nov. 24, 1985.

52. Pedro Lain Entralgo, *The Therapy of the Word in Classical Antiquity* (New Haven: Yale University Press, 1970), p. 66. See also Edwin Hatch, *The Influence of Greek Ideas on Christianity* (New York: Harper & Row, 1957), pp. 55ff.

53. Kelber, *The Oral and the Written Gospel*, pp. 166–67.

54. David L. Barr, "The Apocalypse of John as Oral Enactment." A paper read at the Annual Meeting, Society for Biblical Literature, Anaheim, Calif., Nov. 24, 1985.

55. Ibid., p. 15. Of course, the text also says, in 22:7, "Blessed is he who keeps the words of the prophecy of this book." The phrase "this book" is stressed again in 22:10 and 22:18. Such passages may be seen as directed toward keeping the text pure and rehearsed, and may not be in conflict with the idea that the primary role of the text is as a script for oral performance.

56. Roger Lapointe, "Tradition and Language: The Import of Oral Expression," p. 133. It should be noted that not all scholars agree on the priority of Mark. W. M. Farmer, e.g., puts Matthew first and Mark last in order of writing. W. R. Farmer, *The Synoptic Problem* (New York: Macmillan, 1964).

57. Kelber, *The Oral and the Written Gospel*, p. 220.

58. Wilder, *Early Christian Rhetoric*, p. 38.

59. F. W. Beare, "The Canon of the N.T.," *The Interpreter's Dictionary of the Bible* (Nashville: Abingdon, 1962), vol. 1, p. 521.

60. Norman Perrin and Dennis C. Duling, *The New Testament: An Introduction*, p.

448. For the Roman Catholic editions, the books of the Apocrypha are not separated out but included in the canonical Bible.

61. Beare, "The Canon of the N.T.," p. 522.

62. Paul J. Achtemeier, "How the Scriptures Were Formed," in *The Authoritative Word*, ed. D. K. McKim (Grand Rapids, Mich.: Wm. B. Eerdmans Publishing Co., 1983), p. 15.

63. Perrin and Duling. *The New Testament: An Introduction*, p. 435. In the following discussion of the collection of the letters of Paul, note there is some debate over 2 Thessalonians and Colossians as well as the use of Ephesians as a covering letter. See Werner G. Kümmel, *Introduction to the New Testament* (Nashville: Abingdon, 1975), p. 481.

64. Beare, "The Canon of the N.T.," p. 523. See also Kümmel, *Introduction to the New Testament*, p. 482

65. Perrin and Duling, *The New Testament: An Introduction*, p. 440. For the sayings and discourse Gospels, see *The Other Bible*, ed. W. Barnstone (New York: Harper & Row, 1984); *The Nag Hammadi Library*, ed. James M. Robinson (Leiden: E. J. Brill, 1985); and Elaine Pagels, *The Gnostic Gospels* (New York: Random House, 1979).

66. Beare, "The Canon of the N.T.," p. 523.

67. Ibid., p. 524.

68. Perrin and Duling, *The New Testament: An Introduction*, p. 442.

69. As quoted by Perrin and Duling, *The New Testament: An Introduction,* p. 444.

70. Ibid., p. 334.

71. Ibid., pp. 438–39. Luther also attempted to relegate some canonical books (Hebrews, James, Jude, and Revelation) to second-class status by grouping them unnumbered at the end of the New Testament because they did not clearly present Christ. See Kümmel, *Introduction to the New Testament*, p. 505.

72. Except in the case of the Apocalypse of John, inspiration was not generally attributed to Christian scripture before the third century. Nor did inspiration constitute a criterion for canonicity, and no early Christian writing gained or failed to gain canonical standing on this basis. Thus the later Christian claim that the books of the New Testament are unique and authoritative because they are inspired is not supported from the actual history of the canon. See A.C. Sunberg, "The Bible Canon and the Christian Doctrine of Inspiration," *Interpretation* 29 (1975), 352–371.

73. The following summary is taken from Henry J. Cadbury, "The New Testament and Early Christian Literature," *The Interpreter's Bible* (Nashville: Abingdon, 1951), vol. 7, pp. 33–34.

74. Ibid., p. 34.

75. The following is abbreviated from "English Versions of the Bible," *The Oxford Annotated Bible*, pp. 1535–39.

76. Ibid., p. 1536.

77. Gamble, "Christianity: Scripture and Canon," p. 51.

78. Paul Tillich's exegetical method of "correlation" is a good example of what is being said. Interpretation has the task of correlating the existential question generated by the circumstances of the moment with God's answer found in the Scriptures. See Paul Tillich, *Systematic Theology* (Chicago: University of Chicago Press, 1951), vol. 1, pp. 59–68.

79. Gamble, "Christianity: Scripture and Canon," p. 60, n. 47. See also J. H. Hayes and C. R. Holladay, *Biblical Exegesis* (Atlanta: John Knox Press, 1982).

80. "Interpretation, History and Principles of," *The Interpreter's Dictionary of the*

Bible, p. 719. This allegorical approach was already observable in Paul's interpretations of the Old Testament, as, e.g., in Galatians.

81. Ibid., p. 721.

82. The following is summarized from "Interpretation, History and Principles of," pp. 721–22.

83. Beryl Smalley, *The Study of the Bible in the Middle Ages* (Oxford, England: Basil Blackwell, 1983), pp. xii, 157.

84. Ibid., p. 161.

85. Ibid., pp. 184–185.

86. As quoted in "Interpretation, History and Principles of," p. 722.

87. Smalley, *The Study of the Bible in the Middle Ages*, p. 331.

88. Ibid., p. 330.

89. See Smalley, *Study of the Bible,* chap. 6, "The Friars."

90. This section is based mainly on "Martin Luther," in "Interpretation, History and Principles of," pp. 722–23.

91. Ibid., p. 723.

92. Willem Jan Kooiman, *Luther and the Bible*, trans. by John Schmidt (Philadelphia: Muhlenberg Press, 1961), p. 52.

93. Ibid., p. 53.

94. Ibid. We must, however, remember that in Luther's view some parts of the New Testament (e.g. Hebrews, James, Jude and Revelation) lacked power because they did not clearly present Christ. See Kümmel, *Introduction to the New Testament*, p. 505.

95. David H. Kelsey, "Protestant Attitudes Regarding Methods of Biblical Interpretation," in *Scripture in the Jewish and Christian Traditions*, ed. by F. E. Greenspahn (Nashville: Abingdon, 1982), p. 138.

96. Ibid., p. 139.

97. Ibid.

98. As quoted by Kelsey, p. 136.

99. Ibid., p. 140.

100. Ibid., p. 137.

101. "Interpretation, History and Principles of," p. 723.

102. Ibid.

103. Ibid. Quoted from Augustine, "Against the Epistle of the Manichaeus Called Fundamental."

104. Ibid. Quoted from "Commonitorium #II."

105. Ibid., p. 724.

106. Bruce Vawter, C. M., "The Bible in the Roman Catholic Church," in *Scripture in the Jewish and Christian Traditions*, p. 116.

107. Ibid., p. 117.

108. Ibid., pp. 117–118.

109. George H. Tavard, *Holy Writ or Holy Church* (London: Burns & Oates, 1959), pp. 1–11.

110. Ibid., p. 11.

111. Ibid., p. 209.

112. Jean Levie, S.J., *The Bible, Word of God in Words of Men* (London: Geoffrey Chapman, 1961), pp. 250–52.

113. Ibid., p. 250.

114. Tavard, *Holy Writ or Holy Church*, p. 247.

115. Vawter, "The Bible in the Roman Catholic Church," p. 131.

116. The following treatment is based on D. S. Wallace-Hadrill, *Christian Antioch: A Study of Early Christian Thought of the East* (Cambridge, England: Cambridge University Press, 1982), chap. 2, "Interpretation of the Biblical Record."

117. The work called *On the Witch of Endor*, against Origen, is cited by Wallace Hadrill, p. 31.

118. Wallace-Hadrill, *Christian Antioch* p. 32.

119. Ibid., p. 36.

120. Ibid., p. 45.

121. Ibid., p. 51.

122. John Breck, "Exegesis and Interpretation: Orthodox Reflections on the Hermeneutic Problem," *St. Vladimir's Theological Quarterly* 27 (1983): 86.

123. Ibid., p. 88.

124. The following is based mainly on "Biblical Criticism, History of," *The Interpreter's Dictionary of the Bible*, pp. 413–18.

125. Immanuel Kant, *Religion within the Limits of Reason Alone* (New York: Harper Torchbooks, 1960).

126. "Biblical Criticism, History of," p. 415.

127. David H. Kelsey, "Protestant Attitudes regarding Methods of Biblical Interpretation," p. 156.

128. "Biblical Theology, Contemporary," *The Interpreter's Dictionary of the Bible*, p. 420.

129. Ibid., p. 421.

130. Ibid., p. 425.

131. Ibid.

132. Ibid., p. 428.

133. Ibid., p. 430.

134. See, e.g., Werner H. Kelber, *The Oral and the Written Gospel*, and the discussion on "Jesus and the Oral Tradition" in this chapter.

135. James Barr, *Fundamentalism* (London: SCM Press, 1977), p. 1.

136. Ibid., p. 40. Of course, fundamentalism is not alone in its stress on the inerrancy of the Bible. Bruce Vawter points out that the notion of biblical inerrancy was common from the beginning of Christian times, and from Jewish times before that. See Bruce Vawter, *Biblical Inspiration* (Philadelphia: Westminster Press, 1972), pp. 132ff.

137. James Barr, *Fundamentalism*, p. 55.

138. Ibid., p. 56.

139. Ibid., p. 33.

140. Harry Gamble, "Christianity: Scripture and Canon," p. 52.

141. Bruce Vawter, *Biblical Inspiration*, p. 154.

142. Ibid., p. 152.

143. See George H. Tavard, *Holy Writ or Holy Church*.

144. Avery Dulles, "Scripture: Recent Protestant and Catholic Views," in *The Authoritative Word*, ed. D. K. McKim (Grand Rapids, Mich.: Wm. B. Eerdmans, 1983), pp. 260–61.

145. Philo, "The Contemplative Life," in *Philo*, trans. by F. H. Coulson (Cambridge, Mass: Harvard University Press, 1960), vol. 9, pp. 159–60.

146. Willem Jan Kooiman, *Luther and the Bible*, p. 200.

147. Martin Luther, "Works," as quoted by Kooiman, *Luther*, p. 201.

148. Ibid., p. 202.

149. Ibid.

150. Kooiman, *Luther and the Bible*, p. 203.

151. Ronald Bond, "The 'Lively Word' and the Books of Homilies: The Preaching and Reading Ministries in Tudor and Stuart England," unpublished paper, p. 2.

152. Ibid., p. 3.

153. Ibid., p. 2.

154. P. T. Forsyth, *Positive Preaching and the Modern Mind* (London: Independent Press, 1909), p. 5.

155. Ibid., p. 8.

156. Paul Ricoeur, "The 'Sacred' Text and the Community," in *The Critical Study of Sacred Texts*, ed. Wendy Doniger O'Flaherty (Berkeley: Berkeley Religious Studies Series, 1979), pp. 274–75.

157. Walter Ong, *The Presence of the Word* (New Haven: Yale University Press, 1967), p. 282.

158. Leander E. Keck, "Toward a Theology of Rhetoric/Preaching," in *Practical Theology*, ed. Don S. Browning (New York: Harper & Row, 1983), p. 135.

159. As quoted by Kooiman, *Luther and the Bible*, p. 89.

160. Ibid., p. 88.

161. Walter Ong, *The Presence of the Word*, pp. 282–83.

162. Bernard W. Anderson, "The Bible," *A Handbook of Christian Theology* (New York: Meridian Books, 1958), p. 40.

163. C. H. Dodd, *The Authority of the Bible*, p. 269.

164. Harry Y. Gamble, "Christianity: Scripture and Canon," p. 38.

165. William Temple, *Nature, Men and God* (New York: Macmillan, 1934), p. 322.

166. Walter M. Horton, "Revelation," *A Handbook of Christian Theology*, p. 328.

167. Karl Rahner, "Christianity and the Non-Christian Religions," in *Christianity and Other Religions*, ed. John Hick and Brian Hebblethwaite (London: Fontana, 1980), p. 63.

168. Ibid., pp. 52–79.

169. *The Documents of Vatican II*, ed. Walter M. Abbott (New York: America Press, 1966), p. 662.

170. Karl Barth, *The Doctrine of the Word of God*, vol. 1, chap. 17, part 2 of *Church Dogmatics*, as reprinted in *Christianity and Other Religions*, p. 32.

171. Ibid., pp. 50–51.

172. As quoted by Waldron Scott, " 'No Other Name'—An Evangelical Conviction," in *Christ's Lordship and Religions Pluralism*, ed. G. H. Anderson and T. F. Stransky (Maryknoll, N.Y.: Orbis Books, 1981), p. 59.

173. For a good discussion of how scripture functions as an authoritative basis for Christian theology, see David H. Kelsey, *The Uses of Scripture in Recent Theology* (Philadelphia: Fortress Press, 1975). Kelsey's conclusion is that it is the *patterns* in scripture, not its "content," that make it "normative" for theology (p. 193).

3. SCRIPTURE IN ISLAM

1. Alford Welch, "Introduction" to "Studies in Qur'an and Tafsir," *Journal of the American Academy of Religion* 47 (1979): 620.

2. Alford Welch, "Al-Kur'ān," *The Encyclopedia of Islam* (new ed. Leiden: E. J. Brill, 1981), p. 403.

3. Kenneth Cragg, *The Mind of the Qur'an: Chapters in Reflection* (London: George Allen & Unwin, 1973), p. 14.

4. Welch, "Introduction," p. 621.

5. Labib as-Said, *The Recited Koran* (Princeton: The Darwin Press, 1975), p. 11.

6. Sūra 42:51/50f., as quoted by Helmut Gätje, *The Qur'an and Its Exegesis* (Berkeley: University of California Press, 1976), p. 45.

7. Kenneth Cragg, *The House of Islam* (Belmont, Calif.: Dickenson, 1969), p. 19.

8. Gätje, *The Qur'an and Its Exegesis,* p. 5.

9. Welch, "Al-Kur'an," pp. 402–3.

10. Ibid., p. 403.

11. Ibid., p. 404. For examples of all of the above, see Welch.

12. Ibid.

13. Ahmad von Denffer, *'Ulūm Al-Qur'ān* (London: The Islamic Foundation, 1983), pp. 28–29.

14. As quoted by von Denffer, p. 25.

15. Ibid., p. 27.

16. See, e.g., John Burton, *The Collection of the Qur'an* (London: Cambridge University Press, 1977), p. 4; and Welch, "Al-Kur'ān," p. 425.

17. Cragg, *The House of Islam,* p. 23.

18. Ibid., p. 31.

19. Welch, "Al-Kur'ān," p. 426.

20. Gätje, *The Qur'an and Its Exegesis*, p. 34.

21. The foregoing is based on von Denffer, *'Ulūm Al-Qur'ān,* pp. 31–42.

22. As quoted by Mahmoud Ayoub, *The Qur'an and Its Interpreters* (Albany: State University of New York Press, 1984), vol. 1, p. 8.

23. Ibid., p. 10.

24. Ibid., p. 9.

25. Ibid., p. 11.

26. Ibid.

27. Ibid., p. 8.

28. Ibid., p. 9.

29. Ibid., p. 8.

30. Ibid., p. 13.

31. Ibid.

32. Ibid., p. 14.

33. Ibid. Wilfred Cantwell Smith adds that in reciting the memorized Qur'an daily in prayers, the Muslim devotee enters into some sort of communion with ultimate reality. See Wilfred Cantwell Smith, "The True Meaning of Scripture: An Empirical Historian's Nonreductionist Interpretation of the Qur'an," *International Journal of Middle East Studies* 11 (1980): 490. See also William Graham's analysis of "The Recited Qur'ān in Everyday Piety and Practice," a section of his chapter "Qur'ān as Spoken Word" in *Approaches to Islam in Religious Studies*, ed. Richard C. Martin (Tucson: University of Arizona Press, 1985), pp. 36ff.

34. See, e.g., Harold Coward, "The Meaning and Power of *Mantras* in Bhartṛhari's *Vākyapadīya*," *Studies in Religion* 11 (1982): 365–76.

35. Labib as-Said, *The Recited Koran*, pp. 65–76.

36. Ibid., pp. 121–25.

37. Ibid., p. 55.

38. Ibid., p. 53. It should be noted that the term *qirāt'āt* is also used to refer to the different versions of the written text.

39. Ibid. Said lists the Ten Readings as those of Nāfi', Ibn Kathīr, Abū Amr ibn al-

'Alā', Ibn 'Amur, 'Aṣim, Hamza, al-Kisā'ī, Abū ja'far, Ya'qūb, and Khalaf.

40. Said., p. 54.

41. Ibid., p. 56.

42. Ibid.

43. Ibid.

44. Ibid., p. 58. In parts of the Muslim world these schools are called *Madrasas*.

45. Ahmad von Denffer, *'Ulūm Al-Qur'ān*, p. 149.

46. Ibid., p. 151.

47. Ibid.

48. Arthur Arberry, *The Koran Interpreted* (London: Allen & Unwin, 1955). Recently, however, more translations are being made.

49. Ibid., p. 28.

50. Cragg, *The House of Islam*, p. 32.

51. Labib as-Said, *The Recited Koran*, p. 19.

52. Ibid.

53. Ibid., p. 22. Not all Muslims would agree with Said's third condition.

54. Ibid.

55. Ibid., pp. 22–23.

56. Ibid., p. 23.

57. Ibid., p. 24.

58. Ibid., pp. 26–27.

59. Welch, "Al-Kur'ān," p. 405.

60. John Burton, *The Collection of the Qur'ān* (Cambridge, England: Cambridge University Press, 1977).

61. John Wansbrough, *Quranic Studies* (London: Oxford University Press, 1977).

62. Alford Welch, "Textual Interpretation: The Qirā'āt Literature." Unpublished paper presented at the Calgary Conference on *Quranic Tafsir*, 1985.

63. Labib as-Said, *The Recited Koran*, p. 33.

64. The following summary of the structuring of the 'Uthmānic text, its orthographic problems and the development of variant readings is based on Helmut Gätje, *The Qur'ān and Its Exegesis*, pp. 25-30.

65. Gätje, *The Qur'ān and Its Exegesis*, p. 29.

66. Cragg, *The House of Islam*, p. 16.

67. Ibid., p. 49.

68. Von Denffer, *'Ulūm Al-Qur'ān*, p. 19.

69. Ibid., p. 21.

70. William A. Graham, *Divine Word and Prophetic Word in Early Islam* (The Hague: Mouton, 1977), p. 15.

71. Ibid. Although Annemarie Schimmel has recently shown how Muslims have followed an *imitatio Muhammadi*, an imitation of Muhammad's action as a model for life. "The Prophet Muhammad as a Centre of Muslim Life and Thought," in *We Believe*

in One God, ed. Annemarie Schimmel and Abdoldjavad Falatūri (New York: Crossroad, 1979), pp. 35–61.

72. See Geoffrey Parrinder, *Avatar and Incarnation* (New York: Oxford University Press, 1982).

73. Graham, *Divine Word and Prophetic Word in Early Islam*, p. 18.

74. Gätje, *The Qur'ān and Its Exegesis*, p. 16. For a nontraditional understanding of *tafsir*, see A. Rippin, "Al-Zuhrī, *Naskh al-Qur'ān* and the Problem of Early *Tafsir* Texts," *Bulletin of the School of Oriental and African Studies* 47 (1984): 22–43. A. Rippin also provides a bibliographic review in his article, "The Present Status of *Tafsīr* Studies," *The Muslim World* 72 (1982): 224–38.

75. The following summary is based on Graham, *Divine Word and Prophetic Word in Early Islam*, pp. 33–39.

76. Ibid., p. 34.

77. W. A. Graham, *Divine Word and Prophetic Word in Early Islam*.

78. Gätje, *The Qur'ān and Its Exegesis*, p. 32. See also A. Rippin, "The Present Status of *Tafsīr* Studies," pp. 224–38.

79. The following summary is based on Gätje, *The Qur'ān and Its Exegesis*, pp. 34–35.

80. Ibid., p. 37.

81. The following summary is based on von Denffer, *'Ulūm Al-Qur'ān*, pp. 92–103. See also A. Rippin, "The Exegetical Genre *asbāb al-nuzūt*," *Bulletin of the School of Oriental and African Studies* 48 (1985): 1–15.

82. Ibid., pp. 99–100.

83. Gätje, *The Qur'ān and Its Exegesis*, p. 38. For a review of the role of *Sharī'a*, or law in Sunni life, see M. A. R. Gibb, "Islam" in *The Concise Encyclopedia of Living Faiths*, ed. R. C. Zaehner (New York: Hawthorn Books, 1959), pp. 181ff.

84. Graham, *Divine Word and Prophetic Word in Early Islam*, pp. 37–38.

85. The following summary of Shi'ite exegesis is based on Mahmoud Ayoub, *The Qur'ān and Its Interpreters*, pp. 35–40.

86. Gätje, *The Qur'ān and Its Exegesis*, p. 39.

87. Cragg, *The House of Islam*, p. 78.

88. Ibid.

89. Ibid., p. 79.

90. Ayoub, *The Qur'ān and Its Interpreters*, p. 39.

91. Ibid.

92. The following summary is based on Gerhard Böwering, "The Islamic Case: A Sufi Vision of Experience," in *The Other Side of God*, ed. Peter Berger (New York: Doubleday Anchor Press, 1981), pp. 134–36.

93. Ibid., p. 134.

94. Ibid.

95. Ibid., p. 135.

96. Ibid., pp. 135–36.

97. Wilfred Cantwell Smith, "The True Meaning of Scripture: An Empirical Historian's Nonreductionist Interpretation of the Qur'an," p. 498.

98. Wilfred Cantwell Smith, "The Study of Religion and the Study of the Bible," *Journal of the American Academy of Religion* 39 (1971): 133.

99. Wilfred Cantwell Smith, "The True Meaning of Scripture . . . ," p. 505.

100. As quoted by William A. Graham, "Qur'ān as Spoken Word," p. 37.

101. Ibid., p. 38.

102. Ibid., p. 39.

103. As quoted by Graham, "Qur'ān as Spoken Word," p. 40.
104. Ibid.
105. Ibid.
106. For further discussion on this point, see Harold Coward, *Pluralism: Challenge to World Religions* (Maryknoll, N.Y.: Orbis Books, 1985), pp. 55–59.
107. Fazlur Rahman, *Major Themes of the Qur'ān* (Chicago: Bibliotheca Islamica, 1980) p. 164.
108. Ibid., p. 165.
109. Ibid., p. 167.
110. Fazlur Rahman, *Islam* (New York: Doubleday Anchor Books, 1966), pp. 15–16.

4. SCRIPTURE IN HINDUISM

1. See, e.g., the Pūrva *Mīmāṁsā* view of "eternality," Ganganatha Jhā, *Pūrva-Mīmāṁsā in Its Sources* (Varanasi: Banaras Hindu University, 1964), pp. 133, 156. See also Julius L. Lipner, *The Face of Truth* (London: Macmillan, 1986), pp. 8–9.
2. Ganganatha Jhā, *Pūrva-Mīmāṁsā, p. 157.*
3. *T. R. V. Murti, "The Philosophy of Language in the Indian Context," in Studies in Indian Thought*, ed. Harold Coward (Delhi: Motilal Banarsidass, 1983), p. 361.
4. Aurobindo Ghose, *The Secret of the Veda* (Pondicherry: Sri Aurobino Ashram, 1971), p. 8.
5. The Pūrva Mīmāṁsā school is a significant exception to this doctrine. The Pūrva Mīmāṁsā reject the suggestion that the Vedic words and sentences could ever be transcended because that would remove scripture as the one certain, unchanging ground of *dharma* (rules of behavior and duty). The Pūrva Mīmāṁsā could be described as "scriptural fundamentalists" within Hinduism.
6. The following summary is based in part on two articles by J. A. B. van Buitenen: "Hindu Sacred Literature,"*Encyclopaedia Britannica* (3rd ed.) Macropaedia, vol. 8, pp. 932–40; and "The Ancient and Classical Literatures," in *The Literatures of India: An Introduction*, ed. Edward C. Dimock, Jr. (Chicago: University of Chicago Press, 1974), pp. 15–46.
7. Aurobindo Ghose, *The Secret of the Veda*, p. 408.
8. The dating of the various layers varies from scholar to scholar, and is at best speculative. The dates given are taken mainly from David Kinsley, *Hinduism* (Englewood Cliffs, N.J.: Prentice-Hall, 1982), p. 12.
9. Van Buitenen, "Hindu Sacred Literature," p. 935.
10. Ibid.
11. Kinsley, *Hinduism*, pp. 19–20.
12. Van Buitenen, "Hindu Sacred Literature," p. 940.
13. P. K. Chakravarti, *The Linguistic Speculations of the Hindus* (Calcutta: University of Calcutta Press, 1933).
14. Frits Staal, "The Concept of Metalanguage and Its Indian Background," *Journal of Indian Philosophy* 3 (1975): 319.
15. J. G. Arapura, "Some Perspectives on Indian Philosophy of Language," in *Revelation in Indian Thought*, ed. Harold Coward and Krishna Sivaraman (Emeryville, Calif.: Dharma Press, 1977), p. 20.
16. Bhartṛhari, *Vākyapadīya*, trans. K. A. S. Iyer (Delhi: Motilal Banarsidass, 1977). See also Harold Coward, *The Sphoṭa Theory of Language* (Delhi: Motilal Banarsidass, 1980).

17. Klaus Klostermaier, "The Creative Function of the Word," in *Language in Indian Philosophy and Religion*, ed. Harold Coward (Waterloo, Canada: Wilfrid Laurier University Press, 1978), p. 6.

18. Frits Staal, "Rgveda 10.71 on the Origin of Language," in *Revelation in Indian Thought*, pp. 5–6.

19. See *Ṛgveda* 5.10.2 and 10.114.8.

20. *Bṛihadāraṇyaka Upaniṣad* 4.1.2.

21. J. Gonda, "The Indian Mantra," *Oriens*, 16 (1964): 247.

22. Ibid., p. 255.

23. A. S. C. McDermott, "Toward a Pragmatics of Mantra Recitation," *Journal of Indian Philosophy* 3 (1975): 283–98.

24. Ibid., p. 287.

25. Ibid., pp. 288–90.

26. Frits Staal, "Oriental Ideas on the Origin of Language," *Journal of the American Oriental Society* 99 (1979): 9.

27. Ibid., p. 10.

28. J. Gonda, "The Indian Mantra," pp. 261–68.

29. Mircea Eliade, *Yoga, Immortality and Freedom* (Princeton: Princeton University Press, 1958), p. 216.

30. Frits Staal, "Sanskrit Philosophy of Language," *Current Trends in Linguistics* 5 (1969): 508.

31. Bharati acknowledges that this is the view of many European and Indian scholars but argues that this is erroneous. Agehananda Bharati, *The Tantric Tradition* (New York: Doubleday Anchor Books, 1970), p. 102.

32. Ganganatha Jhā, *Pūrva-Mīmāṁsa in Its Sources*, p. 162.

33. There are, of course, exceptions to this dominant modern view of language. Witness, e.g., Michael Polanyi's defense of "tacit knowing" as meaningful. See M. Polanyi, *Knowing and Being* (Chicago: University of Chicago Press, 1969), pp. 152ff.

34. K. Klostermaier, "Man Carries the Power of All Things in His Mouth," in Harold Coward and Krishna Sivaraman, eds., *Revelation in Indian Thought*, p. 88.

35. For a full analysis of how Bhartṛhari's theory of language does this, see Harold Coward, "The Meaning and Power of *Mantras* in Bhartṛhari's *Vākyapadīya*," *Studies in Religion* 2 (1982): 367–73.

36. Thomas B. Coburn, " 'Scripture' in India: Towards a Typology of the Word in Hindu Life," *Journal of the American Academy of Religion* 52 (1984): 452.

37. Bhartṛhari expresses this view well when he says that the *mantra* "AUM" is the source of all scripture, and that the various Vedas are merely manifestations of the one "AUM." Thus "AUM" implicitly contains "everything" as Coburn suggests. See *Vākyapadīya*, 1.9.

38. *Vākyapadīya*, 1.5.

39. Ibid., 1.137. In all Hindu schools, scripture is viewed as a valid source of knowledge, which makes right exegesis important.

40. McDermott, "Towards a Pragmatics of Mantra Recitation," p. 290.

41. *Vākyapadīya*, 1.11–12.

42. W. Wheelock, "*The Mantra in Vedic and Tantric Ritual*," unpublished paper, p. 19.

43. *Vākyapadīya*, 1.89.

44. *Sphoṭasiddhi of Mandana Miśra*, trans. K. A. S. Iyer (Poona: Deccan College, 1966), Kārikā, 19–20.

45. Van Buitenen, *The Literatures of India: An Introduction*, p. 7.

46. See Satyakam Varma, "Importance of the Prātiśākhyas," *Studies in Indology* (Delhi: Bharatiya Prakashan, 1976), pp. 32–52.

47. Satyakam Varma, "Sanskrit: A Living Tradition," *Studies in Indology*, p. 53. Bhartṛhari's definition of grammar is also to the point: "Grammar is a branch of knowledge solely depending on remembrance," as quoted by Varma (p. 54).

48. *Vākyapadīya* 1:46–47 and 1:142. See discussion in Harold Coward, *Bhartṛhari* (Boston: Twayne, 1976), p. 65.

49. See, e.g., the fine critical survey of modern biblical scholarship in Harvey McArthur, *In Search of the Historical Jesus* (New York: Charles Scribner's Sons, 1969).

50. Satyakam Varma, "Sanskrit: A Living Tradition," *Studies in Indology*, p. 59.

51. Space does not allow a detailed recounting of this development, but concise surveys are available. See, e.g., Satyakam Varma, "A Brief History of Sanskrit Grammar," *Studies in Indology*, pp. 103–43.

52. See *Nirukta*, 2.1.1.

53. For a beginner's introduction to his work, see Harold Coward, *Bhartṛhari* (Boston: G. K. Hall, 1976).

54. The following is based upon "The Life of a Text: Tulasīdāsa's *Rāmacaritamānasa* in Oral Exposition" by Phillip Lulgendorf, University of Chicago (unpublished paper presented at the American Academy of Religion Annual Meeting, Chicago, December 1984).

55. Ibid., p. 3.

56. Ibid., p. 7

57. Ibid., p. 11.

58. J. A. B. van Buitenen, "Hindu Sacred Scripture," p. 934.

59. For the above, see C. Mackenzie Brown, "Purāṇa as Scripture: From Sound to Image of the Holy Word in the Hindu Tradition," *History of Religions* 26, no.1 (1986): 68–73. See also Frits Staal, "The Concept of Scripture in the Indian Tradition," in *Sikh Studies: Comparative Perspectives on a Changing Tradition*, ed. Mark Juergensmeyer and N. Gerald Barrier (Berkeley: Berkeley Religious Studies Series, 1979), pp. 122–23.

60. L. Lancaster, "Buddhist Literature: Its Canons, Scribes, and Editors," *The Critical Study of Sacred Texts*, ed. Wendy Doniger O'Flaherty (Berkeley: Religious Studies Series, 1979), p. 224.

61. J. A. B. van Buitenen, "A Brief History of the Languages of South India," *The Literatures of India*, p. 12.

62. L. Lancaster, "Buddhist Literature: Its Canons, Scribes, and Editors," p. 224.

63. J. A. B. van Buitenen, "Written Texts and Their Preservation," *The Literatures of India*, p. 34.

64. For example, when I was last in Madras in 1982, Professor K. Kunjunni Raja had been hired specially by the Indian central government to teach the traditional *paṇḍits* the basic fundamentals of "Higher and Lower Textual Criticism" at the Kuppuswami Sastri Research Institute, Madras.

65. For the paragraph above, see C. Mackenzie Brown, "Purāṇa as Scripture," pp. 76–78.

66. S. Radhakrishnan, *Indian Philosophy* (New York: Macmillan, 1923), vol. 1, p. 125. For the relationship between religious ritual and poetic vision in the Vedas see R. N. Dandekar, "Aspect of Vedic Exegesis," *Kuppuswami Sastri Birth-Centenary Commemoration Volume*, pt. 2, ed. S. S. Janaki (Madras: The Kuppuswami Sastri Research Institute, 1985), pp. 8–11.

67. Ibid., pp. 130–36.

68. Aurobindo Ghose, *The Secret of the Veda*, p. 12.

69. J. Gonda, *The Vision of the Vedic Poets* (The Hague: Mouton, 1963), pp. 245–58.

70. *Bṛihad-Āraṇyaka Upaniṣad* 1.5.3.

71. *Maitri Upaniṣad*, 6.25.

72. See, e.g., *Ṛg Veda* X.168, "The Ātman of the Gods, the germ of the world . . ."; III.54 "One All is lord of . . . this multiform creation"; S.121" . . . the one life-spirit of the Gods . . . the one God above the Gods . . . " and references to *Ṛta*. Translations from *A Source Book in Indian Philosophy*, eds. S. Radhakrishnan and C. A. Moore (Princeton: Princeton University Press, 1976), pp. 15, 22, 25.

73. *Ṛg Veda*, 4.26.1.

74. *Bṛihad-Āraṇyaka Upaniṣad* 1.4.10; for translation, see R. E. Hume, *The Thirteen Principal Upanisads* (London: Oxford University Press, 1968), pp. 83–84.

75. It should be noted here that this *Upaniṣadic* approach was not completely unknown to the Vedic *ṛṣis*. For example, a remarkable symbolization of the real in very abstract terms occurs in Ṛg Veda, 10.129, where the underlying principle of all (including all the gods) is *tad ekaṁ sat*, "that One Being." On the other hand, it is also true that the theistic approach to the real, which is dominant in the Vedic hymns, is also to be found in the *Upaniṣads*. As Dasgupta points out, a minor current of thought in the *Upaniṣads* is that of theism, which looks upon *Brahman* as the Lord controlling the world. It is because of this unsystematized variety of approaches in the *Upaniṣads* that differing schools of philosophy (e.g., Śaṅkara and Rāmānuja) can appeal to the *Upaniṣads* for support. However, the majority of the *Upaniṣadic* approaches give stronger support to Śaṅkara. S. Dasguptà, *A History of Indian Philosophy* (Cambridge, England: University Press, 1963), vol. 1, p. 50.

76. *Bṛihad-Āraṇyaka Upaniṣad* 2.3.6, and *Māṇḍūkya Upaniṣad* 7.

77. See *Muṇḍaka Upaniṣad* 1.2.12 and 13.

78. *Bṛihad-Āraṇyaka Upaniṣad* 2.4.5., Hume's translation.

79. T. M. P. Mahadevan, *The Philosophy of Advaita* (London: Luzac and Co., 1983), p. 57.

80. *Muṇḍaka Upaniṣad* 1.1.3.

81. *Bṛihad-Āraṇyaka Upaniṣad* 4.3.1–6

82. *Chāndogya Upaniṣad* 6.2.1ff. and 6.13–6.15; *Kaṭha Upaniṣad* 1.20ff.

83. *Kaṭha Upaniṣad* 2.23; *Brihad-Āraṇyaka Upaniṣad* 4.4.21 and 3.5.1.

84. *Kaṭha Upaniṣad* 6.10ff.

85. *Taittirīya Upaniṣad* 2.8 and 9.

86. For translation, see J. H. Woods, *The Yoga System of Patanjali* (Delhi: Motilal Banarsidass, 1966).

87. See Gananatha Jha, *Pūrva Mīmāṁsā in Its Sources*.

88. See S. Radhakrishnan, *The Brahma Sūtra* (London: George Allen & Unwin, 1960).

89. For the last two *sūtras*, see *Indian Metaphysics and Epistemology*, ed. Karl H. Potter (Princeton: Princeton University Press, 1977).

90. See *Yoga Sūtra* 1:24, Vachaspati Miśra's commentary as translated in J. H. Woods, *The Yoga System of Patanjali*.

91. *Saṅkara on the Yoga Sūtras*, trans. Trevor Leggett (London: Routledge Kegan Paul, 1981), p. 89.

92. Vyāsa on *Yoga Sūtra* 1:25, as quoted in Śaṅkara's *Vivaran* and translated by Trevor Leggett, *Saṅkara on the Yoga Sūtràs*, p. 89.

93. For an excellent article on the Hindu (specifically Vedānta) view of reason and revelation, see T. R. V. Murti, "Revelation and Reason in Vedānta," in *Studies in Indian*

Thought, ed. Harold Coward (Delhi: Motilal Banarsidass, 1983), pp. 57–71. See also Julius Lipner, *The Face of Truth*, chaps. 1–3.

94. For a full exposition of this Hindu truth claim, see Harold Coward, *Pluralism: Challenge to World Religions* (Maryknoll, N.Y.: Orbis Books, 1985), chap. 4.

5. SCRIPTURE IN SIKHISM

1. W. Owen Cole and Piara Singh Sambhi, *The Sikhs: Their Religious Beliefs and Practices* (New Delhi: Vikas Publishing House, 1978), p. 43.

2. As quoted by W. Owen Cole, *The Guru in Sikhism* (London: Darton, Longman and Todd, 1982), p. 55.

3. Ibid., p. 62.

4. Tendencies to pay too much attention to the Adi Granth as a physical object were rejected in the *Rehat Maryada,* a guide to Sikh life drawn up in 1945. Following the influence of the Singh Sabha movement of the late nineteenth century, the use of ghee lamps, the placing of water near Guru Granth Sahib to ward off evil, etc., are practices rejected as Hindu idolatry. Interestingly, within Hinduism itself reform movements of this same period, e.g., the Arya Samaj, also reject any practices that lead to the worship of the physical objects (Cole, *The Guru,* p. 99).

5. Cole, *The Guru*, p. 89.

6. Ibid., p. 96.

7. Interview with Rev. Pashaura Singh, Calgaray, Jan. 18, 1985.

8. As quoted in Cole and Sambhi, *The Sikhs: Their Religious Beliefs and Practices,* p. 55.

9. Interview with Rev. Pashaura Singh, Calgary, Jan. 18, 1985.

10. C. H. Loehlin, *The Sikhs and Their Scriptures* (Delhi: ISPCK), 1947, p. 53.

11. See Harold Coward, "The Meaning and Power of *Mantras* in Bhartrhari's *Vākyapadīya*," *Studies in Religion* 11 (1982): 365–376, for a Hindu view of this process.

12. Interview with Rev. Pashaura Singh, Calgary, Jan. 18, 1985.

13. Ibid.

14. Interview with Kiran Gill, Calgary, Apr. 14, 1985.

15. Interview with Dr. Ranjit Dhaliwal, Calgary, Feb. 15, 1985.

16. Sahib Singh, *Sir Guru Granth Sahib Darpin*, 10 vols. (1963).

17. Interview with Avtar Gahunia, Calgary, Feb. 16, 1985.

18. Interview with Rev. Pashaura Singh, Calgary, May 30, 1985.

19. Interview with Avtar Gahunia, Calgary, Feb. 16, 1985.

20. Interview with Rajinder and Kiran Gill, Calgary, Apr. 14, 1985.

21. Ibid.

6. SCRIPTURE IN BUDDHISM

1. Yun-Hua Jan, "Dimensions of Indian Buddhism," in *The Malalasekera Commemoration Volume*, ed. O. H. de A. Wijesekera (Colombo, Sri Lanka: 1976), p. 162.

2. Lewis Lancaster, "Buddhist Literature: Its Canons, Scribes, and Editors," in *The Critical Study of Sacred Texts*, ed. Wendy Doniger O'Flaherty (Berkeley: Berkeley Religious Studies Series, 1979), p. 215. While most Buddhists consider scripture to be conventional, some Buddhists consider some texts to contain the truth in its explicit or absolute form (*neyartha*).

3. Richard Robinson, *The Buddhist Religion* (Belmont, Calif.: Dickenson, 1970), p. 13.

4. Ibid.

5. The following is based upon K. N. Jayatilleke, *Early Buddhist Theory of Knowledge* (Delhi: Motilal Banarsidass, 1980), pp. 183ff. See also E. Lamotte, *Histoire du Bouddhism Indian des origines à l'ere Sáka* (Louvain: Bureau du Muséon, 1958), pp. 25–28.

6. T. W. Rhys Davids, trans., *Buddhist Sutras* (New York: Dover Books, 1969), p. 150.

7. Lewis Lancaster, "Buddhist Literature: Its Canons, Scribes, and Editors," p. 216.

8. Mavis Fenn, "Global Theology and Comparative Religion," unpublished M. A. thesis, University of Calgary, 1985, p. 22.

9. Rhys Davids, *Buddhist Sutras*, p. 112.

10. *Entering the Path of Enlightenment by Santideva*, trans. Marion Matics (London: Macmillan, 1970), p. 16.

11. Lewis Lancaster, "Buddhist Literature: Its Canons, Scribes, and Editors," p. 217.

12. Richard Robinson, *The Buddhist Religion*, pp. 36–37.

13. Ibid., p. 37.

14. Ibid., p. 38.

15. Ibid., p. 50. See also Edward Conze, *Buddhist Thought in India* (Ann Arbor: University of Michigan Press, 1970), pp. 198–201.

16. Lewis Lancaster, "Buddhist Literature: Its Canons, Scribes, and Editors," pp. 217–18.

17. Ibid., p. 218.

18. Richard Robinson, *The Buddhist Religion*, pp. 50–51.

19. *Entering the Path of Enlightenment*, p. 17.

20. Joseph M. Kitagawa, *Religions of the East* (Philadelphia: Westminster Press, 1974), p. 178.

21. The following is adapted from Edward Conze, *Buddhism: Its Essence and Development* (New York: Harper & Row, 1959), pp. 31–32.

22. J. A. B. van Buitenen, "The Literatures of South Asia," p. 19 in *The Literatures of India: An Introduction*, ed. Edward C. Dimock, Jr. (Chicago: University of Chicago Press, 1974).

23. Richard Robinson, *The Buddhist Religion*, p. 36.

24. As quoted by Ananda K. Coomaraswamy, *Buddha and the Gospel of Buddhism* (New York: Harper Torchbooks, 1964), p. 262.

25. Frits Staal, "Scripture in the Indian Tradition," in *Sikh Studies*, ed. M. Juergensmeyer and N. G. Barrier (Berkeley: Berkeley Religious Studies Series, 1979), p. 123.

26. Joseph Kitagawa, "Some Remarks on the Study of Sacred Texts," in *The Critical Study of Sacred Texts*, p. 235. See also *The Life and Teaching of Geshé Rabten*, trans. B. A. Wallace (London: Allen & Unwin, 1980).

27. This phenomenon is well presented in Huston Smith's film of Tibetan Buddhism, *Requiem for a Faith*.

28. Although Buddhists denied the eternality of the word, they were influenced by the Hindu discussion of *sábda* and *sphoṭa*. Thus the Buddhist attitude toward language is ambiguous. For example, the founder of Japanese Esoteric Buddhism, Kūkai, says: "As the performer of the mantra meditates on the syllables *Ma* and *Ta*, the Buddha's nature shines forth and dispells the darkness of ignorance." *Sources of Japanese Tradition*, ed. R. Tsunoda, W. T. de Bary, D. Keene (New York: Columbia University Press, 1969), vol. 1, p. 149.

29. David J. Goa and Harold G. Coward, "Sacred Ritual, Sacred Language: Jodo

Shinshu Religious Forms in Transition," *Studies in Religion* (1983), 363–79.

30. Ibid, p. 375.
31. Ibid.
32. Ibid.
33. Edward Conze, *Buddhism: Its Essence and Development*, p. 30.
34. Ibid., p. 31.
35. Ibid.
36. Lewis Lancaster, "Buddhist Literature: Its Canons, Scribes, and Editors," p. 219.
37. Ibid.
38. Ibid., p. 220.
39. Ibid., p. 221.
40. Ibid.
41. Ibid., p. 222.
42. Ibid., p. 224.
43. Ibid., p. 226.
44. Eva M. Dargyay, *The Rise of Esoteric Buddhism in Tibet* (Delhi: Motilal Banarsidass, 1979), p.7.
45. Ibid., p. 10.
46. Leslie Kawamura, "Is Reconstruction from Tibetan into Sanskrit Possible?" in *"Language" in Indian Philosophy and Religion*, ed. Harold Coward (Waterloo, Canada: Wilfrid Laurier University Press, 1978), p. 90.
47. Lewis Lancaster, "Buddhist Literature: Its Canons, Scribes, and Editors," p. 228.
48. Richard Robinson, *The Buddhist Religion*, p. 28.
49. Ibid.
50. L. Schmithausen, "On Some Aspects of Descriptions or Theories of 'Liberating Insight' and 'Enlightenment' in Early Buddhism," *Studien Zum Jainismus und Buddhismus* 23 (1983): 200–201.
51. Richard Robinson, *The Buddhist Religion*, p. 19.
52. Ibid., p. 31.
53. Winston King, *Theravāda Meditation: The Buddhist Transformation of Yoga* (University Park and London: Pennsylvania State University Press, 1980), p. 23.
54. Ibid.
55. As quoted by Winston King, "The Existential Nature of Buddhist Ultimates," *Philosophy East and West* 33 (1983): 263.
56. Ibid.
57. *Dharmapada* 197–200, as quoted by Richard Robinson, *The Buddhist Religion*, p. 31.
58. Yun-Hua Jan, "Dimensions of Indian Buddhism," p. 159.
59. Ibid.
60. Ibid., p. 160.
61. Ibid.
62. Ibid. For an excellent description of the rigorous discipline involved in such memorization, see *The Life and Teaching of Geshé Rabten*, trans. B. Allan Wallace (London: Allen & Unwin, 1980), pp. 45–56. Geshé Rabten comments, "In the Western academic tradition, note taking plays a vital role, and much of one's knowledge tends to be confined between the covers of one's textbooks. Our corresponding stores of knowledge were held in our minds, through memorization" (p. 53). Just as an old man might need the help of a stick to get up, so one needs to memorize the words of scripture to experience their meaning.

63. Ibid., p. 161. If one wishes to practice the meaning of the scriptures and is attached to the words, then the word constitutes a distraction. See *The Large Sūtra on Perfect Wisdom*, trans. E. Conze (Berkeley: University of California Press, 1975), pp. 332–37.

64. Ibid.

65. As quoted by Y.-H. Jan, "Dimensions," pp. 161–62.

66. As quoted by Y.-H. Jan, "Dimensions." p. 163.

67. The *Samādhirājasūtra* puts it clearly:

> If he, that has become well-versed in numerous works on the Doctrine,
> Is proud of his knowledge and does not preserve his morals,
> He will not be able to save others by his great learning,
> And, morally impure, he is doomed to hell.
>
> Quoted from Y.-H. Jan, "Dimensions," p. 164.

68. Yun-Hua Jan, "Dimensions," p. 161.

69. Ibid., pp. 166–67.

70. As quoted by Giuseppe Tucci, *Minor Buddhist Texts: Part II* (Rome: Instituto Italiano Peril medio et Estremo Oriente, 1958), p. 158.

71. Ibid., p. 160.

72. Ibid.

73. See *Sources of Japanese Tradition*, for section "Amida and Pure Land," pp. 184–212.

74. See the way in which other religions are judged in the *Sandaka Sutta*.

75. Cited by K. N. Jayatilleke, *The Buddhist Attitude to Other Religions* (Kandy, Sri Lanka: Buddhist Publication Society, 1975), p. 24.

76. Ibid., p. 29.

77. Buddhadāsa, *No Religion* (Bangkok: Sublime Life Mission, n.d.).

78. Ibid., pp. 16ff.

7. SCRIPTURE AND THE FUTURE OF RELIGIONS

1. Walter J. Ong, *The Presence of the Word* (New Haven: Yale University Press, 1967), p. 314.

2. *The Collected Dialogues of Plato*, ed. Edith Hamilton and Huntington Cairns (Princeton: Princeton University Press, 1961), pp. 475–525.

3. *Phaedrus*, in *Collected Dialogues*, p. 520. This position is not without several ironies, which must be acknowledged. We likely would not know today what Socrates said against writing if Plato or someone else had not written it down. Also Socrates earlier in the dialogue prefers to have Lysias' speech *read* to him rather than orally recounted.

4. Ibid., p. 521.

5. George Steiner, *The Portage to San Cristóbal of A.H.* (New York: Simon and Schuster, 1982). See the interview in *Time*, March 29, 1982.

6. Nāgārjuna, *Mūlamadhyamakakārikā*, trans. Kenneth K. Inada (Tokyo: Hokuseido Press, 1970).

7. See "editorial" by Pamela McCallum, *Ariel* 15 (1984):3–4.

8. Susan Handelman, *The Slayers of Moses* (Albany: State University of New York Press, 1982), presents a controversial analysis of this point. For an example of a

genuinely oral type of Judaism, see Gershom G. Scholem, *Major Trends in Jewish Mysticism* (New York: Schocken Books, 1971).

9. Klaus Klostermaier, "The Creative Function of the Word" in *Language in Indian Philosophy and Religion*, ed. Harold Coward (Waterloo, Canada: Wilfrid Laurier University Press, 1978), p. 6.

10. George Cardona, *Panini* (Delhi: Motilal Banarsidass, 1980).

11. A. S. C. McDermott, "Toward a Pragmatics of Mantra Recitation," *Journal of Indian Philosophy* 3 (1975): 290.

12. Harold Coward, *Bhartṛhari* (Boston: Twayne, 1976), see chap. 4, "Bhartrhari's *Dhvani* as Central to Indian Aesthetics."

13. Bhartṛhari, *Vākyapadīya*, I:11–12.

14. Heinrich Dumoulin, *A History of Zen Buddhism* (Boston: Beacon Press, 1969), p. 135.

15. See Ananda K. Coomaraswamy, *Buddha and the Gospel of Buddhism* (New York: Harper Torchbooks, 1964), pp. 246ff.

16. Philo, "The Contemplative Life" in *Philo*, trans. F. H. Coulson, vol. 9 (Cambridge, Mass.: Harvard University Press, 1960), pp. 159–60.

17. Willem Jan Kooiman, *Luther and the Bible* (Philadelphia: Muhlenberg Press, 1961), p. 201.

18. Jacob Neusner, *The Memorized Torah: The Mnemonic System of the Mishnah* (Chico, Calif.: Scholars Press, 1985), p. 114.

19. Noam Chomsky, *Language and Mind* (New York: Harcourt, Brace and World, 1968).

20. Jacob Neusner, *The Memorized Torah*, p. 121.

21. Harold Coward, *The Sphoṭa Theory of Language* (Delhi: Motilal Banarsidass, 1980), pp. 71–88.

22. *Saint Augustine, Confessions*, translated by Vernon J. Bourke (Washington: Catholic University of America Press, 1966) VIII:8, "The Fathers of the Catholic Church Series." All references below to Augustine's writings are to this series.

23. *Confessions*, VIII: 8.

24. *Confessions*, VIII: 10–11.

25. *Confessions*, VIII: 12.

26. *The Trinity*, XIV: 8.

27. *Confessions*, X:2.

28. *The Collected Dialogues of Plato*, ed. Edith Hamilton and Huntington Cairns (Princeton: Princeton University Press, 1965), "Meno" 80d, p. 363.

29. *The Trinity*, XIV:8.

30. *The Trinity*, XI:7.

31. *Confessions*, III:5.

32. *The Trinity*, XI:8.

33. Werner H. Kelber, *The Oral and the Written Gospel* (Philadelphia: Fortress Press, 1983), pp. 62–76.

34. Mahmoud Ayoub, *The Qur'an and Its Interpreters* (Albany: State University of New York Press, 1984), pp. 35–40.

35. Gerhard Böwering, "The Islamic Case: A Sufi Vision of Experience," in *The Other Side of God*, ed. Peter Berger (New York: Doubleday Anchor Press, 1981), pp. 134–136.

36. Phillip Lutgendorf, "The Life of a Text: Tulsīdāsa's *Rāmacaritamanasa* in Oral Exposition." Unpublished paper presented at American Academy of Religion, Decem-

ber 1984. While Lutgendorf gives a good description of the Hindi *kathā* of Tulsīdāsa's *Rāmacaritamānasa*, much older and more widespread is the training in *kathā* of the Sanskrit *Bhagavatam Purāṇa*. In Vrindaban, India, for example, there is a school in which kathā-singers are trained in a three-year course.

37. Richard Robinson, *The Buddhist Religion* (Belmont, Calif.: Dickenson, 1970), p. 36.

38. Norman Perrin, *The New Testament: An Introduction* (New York: Harcourt, Brace, Jovanovich, 1974), p. 332.

39. Werner H. Kelber, *The Oral and the Written Gospel*, p. 220.

40. Kelber has further argued this point in "Narrative as Interpretation and Interpretation as Narrative," *Semeia* 39 (1987): 107–33.

41. C. Mackenzie Brown, "Purāṇa as Scripture: From Sound to Image of the Holy Word in the Hindu Tradition," *History of Religions* 26 (1986): 76.

42. Ibid.

43. Ibid. Brown goes on to show how the copying and giving of books even becomes a religious act. Scriptual texts even become objects of worship, or *puja*, for some Hindus. The sacred word is transformed from sound to image, from *mantra* to *mūrti* (p. 82).

44. See R. N. Dandekar, "Aspects of Vedic Exegesis," *Professor Kuppuswami Sastri Birth Centenary Commemoration Volume*, edited by S. S. Janaki (Madras: Kuppuswami Sastri Research Institute, 1985), pt. 2, p. 11: "The religious efficacy of the Ṛgvedic *mantras* lies in their utterance."

45. *The Yoga System of Patanjali*, trans. J. H. Woods. Harvard Oriental Series, vol. 17 (Delhi: Motilal Banarsidass, 1966); see I:27–28, 42–44, and II:32.

46. Joseph Kitagawa, "Some Remarks on the Study of Sacred Texts," in *The Critical Study of Sacred Texts*, ed. Wendy Doniger O'Flaherty (Berkeley: Religious Studies Series, 1979), p. 235.

47. See the film "Requiem for a Faith" by Huston Smith.

48. "Torah, Reading of," *Encyclopedia Judaica* (New York: Macmillan 1971), p. 1254.

49. Mahmoud Ayoub, *The Qur'an and Its Interpreters* (Albany: State University of New York Press, 1984), vol. 1, pp. 8–11.

50. David J. Goa, Harold G. Coward, Ronald Neufeldt, "Hindus in Alberta: Continuity and Change," *Canadian Ethnic Studies* 16 (1984): p. 103. Whereas traditional chanting of sacred scripture in India depended upon long periods of memorization and repetition in early childhood—a practice not likely to occur in Canada or even in modernized families in India—the *guru mantra,* so it claims, requires no training in childhood for it to function in later life. It is said to fulfill the same spiritual role of keeping the mind controlled and focused on the divine. Since the guru is merely a channel to the divine, the *mantra* he or she gives is the psychological device for opening that channel and keeping it open. In traditional Hinduism this function was often fulfilled by the ritual learning and chanting of scripture.

51. David J. Goa and Harold G. Coward, "Sacred Ritual, Sacred Language: Jodo Shinshu Religious Forms in Transition," *Studies in Religion* (1983), p. 376.

52. Jacques Ellul, *The Humiliation of the Word,* trans. Joyce Main Hanks (Grand Rapids, Mich.: Wm. B. Eerdmans Publishing Co. 1985), pp. 1–4.

53. Willem Jan Kooiman, *Luther and the Bible*, p. 52.

54. Martin Luther, *Works,* ed. Jaroslav Pelikan (St. Louis: Concordia Publishing House, 1958), vol. 7, p. 526.

55. *The Oxford Annotated Bible,* ed. H. G. May and B. M. Metzger (New York: Oxford University Press, 1962), p. 1537.

56. Ronald Bond, "The 'Lively Word' and the Book of Homilies: The Preaching and Reading Ministries in Tudor and Stuart England," unpublished paper, p. 2.

57. Walter J. Ong, *Orality and Literacy: The Technologizing of the Word* (New York: Methuen, 1982), pp. 8–9, 14–15.

58. See "Bibliolatry," *Encyclopaedia of Religion and Ethics,* ed. James Hastings, et al. (New York: C. Scribner's Sons), as well as C. Mackenzie Brown, "Purāṇa as Scripture."

59. G. van der Leeuw, *Religion in Essence and Manifestation,* trans. J. E. Turner, with additions by Hans Penner (New York: Harper & Row, 1963), pp. 435–36.

60. Unless, of course, literary analysis brings us full circle to a kind of second naïveté and so opens us to a recovered sense of awe for the complexity and power of the text, which is what the best literary criticism does do.

61. Bernard C. Lategan, "Reference: Reception, Redescription and Reality," in *Text and Reality: Aspects of Reference in Biblical Texts* by Bernard C. Lategan and Willem S. Vorster (Atlanta: Scholars Press, 1985), p. 67.

62. Bernard C. Lategan, "Some Unresolved Methodological Issues in New Testament Hermeneutics," in *Text and Reality*, p. 12.

63. I say "usually" because there are exceptions as, e.g., when the poet through nervousness or lack of skill is not a good reader. It is also possible to read sermons that are more enlivening than the ones we may hear "in the flesh" (e.g., the written sermons of John Donne, or, to take a more recent example, Paul Tillich).

64. The term "transcendent" is used in this discussion rather than "God" because the latter is inappropriate for Buddhism and nontheistic Hinduism. The term "transcendent," however, does include both the theistic religions (Judaism, Christianity, Islam, and parts of Hinduism) as well as Buddhism and the nontheistic aspects of Hinduism. In all religions there is experience of a reality that transcends ordinary human conception—thus the use of the term "transcendent." For more discussion, see Harold Coward, *Pluralism: Challenge to World Religions* (Maryknoll, N.Y.: Orbis Books, 1985), p. 106.

65. William Barclay, *Epilogues and Prayers* (London: SCM Press, 1963), p. 9.

66. Words in Buddhism can work in a positive way, as in Tibetan or Jodo Shinshu chanting, or in a negative way, as in Madhyamika philosophy or in Zen *kōan* meditation. In both cases, however, the aim of the word-use is to sensitize the devotee to the transcendent (*sunya* or *satori*) experience. And when the written, following Luther, functions in a relational context, it then shares in the revealing power of the oral.

67. This distinction in function between rational and nonrational psychological processes has been argued in different ways in the following examples: within Christianity, F. Schleiermacher, *On Religion,* and Rudolf Otto, *The Idea of the Holy*; in Hinduism, Bhartṛhari, *Vākyapadīya;* in Buddhism, Nagarjuna, *Mulamadhyamakakarika*; and in modern psychology, William James, *Varieties of Religious Experience*, and Carl Jung, *Collected Works.* It must also be admitted that at the further end of the religious-experience spectrum—in the mystical experience of sacred words—it is often unfamiliar words that at times have power, e.g., the Kabbala, Sufism, or speaking in tongues. But this analysis is directed toward the beginning side of the religious-experience spectrum.

68. One might go so far as to say that to speak words, in the consciousness that others have spoken the same words for generations, is already to be lifted beyond oneself.

69. Jacques Ellul, *The Humiliation of the Word.* It is of interest to note that nurses in intensive care units report that "hearing is the last sense to go." This supports Ellul's

contention that "hearing" is the sensory modality with the deepest impact upon our psyche. It is thus appropriate that the sacred should be grounded in the aural sensory channel.

70. See Friedrich Heiler, *Prayer: A Study in the History and Psychology of Religions* (New York: Oxford University Press, 1958), pp. 354–55.

71. See Peter Craigie, "Some Biblical Perspectives on Education in the Faith," *Touchstone* 4 (1986): 11.

72. We recall here Jacob Neusner's description of how the memorized Mishnah does this for Jews (*The Memorized Torah* [Chico, Calif.: Scholars Press, 1985]); and Northrop Frye's description of how the early reading and hearing of the Bible, as the only book in the pioneer household, provided the grounding in consciousness for the thought forms reflected in much literature (*Divisions on a Ground,* ed. J. Polk [Toronto: Anansi, 1982]).

73. See "Mysticism in Jung and Yoga," in Harold Coward, *Jung and Eastern Thought* (Albany: State University of New York Press, 1985), chap. 7, and "Can Jungian Psychology Be Used to Interpret Indian Devotional Poetry?" by Harold Coward, *Studies in Religion* 8 (1979): 177–90.

74. See *Patanjali's Yoga Sutras,* trans. Rama Prasada (New Delhi: Oriental Books, 1978), I:27 and II:32.

75. See, e.g., Bṛhadāraṇyaka Upaniṣad 4.5.15.

Index

A boldfaced number indicates the page upon which the definition of a term is given.